Whether you succeed or fail in your first attempt as CEO, the best is yet to come. **The Organization Game**'s unique "what if" approach lets you replay your choices again and again to explore the outcome of different decisions. In all, the book offers more than 75 decision points, and 30 different outcomes, for hour after hour of provocative reading.

Part choose-your-own-adventure novel, part innovative business manual, this always entertaining book provides expert insight into organizational theory and practice in corporate America today. It will sharpen your own thinking and decision-making skills when initiating or responding to organizational change in your company.

ABOUT THE AUTHOR

Craig R. Hickman is the bestselling author of *The Strategy Game; Mind of a Manager, Soul of a Leader; The Oz Principle; Creating Excellence; The Future 500; Practical Business Genius* and other influential business books and articles.

Mr. Hickman currently conducts workshops for organizations, businesses, and management groups worldwide. He holds an MBA with honors from Harvard.

THE ORGANIZATION GAME

An
Interactive
Business
Game
Where
YOU
Make
or
Break
the
Company

REENGINEERING
TEAMS
INNOVATION
BEST PRACTICES
REVOLUTIONARY CHANGE
EMPOWERMENT &
ACCOUNTABILITY

CRAIG R. HICKMAN

Bestselling Author of
The Strategy Game

PRENTICE HALL
Englewood Cliffs, New Jersey 07632

Prentice-Hall International (UK) Limited, *London*
Prentice-Hall of Australia Pty. Limited, *Sydney*
Prentice-Hall Canada, Inc., *Toronto*
Prentice-Hall Hispanoamericana, S.A., *Mexico*
Prentice-Hall of India Private Limited, *New Delhi*
Prentice-Hall of Japan, Inc., *Tokyo*
Simon & Schuster Asia Pte. Ltd., *Singapore*
Editora Prentice-Hall do Brasil, Ltda., *Rio de Janeiro*

© 1994 by Craig R. Hickman

10 9 8 7 6 5 4 3 2 1

Library of Congress Cataloging-in-Publication Data

Hickman, Craig R.
The organization game : an interactive business game where you
make or break the the company / by Craig R. Hickman.
   p. cm.
   ISBN 0-13-039066-6
   1. Decision-making. 2. Management games. 3. Organizational
effectiveness. I. Title.
HD30.23.H533 1994
658.4′03—dc20   94-5924
                                                                          CIP

If you would like to receive information on any of the following:
The Organization Game Software, The Organization Game
Leader's Guide, or The Organization Game Workshop, please
call 801-221-7715 or write to The Organization Game, P.O. Box
50148, Provo, Utah 84605-0148.

ISBN 0-13-039066-6

PRENTICE HALL
Career & Personal Development
Englewood Cliffs, NJ 07632

Simon & Schuster, A Paramount Communications Company

Printed in the United States of America

Dedication

To Sherm Hibbert, Peter Drucker, Paul Thompson, Paul Lawrence, Bill Ewing, and Jay St. Clair, who awakened and fueled my enduring interest in organizational effectiveness and design.

ACKNOWLEDGMENTS

As always, there are many people who helped me write this book:

- First, my literary agent and collaborator, Michael Snell, has provided his usual valuable input.
- Mary H. Kowalczyk and the people at Word Masters have expeditiously and carefully handled all aspects of getting the manuscript into its final form.
- The many readers of *The Strategy Game* have offered encouragement, tips, and input that have made *The Organization Game* an even better choose-your-own-adventure experience.
- Karen Hansen, senior editor at Prentice Hall, who originally acquired the manuscript of The Strategy Game while she was at McGraw-Hill, continued to be a constant visionary voice throughout the development of this book.
- My wife, Pam, who has always been a great support in my writing endeavors, especially encouraged me to continue this series of game books.
- My son, Jared Hickman, who first sparked the idea for *The Strategy Game* assisted me as I traveled across the country producing the initial draft of *The Organization Game*.
- Other members of my family, my two daughters, Kimberly and Leigh, as well as my mother and father, Winston and Verla Hickman, and my brothers, Larry and Mark, and my sister, Debbie, along with their spouses, have provided great inspiration and support.

- Joe Cannon and Stan Varner, who have stimulated my thinking for years, continued to provide their uniquely insightful perspectives during this project.
- Finally, I want to thank those unmentioned others who have contributed in countless ways to my writing and to this book—to them, I am most grateful.

BIBLIOGRAPHY

Sources Referred to in
The Organization Game

Block, Peter. *Stewardship: Choosing Service Over Self-Interest.* San Francisco, California: Group West, 1993.

Block, Peter. *The Empowered Manager: Positive Political Skills at Work.* San Francisco, California: Jossey-Bass Publishers, 1987.

Covey, Stephen R. *First Things First.* New York: Simon & Schuster, 1994.

Connors, Roger, Smith, Tom, and Hickman, Craig. *The Oz Principle: Getting Results Through Individual and Organizational Accountability.* Englewood Cliffs, New Jersey: Prentice Hall, 1994.

Gilder, George. *Life After Television: The Coming Transformation of Media and American Life.* New York: W.W. Norton & Company, 1992.

Hammer, Michael, and Champy, James. *Reengineering the Corporation: A Manifesto for Business Revolution.* New York: Harper Business, 1993.

Jung, Carl G. *Modern Man in Search of a Soul.* New York: Harcourt Brace Jovanovich, 1933.

Katzenbach, Jon R., and Smith, Douglas K. *The Wisdom of Teams:*

Creating the High-Performance Organization. Boston, Massachusetts: Harvard Business School Press, 1993.

Mintzberg, Henry. *Mintzberg on Management: Inside Our Strange World of Organizations.* New York: The Free Press, 1989.

Nanus, Burt. *Visionary Leadership: Creating a Compelling Sense of Direction for Your Organization.* San Francisco, California: Jossey-Bass Publishers, 1992.

Peck, Scott. *Further Along the Road Less Traveled.* New York: Simon & Schuster, 1993.

Peters, Tom. *Liberation Management: Necessary Disorganization for the Nanosecond Nineties.* New York: Alfred A. Knopf, 1992.

Shekerjian, Denise. *Uncommon Genius: How Great Ideas Are Born.* New York: Viking Penguin, 1990.

Tichy, Noel M., and Sherman, Stratford. *Control Your Destiny or Someone Else Will: How Jack Welch Is Making General Electric the World's Most Competitive Company.* New York: Currency-Doubleday, 1993.

Toffler, Alvin. *Powershift: Knowledge, Wealth, and Violence at the Edge of the 21st Century.* New York: Bantam Books, 1990.

Waterman, Robert H., Jr. *Adhocracy.* New York: W.W. Norton & Company, 1991.

Zenger, John H., Musselwhite, Ed, Hurson, Kathleen, and Perrin, Craig. *Leading Teams: Mastering the New Role.* Homewood, Illinois: Business One Irwin, 1994.

CONTENTS

PREFACE

My purpose in writing *The Organization Game* is two-fold: first, to entertain readers by engaging them in a highly interesting and suspenseful exploration of the myriad of organizational forms, approaches, and alternatives facing today's businesses throughout corporate America and the world, and second, to stimulate learning by exposing readers to a broad range of organizational theories and ideas that can inform their own thinking and decision making while initiating or responding to organizational change.

On the entertainment side, *The Organization Game* is much like a novel that introduces readers to a new world: new circumstances, interesting characters, and intriguing perspectives.

On the learning side, *The Organization Game* offers readers a whole-picture view of what's happening in business organizations today, an opportunity to develop more accountability for initiating and implementing successful organizational change, and a challenge to improve thinking and decision making when revolutionizing, reengineering, redesigning, or revitalizing organizations.

In the era of new management, people are expected to assume responsibility for overall results. To do so successfully, they must become much more savvy about organizational change and the effective deployment of people. This book is designed to help readers develop such savvy.

Just as I did in the beginning of *The Strategy Game,* I would like to offer some cautionary words of advice before you begin playing *The Organization Game.* You are being asked to make organizational decisions that will shape the future of fictitious CyTech. The choices you face are intended to simulate real life;

however, you may occasionally be presented with choices you consider to be extreme, inflexible, or contrived. Remember, this is only a game. I suggest that you consider any such circumstances as mere constraints, not unlike many similar circumstances and conditions that compose the world of today's CEO's. You may also feel there is a lack of sufficient information for you to make the best decision. As this occurs all too often in real life, use what you do know to stretch your thinking and make the best decision. Keep in mind that the negative outcomes you encounter throughout the book are designed to stimulate your thinking and test your decision making. You may be able to make those choices that turn out negative in the book successful and productive in real life. However, if you read the other alternatives available to you at each of the decision points, you will discover why the author considered one or more of the other alternatives a better choice. You are now ready to begin your organizational shaping experience at CyTech Corporation.

I hope you find this book enjoyable and useful.

Craig R. Hickman

Imagine that you have just come aboard as the CEO of CyTech (Cybernetic Technologies, Inc.), a $4 billion computer and consumer electronics company. When Bill Anderson, founder and CEO of CyTech, died suddenly three months ago without grooming a successor, the board of directors picked you for the job because of your stellar track record at AT&T, where you guided the development and introduction of the *EO Communicator*, a wireless computer/ communicator that can read handwriting. Now CyTech's board of directors expects you to reshape the company's organization and work culture for the twenty-first century. If you succeed, you could literally revolutionize the world of personal and corporate communications, gain an ownership position worth millions of dollars, and, as the leader of one of the most admired companies of the twenty-first century, influence the practice of management for decades to come. If you fail, you could destroy CyTech, jeopardize the livelihoods of tens of thousands of employees, and find your own career in a tailspin. The challenge is daunting, but intoxicating.

1

THE CURRENT SITUATION

CyTech, formed five years earlier in a joint venture between Compaq Computer and Teledyne, gained overnight prominence three years ago when it introduced *PowerBase,* a hand-held "phone-fax-computer" that eclipsed Apple's second-generation Newton technology, *PowerPad,* and outperformed AT&T's *EO Communicator. PowerBase* is a multipurpose machine, slightly larger than the typical laptop computer, with all the capabilities of a powerful PC; but, in addition, it has features that allow the users to place telephone calls from almost anywhere in the world, receive or send fax messages, connect easily with other home or office PC systems, and link into all major computer communications services.

In the three years since *PowerBase's* introduction, the company has grown from $800 million to $4 billion. A brief summary of selected financial and stock information appears in the following table:

Selected Financial and Stock Information
(Dollars in millions, except stock price in actual dollars)

	Year ended March 31				
	Current Year	———————	Previous Years	———————	
Sales	$4,083	$2,542	$1,389	$798	$418
Profits	242	127	42	24	8
Profits as a % of:					
Sales	6%	5%	3%	(3%)	2%
Assets	9%	7%	4%	(6%)	3%
Common Equity*	17%	11%	8%	(12%)	7%
Market Value**	6,123	3,106	1,763	86	376
Stock Price	24 ¾	15	11 ¼	$^{11}\!/_{16}$	3 ⅛

* Total stockholders' equity includes capital stock, surplus, and retained earnings at the company's year end. For purposes of determining profits as a percent of common stockholders' equity, all preferred stock is excluded.

** Calculated by multiplying the number of common shares outstanding by the price per common share as of March 31.

CyTech is a NASDAQ-traded stock, national market issue, with 25 percent owned by Compaq Computer, 25 percent owned by Teledyne, and 50 percent owned by a variety of institutional and individual investors. Outstanding shares of common stock increased from 125 million to 255 million over the five-year period.

On the negative side, CyTech's rapid growth has created overnight a fragmented and confused organizational culture and work environment that a psychiatrist might compare to multiple-personality disorder. The organization's freewheeling innovation personality constantly comes into conflict with the work force's natural tendency toward stabilization; the "wizards" in R&D distrust "the suits" in accounting; the accountants can't understand why marketing and sales budgets look like the national debt; marketing accuses R&D of caring more about "techno junkies" than business customers; and the senior-management team embodies all the diversity and displays all the tensions that run rampant throughout the organization.

In your first eye-opening weeks on the job, you spend a lot of time getting to know your senior team:

The Senior Team

John Solo	*Executive Vice President of Worldwide Sales and Marketing*
Bob Kiechel	*Senior Vice President of Product Development*
Hal McPhee	*Chief Financial Officer*
Nan Thurow	*Senior Vice President of Worldwide Operations*
Karen Walsh	*Vice President of CyTech's Advanced Technology Lab*
Morris Strandmeyer	*Vice President of Production*

John Solo, age 43, married with four children, has been executive vice president for worldwide sales and marketing for almost a year. A down-to-earth, easygoing Australian, he relishes the extreme pressures to keep CyTech's sales growing, instinctively focusing on present circumstances and functions and brilliantly handling every crisis that demands immediate action. He's pragmatic and realistic in assessing competitive issues and marketing problems, but he often ignores policies and procedures in order to take decisive action, sometimes with dire consequences later. John Solo thrives on change and resists any and all planning efforts because he sees them as a waste of time. He views himself as the ultimate realist, forever adaptable to current realities, particularly when it means concocting an *ad hoc* plan. The motto *carpe diem* adorns his office wall. In his year at CyTech, he has won a reputation for working hard and playing hard, always exhausting his troops in the field and his teammates on the intercompany softball team: "Go for the ball." Extremely capable at turning things around (or upside down), John Solo charges ahead and never looks back.

Bob Kiechel, 48, divorced with two children, has been senior vice president of product development for four years. An ex-Apple executive, he has become the company's most inventive leader. Both logical and resourceful, he provides a constant catalyst for change at CyTech by constantly developing new products. He enjoys a wide-ranging scope of interests and reads Russian literature in the original language. Driven by a strong need to be viewed as a supremely competent individual, Bob continually searches for new possibilities and opportunities. He knowingly rebels against established norms and procedures whenever he perceives them as no longer logical or useful. Seeing more possibilities than the company could ever possibly implement, he loves experimenting with change, demands ingenuity from his people, and bristles when too much structure seems to get in the way. When it comes to getting results, Bob doesn't consider any outcome worthwhile unless it's unique and innovative. Constantly asking the question, "What if?," Bob perpetually shapes and reshapes the puzzle of CyTech's future.

Hal McPhee, 46, married with no children, has served as chief financial officer for a little less than two years. An ex-IBM executive who enjoys a reputation for objectivity and realism when addressing all issues facing the company, Hal scrutinizes every new strategic initiative to make sure the facts support it. He always pays attention to the smallest details. Conservative by nature, he favors caution and carefulness, constantly seeking to establish order in an otherwise chaotic environment. Bob rarely initiates change but reacts to it responsibly, at least from his own point of view. While he acknowledges current management trends toward highly dynamic organizations, he prefers hierarchical structures in which everyone knows his or her position in the scheme of things and conforms to established operating practices. When it comes to getting results, Hal works tirelessly toward tangible goals and objectives while asking the question, "What level of results should we get from current managerial and technical capabilities?"

Nan Thurow, 41, married with two children, has been senior vice president of worldwide operations for 18 months. During that time she has developed a well-earned reputation as a savvy outsourcer of secondary business activities, such as contracting with suppliers for telephone, fax, and computer component manufacturing, as well as packaging, shipping and technical service. She has even helped employee groups who might otherwise have been laid off establish their own independent companies to perform contract services for CyTech. She is introspective and by her own admission, rather scholarly, but perfectly capable of generating innovative approaches at the blink of an eye. She enjoys looking at things in new and different ways, but always operates purposefully and tactfully. Nan places a high premium on beliefs and values and steadfastly encourages individual learning and development. Uncannily aware of what others are thinking and feeling, she prefers planning for change, developing blueprints for future possibilities and charting people-sensitive pathways to their attainment. Since she never believes the present is good enough, she persists in bringing about constant improvements. When it comes to getting results, Nan focuses on aligning the purposes and capabilities of people throughout the organization, including suppliers and affiliates, to reach superior performance.

Karen Walsh, 38, married with one child, has run CyTech's advanced technology lab for over two years and easily enjoys the highest I.Q. of any member of CyTech's senior management team. Both objective and visionary, she can immediately identify the subtlest flaws in another person's thinking. Her quest for logical purity drives her every action, and while she often comes across as rather absent-minded in day-to-day activities, people who work with her consider her a brilliant futurist. She lives in a world of thoughts and concepts, rarely showing emotion, but adapts ingeniously to externally driven and internally planned change. Always grasping the big picture with perfect clarity, Karen can, at times, become impatient with others who don't see the breadth and depth of her vision or who don't even understand what she's talking about. At CyTech, she constantly explores possibilities within a holistic and futuristic framework. When it comes to getting results, she doggedly pursues her own logical pathways even when they appear intangible and impractical to others.

Morris Strandmeyer, 49, married for the second time with five children, has overseen production since the company came into existence five years ago. As a former Compaq Computer executive, Morris has brought a penchant for continuity and discipline to the free-spirited CyTech organization. Highly organized and decisive, he works hard to get the most out of the company's current strengths and capabilities. Morris usually advocates strong organizational policies and always prefers logical, well-planned approaches to address company issues and situations. A firm believer in control, he jealously guards the highly technical manufacturing process that produces the core elements of *PowerBase*'s revolutionary operating system. Morris believes that all organizations must drive toward consistency and predictability in order to realize the best results. When it comes to getting those results, he pursues short-term, tangible progress and frequently asks, "Can we actually achieve the expected results with our current assets and capabilities?"

Together with this diverse team of senior executives, you review CyTech's current situation. Within the last few years, new technologies, such as digital cellular phones and personal communications networks, have brought explosive growth to the wireless communications market. At the dawn of the cellular phone era, 15 years earlier, AT&T's market researchers predicted that by the turn of the century about 900,000 mobile phones would be in use in the United States. Today there are 20 times that number in use, and the turn of the century still lies a few years away. America's rapid adoption of cellular technology, a phenomenon now repeating itself around the globe, has created a $30 billion-plus industry. The giant companies in communications, computers, consumer electronics, and information services around the globe are attempting to dominate the burgeoning market by investing billions in technology development, acquisitions, marketing, and manufacturing. Driving this whirlwind of activity is the vision of "anytime, anywhere communication." The emerging hand-held phone-fax-computer hybrids are altering the way people live and work, permanently redefining the work place, the store, the library, the school, and every other institution. People can buy stocks while riding a train, order a pair of gloves from an electronic L. L. Bean catalog while sitting in a ski-lift chair, or look up a legal precedent from a computerized law library while reclining on a lounge chair in the backyard. When Apple Computer first introduced its new personal digital assistant, the *Newton,* analysts didn't believe that it would ever become a big hit, and the first *Newton* seemed to prove them right. However, when Apple's second-generation *PowerPad* hit the market simultaneously with AT&T's upgraded *EO Communicator,* IBM/Bell South's *Super Simon,* and other similar products from Motorola, Sony, and Matsushita, consumers fell in love with the devices and sales soared.

Today most analysts agree that the shift to wireless communications has become inevitable and irresistible, comparing the trend toward the phone-fax-computer to the earlier migrations from trains to airplanes or from main frames to PCs. As the variety of wireless communication products proliferates, observers have dubbed the next millennium "The Wireless Century." In addition to the staggering technological developments in recent years, two events have ignited the wireless communications market explosion and CyTech's phenomenal growth: the FCC's allocation of a broad radio spectrum for personal communications networks and the elimination of any health risk associated with the use of cellular technology. However, with a myriad of new and old competitors aggressively searching for new ways to improve computing power with advanced chip design, to redesign products for easier use, to add visual features, to enhance screen images, to upgrade printing quality, to cut costs, or to develop a variety of other features including voice-command systems and multimedia adaptations, the future possibilities all but boggle the mind. Deciding just how CyTech should organize itself to create its own future dominates your every thought as you take the helm at CyTech.

To set the stage for a series of discussions on this topic with your senior team, you circulate a well-known article from *Fortune Magazine* that discusses the new communications revolution and proposes five basic principles for success, which your own experience and study confirm:

- You can't say it often enough: don't lose touch with the customer.
- Even in a high-tech industry, management skills make more of a difference than technology.
- Today's successes often obscure the first signs of tomorrow's failure.
- The company with the highest unit volume almost always wins.
- You find unit volume at the bottom of the market, where low prices create new customers.

Over the next several weeks you conduct eight intense management meetings with your team in an effort to nail down CyTech's approach to its future. In open-ended discussions, your team delineates and debates all the latest organizational ideas, concepts, philosophies, processes, and programs until six major thrusts emerge as the most viable possibilities for CyTech. These range from radical revolution on one extreme to rather continuous improvement on the other:

1. A Classic Innovative Organization
2. A Synthesis of Best Practices
3. A Focus on Empowerment and Accountability
4. A Work Team Approach
5. A Reengineering of Work Processes
6. A Revolutionary New Perspective

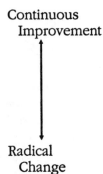

Continuous Improvement

Radical Change

You review each of these organizational possibilities in detail over several weeks, trying to decide which approach makes the most sense. Your decision will establish the pattern of your leadership, guide the company's organizational culture, and set the stage for success or failure. It's a tough call.

The *innovative organization,* which has gained a good deal of favor among certain organization-development theorists, ranks as one of seven major organizational forms in Henry Mintzberg's book *Mintzberg on Management.* In his book the McKinsey-award-winning author and McGill University business professor clearly explains the classic innovative organization: "Some people refer to this type [of organization] as high technology and to its basic orientation as intra-preneurship. Whereas the entrepreneurial configuration innovates from a central individual at the top, this one depends on a variety of people for its strategic initiatives." According to Mintzberg, the innovative organization is fluid, organic, and selectively decentralized to promote ad hocracy. With it an organization deploys functional experts in multidisciplinary teams of staff, operators, and managers to carry out innovative projects. Coordination in such organizations occurs by mutual adjustment encouraged by liaison personnel and by integrating managers through a matrix-style structure. Strategy gets developed through learning and grass-roots discussions and usually evolves through a variety of bottom-up processes. In general, management facilitates rather than dictates strategy. To promote innovation, the innovative organization relies on more democracy and less bureaucracy. Because this approach achieves effectiveness at the expense of efficiency, however, human problems associated with ambiguity can proliferate and lead to inappropriate transitions to other organizational configurations. According to Mintzberg, "This configuration is found in environments that are both dynamic and complex. A dynamic environment, being unpredictable, calls for organic structures; a complex one calls for decentralized structure. This configuration is the only type that provides both. Thus, we tend to find the innovative organization wherever these conditions prevail, ranging from guerilla warfare to space agencies. There appears to be no other way to fight a war in the jungle or to put the first man on the moon." This organizational solution most closely resembles CyTech's current approach and represents the least radical of the six options, building on traditional organizational theory that embraces the realities of dynamic markets and changing technologies.

The next option, a *synthesis of best practices,* while less traditional than the first, demands relatively little in the way of radical change because it represents a combination of tried and proven contemporary practices. To implement the option you could combine several "best in world" practices, possibly including Motorola's total quality management process, Xerox's systematic bench-marking, 3M's autonomy and decentralization, General Electric's process mapping and workout programs, Corning's training and development orientation, Wal-Mart's service philosophy, Hewlett Packard's work teams, and other proven practices dealing with quality, cost, service, and speed to market. This organizational approach would require an immediate and intense study of "best in world" practices. Over the course of several weeks, you could sift through all the best practices, searching for the ones that offer the greatest promise for CyTech. Thereafter, an ongoing search for and incorporation of "best in world" practices would permeate the corporate culture and drive CyTech's organizational change agenda. The best argument for this option stems from a belief that you can benefit from the accumulated knowledge and wisdom of outstanding organizations and management teams. You must assume that the state-of-the-art firms have reached an apex, and all you need now is to synthesize and refine what others have already done.

Near the middle of the spectrum of organizational choices lies a program of empowerment and accountability. Drawing on themes developed in the books *The Empowered Manager and Stewardship* by Peter Block and *The Oz Principle: Getting Results Through Individual and Organizational Accountability* by Roger Connors and Tom Smith, this organizational approach focuses on developing each individual and his or her productivity within the organization. According to Block, "The universal question is, how do we empower others? How do we get other people to take responsibility for their actions and our business? The answer is, you don't empower other people. You don't give other people their freedom. You don't legislate self-esteem. You begin with yourself. You cannot give to others what you have not claimed for yourself. Claim your autonomy, your vision; declare the organization you wish to create. Live that out at every moment. Then, and only then, make it easy for others to do the same." Connors and Smith add that "a thin line separates success from failure, the great companies from the ordinary ones. Below that line lies excuse making, blaming others, confusion, and an attitude of helplessness, while above that line lies a sense of reality, ownership, commitment, solutions to problems, and determined action. While losers languish below the line, preparing stories that explain why past efforts went awry, winners reside above the line, powered by commitment and smart work." Implementation of this option would require getting 20,000 CyTech employees worldwide operating as accountable individuals. By combining empowerment with accountability, this option would ideally turn every manager within the CyTech organization into an empowering leader capable of tapping the talents of every employee, helping each to maintain individual accountability for results and to achieve peak performance. According to Jack Welch, CEO of General Electric, as recorded in the influential book *Control Your Own Destiny or Someone Else Will: How Jack Welch Is Making General Electric the World's Most Competitive Company*, "If you're not thinking all the time about making every person more valuable, you don't have a chance."

The next alternative, a *work team* approach, also lies near the center of the spectrum of choices, though it does imply a bit more radical change. John Katzenbach and Douglas Smith, two McKinsey consultants and authors of *The Wisdom of Teams*, describe how teams are transforming many American organizations into high-productivity work environments. And a group of Zenger-Miller principals, led by John Zenger, authors of *Leading Teams*, show people how to implement the new management by moving from traditional hierarchical leadership to team leadership. According to an American

Society for Training and Development executive survey, 230 human resource executives indicated that increased organizational emphasis on teams made big differences in performance and results: productivity increased in 77 percent of the respondents' companies, quality improvements due to teamwork occurred in 72 percent, waste declined in 55 percent, job satisfaction rose in 65 percent, and customer satisfaction improved in 57 percent. *Fortune* magazine recently reported that productivity increased 40 to 50 percent at General Mills plants using teams compared to zero increases at plants not using teams. In another example cited in an article from *Training and Development,* written by Anthony Montebello and Victor Buzzotta, a division of 3M that formed a network of cross-functional teams to develop new products became one of the company's most innovative and fastest growing divisions. The same article indicates that teams at one of Ingersol Rand's manufacturing plants reduced scrap from 15 percent to 3 percent. According to Montebello and Buzzotta, "Many thinking executives have concluded that, given today's productivity and quality objectives, traditional job designs oversimplify the work process. They found that changing the traditional structure, in which employees perform specialized job functions, to a team structure, in which team members share a core of functions, improves efficiencies and effectiveness." If CyTech pursues this solution, the company must move through four stages of team development: (1) cautious affiliation, during which team members assess each one another's abilities and attitudes and then try to determine how and where they fit, (2) competitiveness, where the team often gets frustrated with progress because of the gap between expectations and reality and begins pointing fingers and suffering strained relationships, (3) harmonious cohesiveness, in which members of the team actually find that they enjoy being part of the team and realize that they can accomplish much more as a group than as individuals, and (4) collaborative team work, where the group truly becomes a team that makes decisions about tasks and processes, solves problems, and initiates change. Clearly, the process would take time, and it would require a fairly major change in CyTech's existing organizational structure.

The fifth potential organizational solution, a *reengineering of work processes,* would apply the philosophies of recently popular business books, including *Re-Engineering the Corporation: A Mani-*

festo for Business Revolution by Michael Hammer and James Champy, and *Liberation Management: Necessary Disorganization for the Nanosecond Nineties* by Tom Peters. The authors of these books proclaim the need for a brand new way of doing things, a real departure from all the traditional organization and management theories and practices. According to Hammer and Champy, Adam Smith's idea about breaking down industrial work into simple and basic tasks has out-grown its usefulness in the post-industrial age which requires the reunifying of basic tasks into coherent *business processes*. At the heart of this organizational solution rests a simple idea: that an organization must rethink and redesign all its processes in fundamental, radical, dramatic, and revolutionary ways, basically a "start from scratch" approach to organization development. Hammer and Champy argue, "Today's airlines, steel mills, accounting firms, and computer chip makers have all been built around Adam Smith's central idea—the division or specialization of labor and the consequent fragmentation of work. The larger the organization, the more specialized is the work and the more separate steps into which the work is fragmented. This rule applies not only to manufacturing jobs. Insurance companies, for instance, typically assign separate clerks to process each line of a standardized form. They then pass the form to another clerk, who processes the next line. These workers never complete a job; they just perform piecemeal tasks." This outmoded method of work must change, argue the authors: "The reality that organizations have to confront is that the old ways of doing business simply don't work anymore. In today's environment, nothing is constant or predictable—not market growth, customer demand, product life-cycles, the rate of technological change, or the nature of competition. The overall process of producing or delivering a good or service inevitably has become increasingly complicated, and managing such processes has become more difficult. The time has come, then, to retire those principles and adopt a new set we call re-engineering." According to this line of thinking, if people in organizations do not see the whole picture, they cannot address the necessary processes. Most workers tend to lose sight of the larger picture while focusing myopically on their individual tasks. Changing that tendency would require CyTech to rethink and redesign everything it does. That, of course, would be a more massive undertaking than the preceding options.

The final choice, a *revolutionary new perspective,* represents the most radical possibility. Here, you assume that modern organizations have traveled upward on a single "S"-shaped learning curve that began in the late 1800s and reached its peak in the 1900s. Now, many organizations are beginning to decline as they frantically attempt to combine, integrate, and balance the many aspects of managerial thought and practice accumulated over the 100-year-old learning curve. If so, success in the future depends on embarking on a whole a new learning curve, abandoning everything on the current curve, including a reengineering of existing work processes. The new curve must represent a totally new and different conception of individual and collective work. Moving far beyond reengineering processes or any of the other organizational options, the new curve, to be conceived by your management team, would focus on identifying and deploying motivations. Whereas the last 100-year learning curve focused on controlling, influencing, and directing action, the next 100-year curve should encompass identifying, developing and deploying desires, the natural desires of individuals. Using the book, *Powershift* by Alvin Toffler as a catalyst for their thinking, the conceptual giants on your management team, Bob Kiechel, Nan Thurow, and Karen Walsh, might develop such a new learning curve. Can your people identify, test, shape, educate, facilitate, and deploy your people's motivations in concert with other similarly motivated people to achieve a new kind of alignment based on inherent common purpose, as opposed to managed, engineered, or contrived common purpose? This organizational solution would move beyond humanism, individualism, and behaviorism to the core concepts of knowledge, beliefs, and attributes, with individual motivation as its core principle. Implementing this option would require a fundamental change in the way people think about and perceive everything that goes on at CyTech.

Having mulled over and discussed each of these six organizational approaches in detail over several weeks, you grow more and more anxious to make a decision that will set the wheels in motion. Three months have elapsed since you took over, and the board has grown impatient for you to choose an organizational direction and agenda. To facilitate your decision making, you and your senior team summarize the strengths and weaknesses of each of the six organizational approaches, as follows:

Alternative Organizational Approaches	Strengths	Weaknesses
A Classic Innovative Organization	Easy to implement Requires minor change Allows for evolutionary development	Too traditional and conventional Ignores inefficiencies Still too bureaucratic
A Synthesis of Best Practices	Draws on proven practices Focuses on "best in world" Combines the best of the best	Looks to the past and present, not future Relies on successes of other organizations Assumes synthesis of practices can work Costly to implement
A Focus on Empowerment and Accountability	Gives people more power to act Makes people more accountable for results Doesn't require massive reorganization	Depends too much on individual education and motivation Too soft and fuzzy Takes too long to produce results
A Work Team Approach	Reduces need for elaborate hierarchies Improves communication and productivity Addresses complexity of CyTech's organization	May represent nothing more than a passing fad Not everyone can or should work in a team Too indirect and abstract Work teams don't necessarily guarantee improved performance
A Reengineering of Work Processes	Discards old, worn-out practices Promotes whole-picture view Redesigns everything to meet twenty-first-century challenges	Too theoretical Turns the organization upside down Too little evidence of results
A Revolutionary New Perspective	A truly revolutionary approach Far-sighted solution Anticipates the near future and beyond	Too outlandish and off the wall Too idealistic and impractical, unimplementable Untried and unproven

Not surprisingly, given their diversity and individuality, your senior team cannot reach a consensus. In fact, each member of your team champions a different alternative. Since you respect them so much, you find yourself moved by their eloquent arguments. Hal McPhee favors the classic innovative organization; Morris Strandmeyer feels most comfortable with a synthesis of best practices; John Solo prefers a focus on empowerment and accountability; Nan Thurow would love to adopt work teams; Bob Kiechel argues aggressively for reengineering work processes; and Karen Walsh feels energized by the challenge of formulating a revolutionary new perspective. Each member of the team expresses a willingness to compromise, to a certain degree, provided the chosen path reflects his or her own preferences. Obviously, you will not be able to satisfy everyone because one and only one of the six alternatives should drive change at CyTech.

During a three-day retreat at Pebble Beach, California, each member of your team summarizes his or her ideas, then, one by one, each yields the final decision to you. However, before you make your decision, you ask your senior team to review two more items. First, you hand out copies of another highly regarded *Fortune* magazine article written by executive editor Walter Kiechel III entitled, "How We Will Work in the Year 2000"; then you circulate an industry white paper by futurist George Gilder, *Life After Television: The Coming Transformation of Media and American Life*, published in book form by Norton & Company. In the *Fortune* article, Kiechel identifies six trends that will reshape the work place: (1) the average company will become smaller, employing fewer people; (2) the traditional hierarchical organization will give way to a variety of organizational forms, the network of specialists foremost among these; (3) technicians, ranging from computer repairmen to radiation therapists, will replace manufacturing operatives as the worker elite; (4) the vertical division of labor will be replaced by a horizontal division; (5) the paradigm of doing business will shift from making a product to providing a service; and (6) work itself will be redefined as constant learning with more high-order thinking and less nine-to-five clock-punching.

In *Life After Television*, Gilder claims that the United States "has only to unleash its industrial resources to command the tele-future, in which new technology will overthrow the stultifying influence of mass media, renew the power of individuals, and promote democracy throughout the world." You ask your senior team to think about these issues as preparation for aligning themselves behind whichever alternative you select. You promise that you will make your decision within the next two weeks, and you urge each of your executives to give you any additional input privately. Over the next two weeks, John, Bob, Hal, Nan, Karen, and Morris each approach you to lobby for their respective position, convincing you that they each genuinely want the best possible future for the company. Nothing new comes to your attention except the fact that each of your people will react to your ultimate decision more "flexibly" than their public arguments may have indicated. It's clear everyone is waiting for you to exert your leadership. Now you must make your first major, and possibly your most important, decision as CEO of CyTech.

- *If you choose to build a classic innovative organization, turn to Chapter 2.*

- *If you prefer a synthesis of best practices, turn to Chapter 14.*

- *If you decide to focus on empowerment and accountability, turn to Chapter 26.*

- *If you find yourself drawn to work teams, turn to Chapter 38.*

- *If you opt to reengineer work processes, turn to Chapter 50.*

- *If you wish to formulate a revolutionary new perspective, turn to Chapter 62.*

Having chosen the organizational option that requires the least wrenching changes for CyTech, you call your senior team together to discuss building a classic innovative organization structure. When you sense some hesitation from the future-minded Karen Walsh and the always inventive Bob Kiechel, you decide to explain your logic more fully than you had planned: "Remember, the innovative organization approach, as we've discussed, represents a highly organic structure. There's little formalization here. It will allow us to strengthen our emphasis on project teams, particularly cross-functional teams, and help all of our managers act more like integrators and coordinators. In addition, it will provide more staff support to the operating groups, something I know we can do more effectively than we have in the past. We can't rely on any standardized form of coordination, and we must avoid the encroachment of administrative bureaucracy as we implement this structure. In particular, I want to make sure we avoid any sharp divisions of labor or severe organizational unit differentiation, because any highly formalized behaviors will undermine our efforts to constantly innovate. This organizational approach cannot emphasize planning or control, which should make some of you very happy."

2

BUILDING A CLASSIC INNOVATIVE ORGANIZATION

Bob Kiechel shakes his head. "I must admit you've really surprised me. I expected you to land somewhere in the middle or more toward the radical end. Instead, you've chosen the path of least resistance. I'm confused." Nan nods her agreement.

Though you hesitate momentarily, wondering whether you should expose your deepest thoughts and feelings about this decision, you quickly decide to put all your cards on the table. "First of all, I don't believe we should throw away everything we've learned in the last hundred years about management and organization. Why reinvent the wheel? Instead, I think we should simply modify our current organizational structure to incorporate principles of the classic innovative organization because those principles will enable us to meet the needs of our rapidly changing environment, industry, and marketplace. We could waste months trying to reengineer or invent some new kind of organization, each day losing our position in the marketplace, neglecting our customers, and squandering our current strengths. Look, we know our business, and I don't want to overcomplicate things by spending a lot of time worrying about structure and process. Also, my gut tells me that we're better off at one extreme or the other, and, frankly, I'm not ready to risk the future of this company on some unproven fad or radical new perspective. I'm not interested in using CyTech as an experimental guinea pig for the rest of the industry and corporate America. If a company really could reinvent the wheel, it might reap huge dividends, but that's not our business right now. Let's take advantage of what we have already learned about management and organization at CyTech, making sure we allow for sufficient innovation to move us forward and more fully satisfy our customers' needs now and in the future."

John Solo, the executive vice president for worldwide sales and marketing who hates planning and favored the empowerment and accountability option, responds, "People, let's remember that of all the options we've weighed, the innovative organization requires the least change, but it still excludes excessive planning and control. This approach will give us plenty of flexibility and informality while still allowing us to focus on what's really important: meeting the needs of our customers."

When you finally ask your senior team to support your decision, they all indicate that they can, though Bob and Nan seem, judging by the looks on their faces, less than thrilled to do so. During the next six months, you take several steps to implement the innovative organizational structure with a number of rather important changes. Ad hocracy, the notion that ideas can and should emerge from the ranks of those closest to the customer, becomes the new corporate buzz word, and support staff throughout CyTech emerge as the premier players in the firm's ongoing operations as they organize project teams, set schedules, and communicate and coordinate with other project teams, task forces, and functional entities. In order to minimize the boundaries that often develop between projects and functions, you work hard to blend administrative and operating work into a single effort. Integrative managers, nicknamed "border guards" and the front-line leaders among support staff, begin to form the new power elite in the new organization, keeping channels of communications and coordination open and making sure no one establishes unnecessary boundaries. At the same time, the marketplace heats up as competitors develop new features for their own phone-fax-computers. A Japanese competitor, Tanji, substantially improves its product's fax capabilities by increasing electronic storage to 100 pages, AT&T develops a new powerful chip to enhance its next generation of *EO Communicators*, and IBM announces the imminent introduction of a multimedia, CD-ROM version of the phone-fax-computer, also using a more powerful chip. All the while, CyTech has been working feverishly to improve *PowerBase*'s design and screen image and to add a CD-ROM port. However, as a host of new competitors enter the market with astonishing new product developments, you find yourself losing sleep at night. While the board seems happy with your performance and CyTech's new innovative organizational approach, some members of your senior team increasingly call your attention to the coming mass market, which argues for less focus on innovation and more attention to production and sales.

In a day-long management meeting, Hal McPhee, your chief financial officer, pulls out his latest analysis of CyTech and its competitors, identifying the strong growth in sales for each company and extrapolating trends to project a huge mass market where volume of production, operational efficiencies, and aggressive marketing and sales will win the day. He argues that given the rapidly evolving marketplace CyTech should be moving more toward what he calls a "Mass-Market Organization," requiring more formalized procedures, division of labor, functional groupings, and a more clearly established hierarchy. "We need more standardization of work around here if we're going to come out on top," insists McPhee.

Karen Walsh counters, "That's exactly the kind of organizational structure we've been trying to avoid. In fact, you argued for the innovative organizational choice from the beginning. Why are you changing your mind?" *

McPhee rebuts, "I'm not changing, the market's changing. We're very rapidly moving from a high-growth, high-innovation environment to a maturing mass market one. We must respond accordingly and that means turning our innovative organizational approach into a mass marketing and producing structure."

This debate rages for over an hour, with other members of the team adding their voices. At the end of the day, you ask everyone to come back in one week with recommendations for CyTech's next steps.

It's been 14 months since you assumed the reigns, and CyTech has certainly made impressive progress, but you do recognize the onrushing mass market and wonder how CyTech should respond. At year's end, CyTech's sales reach $5.4 billion and the stock price climbs to 32 ^{1}/16, as shown in the following table:

Selected Financial and Stock Information
(Dollars in millions, except stock price in actual dollars)

	Year ended March 31	
	First Year	Previous Year
Sales	$5,435	$4,083
Profits	326	242
Profits as a % of:		
Sales	6%	6%
Assets	10%	9%
Common Equity*	19%	17%
Market Value**	8265	6123
Stock Price	32 ^{1}/16	23 ^{3}/4

* Total stockholders' equity includes capital stock, surplus, and retained earnings at the company's year end. For purposes of determining profits as a percent of common stockholders' equity, all preferred stock is excluded.
** Calculated by multiplying the number of common shares outstanding by the price per common share as of March 31.

Early in April, you hold a "mass market summit meeting," during which three new organizational alternatives emerge from your senior team. One suggests constructing a mass market organization that would focus on standardizing work and more greatly formalizing tasks and functions, in general moving the organization toward a more traditional, hierarchical structure. Hal McPhee, CFO, and Morris Strandmeyer, VP of production, particularly like this alternative.

The next possibility, put forth by Karen Walsh, VP of the advanced technology lab, and Bob Kiechel, senior VP of product development, suggests a more horizontal organization, one that achieves the purest form of decentralization wherein individuals can decide and act for the overall good of the organization. Such a structure would maintain the philosophy of continuous innovation and product breakthroughs as the dominant force within CyTech, regardless of what mass marketing opportunities materialize. Karen argues that CyTech should, first and foremost, remain on the razor's edge of research and development, and any full-blown attempt to convert the company into a mass market organization could destroy that position overnight. "Besides," she concludes, "the mass market idea is an illusion. There aren't any mass markets, just lots of micromarkets."

The third alternative, presented and supported by Nan Thurow, senior VP of worldwide operations, and John Solo, executive VP of worldwide sales and marketing, recommends staying with the innovative organizational form while working to streamline some aspects of the organization to obtain additional efficiencies, but carefully avoiding the danger of reverting to a more bureaucratic form. They argue that CyTech has done an excellent job with continuous innovation, steadily devising new product developments to keep *Power-Base* ahead of the pack.

After weeks of discussion, the positions of your management team don't change, with two still favoring the mass market organization, two preferring the horizontal structure, and two wanting to maintain the current course. Once again, it's your call. To help clarify the pros and cons of each alternative, you create the chart on page 22.

The moment of truth has arrived. What will you do?

- *If you decide to move CyTech toward a mass market organization, turn to Chapter 3.*

- *If you want to adopt a horizontal form of organization, turn to Chapter 4.*

- *If you choose to remain with the current innovative organization structure, turn to Chapter 5.*

	Coordinating Mechanism	Key Aspect of the Organization	Type of Decentralization	Advantages	Disadvantages
Mass Market Organization	Standardization of Work Processes	Techno-Structure	Limited Horizontal Decentralization	Mass Market Efficiency	Bureaucratic Red Tape
Horizontal Organization	Standardization of Norms	Ideology (of innovation)	Highly Decentralized	Continuous Innovation	Inability to Fully Exploit Breaktroughs
Innovative Organization	Mutual Adjustment	Support Staff	Selected Decentralization	Integration	Inefficiency

Not surprisingly, Hal McPhee, your chief financial officer, and Morris Strandmeyer, your vice president of production, enthusiastically endorse your decision and assume aggressive roles in selling the idea to the rest of the senior team. At an early morning staff meeting, Hal exclaims, "Of course the mass market organization has gotten a lot of flak because people associate it with bureaucratic red tape, rigidity, and control, but that's all stereotypical. Just look at McDonald's, Levi's, the Swiss Railroad, and Blockbuster Video. They make it work in the mass market. Their organizations meet the needs of mass customers, day in and day out, without skipping a beat. That's where our market is going."

3

MOVING TOWARD A MASS MARKET ORGANIZATION

Then Morris Strandmeyer applauds Hal's point, adding, "Look, we're not going back to Max Weber's or Frederick Taylor's narrow, scientific definitions of the machine organization that emerged in the early 1900s. We don't want to dehumanize our workers or treat them like interchangeable parts, but this organization does need to function more like a mass production and marketing machine to take advantage of the enormous opportunities coming our way."

Once again, when you ask for full support of this decision from all your senior team members, they concur on the surface, yet you know that not everyone feels good about moving in this direction. Within two months, your misgivings are proven accurate when Karen Walsh and Bob Kiechel leave CyTech to form their own company funded by Ross Perot to the tune of $50 million. Devastated by the blow, the board of directors raise their first serious questions about your competence and begin scrutinizing your decision to move toward a mass market organization. However, within 90 days of Walsh's and Kiechel's departure, a raging price war, ignited by a few foreign competitors, drops the price of phone-fax-computers to below $500. A frenzy sweeps through the marketplace as consumers throughout the world scramble to buy *PowerBases, PowerPads, EO Communicators,* and other personal computing and communicating products. Thankfully, CyTech's installation of new work procedures, operational standardization, and cost-conscious out-sourcing contribute greatly to the company's successful response to this predicted turn of events. In fact, because CyTech has increased production, streamlined supplier relationships, and disciplined its marketing and sales effort, *PowerBase 3,* the company's third-generation phone-fax-computer, soon becomes the number one product in the market, with a 32 percent market share. In addition, your competitive intelligence suggests that *PowerBase 3* generates more profit than AT&T's or Motorola's latest rivals.

The numbers quickly cause the board of directors to forget about the departures of Kiechel and Walsh and to praise you for your wise leadership. At the end of your second year as CEO, CyTech's stock climbs to $51 as the company grows to over $8 billion in annual revenues, as shown in the following table:

Selected Financial and Stock Information
(Dollars in millions, except stock price in actual dollars)

	Year ended March 31	
	2nd Year	1st Year
Sales	$8,061	$5,435
Profits	564	326
Profits as a % of:		
Sales	7%	6%
Assets	12%	10%
Common Equity*	28%	19%
Market Value**	13,128	8,265
Stock Price	51 $\frac{1}{4}$	32 $\frac{1}{16}$

* Total stockholders' equity includes capital stock, surplus, and retained earnings at the company's year end. For purposes of determining profits as a percent of common stockholders' equity, all preferred stock is excluded.

** Calculated by multiplying the number of common shares outstanding by the price per common share as of March 31.

However, a nagging concern grows inside you as you watch CyTech grow more and more focused on operational efficiency and sales maximization and less concerned with innovation and product development. While you foresaw and took this risk, you now begin to realize how much of CyTech's innovating life blood has seeped away. Many of the people who worked for the innovative and future-minded departed executives have also jumped ship during the last several months, some to join the new Kiechel-Walsh venture, others to work for smaller companies more dedicated to product development. You suppress a chilling fear that one of these nimble competitors will come up with a product breakthrough that will knock CyTech off its number one perch before you can reignite CyTech's new product fires.

As the months roll on, CyTech's market dominance mounts but does nothing to abate the chilling fear inside. As you hear rumors of one competitor after another preparing monumental break-throughs, you begin to feel downright paranoid. However, CyTech's sales success intoxicates you, enough to lull you into a false, though euphoric, sense of security. CyTech's PR department does such a wonderful job communicating the consumer benefits of *PowerBase 5*, the company's latest generation of products, only slightly modi-fied from *PowerBase 4*, that it easily becomes the world's premier phone-fax-computer. Its market share increases to 48 percent, convincing most people inside CyTech that the company can do nothing wrong. Hal McPhee goes so far as to predict that even a smashing product breakthrough won't displace CyTech as the phone-fax-computer leader: "We're just too big and strong," he boasts. Although you inwardly discount McPhee's cockiness, his words do make it easier for you to suppress the chilling fear, especially when year-end results hit Wall Street. CyTech's year-end results win front page coverage in *The Wall Street Journal*, which interviews both you and Hal McPhee. When your picture appears on the cover of *Fortune,* the board of directors exults over the company's performance, especially the $91 price of its stock. The table on page 26 summarizes CyTech's success.

At the beginning of your fourth year as CEO, your worst fear finally materializes when Bob Kiechel and Karen Walsh's company, VIP Systems, introduces a voice-operated phone-fax-computer. The same media that heaped such accolades on CyTech now proclaims

Selected Financial and Stock Information
(Dollars in millions, except stock price in actual dollars)

	Year ended March 31	
	3rd Year	2nd Year
Sales	$12,672	$8,061
Profits	1,014	403
Profits as a % of:		
Sales	8%	5%
Assets	15%	9%
Common Equity*	31%	17%
Market Value**	23,688	13,128
Stock Price	90 ⅞	51 ¼

* Total stockholders' equity includes capital stock, surplus, and retained earnings at the company's year end. For purposes of determining profits as a percent of common stockholders' equity, all preferred stock is excluded.

** Calculated by multiplying the number of common shares outstanding by the price per common share as of March 31.

the VIP product as the breakthrough of the century, one that will change the life of every human being in the world. VIP's product, *Voicepower 1*, runs on a new, high-powered Intel chip with the capacity to operate a 50,000 word vocabulary-recognition program in 20 different languages with immediate translation. Once the purchaser has worked through a voice-testing exercise that takes less than an hour, he or she can count on 99 percent voice recognition. *Voicepower 1* sells for $1,000, almost double the price of *PowerBase 5*, but it immediately takes the market by storm, stalling CyTech's *PowerBase 5* sales almost overnight. As a result, at mid-year, CyTech's stock plummets from $91 to $11 a share, a loss in market value of over $20 billion.

    With no concrete plans for product breakthroughs on the drawing board and insufficient in-house expertise to match VIP's breakthrough, CyTech cannot recover in the foreseeable future. To appease disgruntled shareholders, CyTech's board of directors asks for your resignation, which you submit without argument.

- *You may have been able to make the mass market innovative organizational approach work in real life, avoiding the loss of CyTech's innovation capabilities; however, if you'd like to discover why the author considers other approaches more preferable, turn to Chapter 4 or 5.*

- *If you would like to choose one of the other primary alternatives identified at the end of Chapter 1, turn to one of the following:*

  Chapter 14, Developing a Synthesis of Best Practices;

  Chapter 26, Imbuing the Culture with Empowerment and Accountability;

  Chapter 38, Pursuing a Work-Team Approach;

  Chapter 50, Reengineering Work Processes; or

  Chapter 62, Embracing a Revolutionary New Perspective.

Expressing their surprise at your decision, Bob Kiechel, senior VP of product development, and Karen Walsh, VP of the advanced technology lab, also seem elated over the opportunity to create a more horizontal organization. These two creative and forward-looking executives firmly believe CyTech must evolve into a more committed and entrenched innovator. Never really comfortable with the more conventional forms of organization, Bob and Karen consider the horizontal organization appropriate because it maximizes decentralization, depends on cultural norms, and, most important, enshrines the ideology of innovation. Had you not selected this option, the two could very well have left the company for an environment more to their liking. You're glad to have won their enthusiastic support.

4

ADOPTING A HORIZONTAL ORGANIZATION

Nevertheless, you point out in a management meeting that the board of directors will find it hard to let go of the short-term profits a mass market organization would likely produce, but reiterate your belief that CyTech must, at all costs, remain on the innovation edge. You reassure your senior team that you can manage the expectations of the board and the company's shareholders.

Hal McPhee, CFO, and Morris Strandmeyer, VP of production, raise their predictable objections, observing that "horizontal organizations don't belong in the high-tech industry. This is a manufacturing business, not a service company or some nonprofit institution."

You respond by saying, "That's precisely why making innovation the driving force and unifying ideology at CyTech makes so much sense. We will do something that no other competitor in our industry has fully accomplished. When every activity here revolves around innovation and product development, regardless of people's locations, the nature of their functions, or their daily tasks, we will have built an organizational culture capable of sustaining an innovation advantage indefinitely. That's what I want."

Long arguments ensue during management meetings over the next several weeks, as McPhee and Strandmeyer remain steadfastly opposed to your decision. When you find out that Hal McPhee has gone directly to members of the board of directors to question your decision, you ask for his resignation. You're not surprised, however, when McPhee appeals to the board for redress. At the next board meeting you communicate your rationale behind adopting a horizontal organization with a constant emphasis on innovation and product development: "Innovation built this company, and the horizontal organization will keep us moving in the right direction." You inform the board that several competitors are working on a variety of breakthroughs that will drastically change the market and industry, making it imperative that CyTech move decisively to become the innovation leader in the industry. The board accepts your arguments and agrees with your decision to remove Hal McPhee.

In the months that follow, every part of the CyTech organization redefines job descriptions, mission statements, and budgets to support product development. As a natural consequence, sales begin to slow, but you reassure the board that the slowdown represents a short-term, but temporary, price that CyTech must pay to assume the undisputed role of innovation leader in the market. As a number of promising R&D projects gain momentum, Karen Walsh reports that within 15 months her lab will unveil a major breakthrough in voice-operated phone-fax-computers.

To your surprise, however, after only four months of aggressively implementing the horizontal organization, a bitter price war initiated by a group of foreign competitors squeezes CyTech's profit margins to zero. This development panics the board, which asks for you to refocus on sales and marketing. Unwilling to abandon your strategy, however, you oppose the board, urging them to take a longer-term view. Your appeal falls on deaf ears, and when word of the conflict between you and the board leaks to the press, CyTech's stock price takes a nosedive. The table on the next page summarizes CyTech's performance for the first six months of the year.

Selected Financial and Stock Information
(Dollars in millions, except stock price in actual dollars)

	Year ended March 31	
	2nd Year (6 months only)	1st Year
Sales	$2,692	$5,435
Profits	135	326
Profits as a % of:		
Sales	5%	6%
Assets	9%	10%
Common Equity*	17%	19%
Market Value**	2,295	8,265
Stock Price	8 $\frac{7}{8}$	32 $\frac{1}{16}$

* Total stockholders' equity includes capital stock, surplus, and retained earnings at the company's year end. For purposes of determining profits as a percent of common stockholders' equity, all preferred stock is excluded.

** Calculated by multiplying the number of common shares outstanding by the price per common share as of March 31.

After reviewing these figures, the board asks for your immediate resignation. You cannot believe what's happening, but you have no choice but to comply with the board's wishes. To your chagrin, Hal McPhee replaces you as CEO of CyTech.

- *You may have been able to make the horizontal organization work in real life, but CyTech's board simply could not live with short-term losses in sales and profits. Any change in organization now would have taken too long to satisfy their demands. If you would like to discover the option that the author considers to be most viable in this situation, turn to Chapter 3 or 5.*

- *If you would like to try your hand at one of the other alternatives at the end of Chapter 1, turn to one of the following:*

    Chapter 14, Developing a Synthesis of Best Practices;

Chapter 26, Imbuing the Culture with Empowerment and Accountability;
Chapter 38, Pursuing a Work Team Approach;
Chapter 50, Reengineering Work Processes; or
Chapter 62, Embracing a Revolutionary New Perspective.

Your decision to remain with the innovative organizational form elicits a certain amount of respect from your senior team as they perceive temperance and seasoning in your decision making. All of them agree that maintaining the innovative organization approach should prevent potential vulnerability from the lost capabilities that could occur if you chose either the mass market or horizontal organization approaches. The mass market organization could never foster the necessary innovation for CyTech to remain ahead of competitors in the long term, and the horizontal organization could never sufficiently exploit all the marketing opportunities created by CyTech's future breakthroughs. Remaining with the innovative organizational form, pushing it forward to the next phase of development, seems the most logical step. You appreciate the alignment of your senior team behind this decision and begin thinking long and hard about the next phase of evolutionary development for your current form of organization.

5

STICKING WITH THE INNOVATIVE ORGANIZATION

Reviewing author Bob Waterman's ideas in his book *Ad Hocracy,* you conclude that the notion of allowing decisions and options to flow from those closest to the customer should guide CyTech's organizational culture development in coming years. However, your new focus on ad hocracy gets tested much sooner than you expected as CyTech finds itself immersed in a price war initiated by a group of foreign competitors who have dropped the price of their phone-fax-computers below $500. Fortunately, CyTech possesses the flexibility and vision to respond immediately by forming several *ad hoc* cross-functional teams to examine issues of production, supplier practices, marketing, distribution, and sales. Acting on

33

recommendations from the *ad hoc* teams, CyTech moves quickly to cut its production costs, improve supplier efficiencies, and beef up selected marketing and sales capabilities.

As sales escalate during the price war, CyTech holds its own against competitors and manages to keep profits constant as a percent of sales. CyTech's stock increases from $32 to $45 per share as you conclude your second year as CEO of CyTech.

Selected Financial and Stock Information
(Dollars in millions, except stock price in actual dollars)

	Year ended March 31	
	2nd Year	1st Year
Sales	$7,648	$5,435
Profits	458	326
Profits as a % of:		
Sales	6%	6%
Assets	11%	10%
Common Equity*	20%	19%
Market Value**	11,475	8,265
Stock Price	44 $^{15}/_{16}$	32 $^{1}/_{16}$

* Total stockholders' equity includes capital stock, surplus, and retained earnings at the company's year end. For purposes of determining profits as a percent of common stockholders' equity, all preferred stock is excluded.
** Calculated by multiplying the number of common shares outstanding by the price per common share as of March 31.

Pleased with your performance, the board of directors congratulates you on successfully walking that fine line between too much organization and too little organization. However, you continue looking for ways to strengthen CyTech's innovative organizational form and its ad hocracy culture. One way to do so might involve separating the operating core of the company from the administrative component to allow for even more ad hocracy in administrative support while maintaining continuity and consistency in production, distribution, and sales. The additional administrative ad hocracy could allow for greater flexibility in deploying cross-functional teams to deal with crucial issues, problems, and changes. In addition to providing administrative ad hocracy, the slightly increased standardization in core operations could facilitate the sort of efficiencies needed for the company to win the price war game.

Another gambit could formally separate product development from all other activities, with the aim of strengthening innovation while disciplining other operations. This would allow the production, distribution, marketing, and sales side of the business to transition toward a mass market organization capable of delivering more efficiencies, while enabling the product development side to adopt a horizontal organization that could create even greater innovation. Earlier you had discarded both these organizational approaches for CyTech as a whole, but a year ago you had not seriously considered separating the company into two major divisions. Now, maybe you should.

Yet a third way to strengthen CyTech's innovative form would involve simply promoting greater levels of flexibility and ad hocracy throughout the organization. This approach poses a problem, however, because the tendency toward bureaucracy grows exponentially with increasing size. Given CyTech's explosive growth, just keeping ad hocracy at its current level will prove difficult. Increasing it could prove impossible.

As you consider these three alternatives, you seek input from your senior management team and with their aid create a chart to help you assess the strengths and weaknesses of each possibility.

Alternative	Strengths	Weaknesses
Separate core operations from administrative support	Allows for more ad hocracy in administration and more standardization in operations	Creates discontinuity between administration and opertions
Separate product development from other operations	Facilitates both innovation and mass production/ marketing	Destroys the flow from product development to production, marketing, distribution, and sales
Increase ad hocracy throughout the organization	Fosters integration and coordination	Becomes more difficult as the orgnization grows ever larger

Your senior team expresses the usual ambivalence over the three alternatives, half-heartedly arguing for one alternative one day, and another the next. You hesitate to embroil them in further discussion since the price war has placed great strain on everybody. Since the strain has taken a toll on you as well, you decide to postpone your decision until after your vacation.

While on vacation in Santa Fe, New Mexico, you leisurely pick up Monday's *Wall Street Journal* to see what's going on. As chance would have it, you read about a company called Thermo Electron, a $1.2 billion diversified technology company, which started out as a small laboratory instrument manufacturer but has used an innovative organizational approach to turn itself into a highly diversified technology factory. Relaxed and reflective, you see a bright possibility in the Thermo Electron story. According to the article, "What fuels Thermo's fertile hothouse for new businesses is its novel equity structure. It is designed like a solar system with planets orbiting a core. When a manager or engineer invents something or finds a new market for technology, Thermo often creates a whole new company in a strategy it calls a 'spin-out.' This strategy differs from the widely used 'spin-off' in two ways: Thermo always retains a majority of the equity in the new company, and, in contrast to a spin-off distribution of stock to existing shareholders, it offers new stock to the public."

In the years ahead, CyTech should develop many new products and exploit their market opportunities to the fullest, and that goal mandates that you adopt an organizational approach that can promote the spin-out of these business opportunities with as much effectiveness and profitability as possible. Thermo Electron seems to have perfected the art of fueling the entrepreneurial engine to motivate employees, maintain very high levels of productivity, and grow new businesses like crazy.

With Thermo Electron in mind, you review, once again, the three alternatives for strengthening CyTech's current organizational thrust. Now you have found another option, the spin-out strategy. Though frustrated by the fact that none of the earlier alternatives has fully captured your imagination, you try to contain your impulsive excitement over Thermo Electron's approach. Sleep on it, you tell yourself.

Over the next few months you continue mulling over the possibilities, but make no changes. The demands of the price war consume most of your thinking and decision making, but you know you'll have to make a move shortly after year's end.

As you complete your third year as CEO of CyTech, the results look good, but not great.

Selected Financial and Stock Information
(Dollars in millions, except stock price in actual dollars)

	Year ended March 31	
	3rd Year	2nd Year
Sales	$8,526	$7,648
Profits	426	458
Profits as a % of:		
Sales	5%	6%
Assets	10%	11%
Common Equity*	18%	20%
Market Value**	10,971	11,475
Stock Price	43 ¼	44 ^{15}⁄₁₆

* Total stockholders' equity includes capital stock, surplus, and retained earnings at the company's year end. For purposes of determining profits as a percent of common stockholders' equity, all preferred stock is excluded.
** Calculated by multiplying the number of common shares outstanding by the price per common share as of March 31.

Before deciding exactly how to strengthen CyTech's innovative organization and ad hocracy culture, you add one more alternative: Hire a consultant to help you figure out what to do. Now, you really must decide.

- *If you decide to divide administrative activities from the operating core, turn to Chapter 6.*

- *If you want to separate product development from all other operations, turn to Chapter 7.*

- *If you choose to increase ad hocracy throughout the organization, turn to Chapter 8.*

- *If you wish to follow the Thermo Electron spin-out path, turn to Chapter 75.*

- *If you would rather hire a consultant to help you figure out what to do, turn to Chapter 11.*

With the price war continuing unabated in the marketplace, this decision turns out to be a good one for you, your senior team, and everyone at CyTech. Hal McPhee was right; CyTech *has* moved into a mass market where it must behave like a mass producer. However, he was wrong when he proposed that the entire organization move into a mass market mode. CyTech still operates within a highly innovative and volatile industry requiring maximum flexibility. Separating out the operating core allows for more standardization, formalization, and division of labor among the operating units, which improves profitability and increases sales. At the same time, increased flexibility and ad hocracy in the administrative support units fuel responsiveness to customers, creativity in problem solving, and adaptiveness to change.

In the months after you make this decision, a myriad of integrative managers and administrative support leaders routinely tap people in all areas of the company to form *ad hoc* cross-functional teams to address a plethora of issues and problems. New product development progresses, operational efficiencies increase, and sales accrue. By year end CyTech surpasses $10 billion in sales, with the price of CyTech's stock climbing to $60 per share (p. 40).

CyTech's steady investment in research and development pays off with the midyear introduction of a multimedia version of the

6

DIVIDING ADMINISTRATIVE ACTIVITIES FROM THE OPERATING CORE

Selected Financial and Stock Information
(Dollars in millions, except stock price in actual dollars)

	Year ended March 31	
	4th Year	3rd Year
Sales	$10,125	$8,526
Profits	608	426
Profits as a % of:		
Sales	6%	5%
Assets	11%	10%
Common Equity*	20%	18%
Market Value**	15,300	10,971
Stock Price	59 ¾	43 ¼

* Total stockholders' equity includes capital stock, surplus, and retained earnings at the company's year end. For purposes of determining profits as a percent of common stockholders' equity, all preferred stock is excluded.
** Calculated by multiplying the number of common shares outstanding by the price per common share as of March 31.

phone-fax-computer, *PowerBase 10*, a major leap forward in technology. The new *PowerBase 10* sends a visual image over the telephone, allowing users to see the person(s) they are talking to on their phone-fax-computer screens. It also lets users create personalized multimedia, CD-ROM programs and disks.

About the same time, however, Motorola introduces a voice-activated phone-fax-computer, *Image Maker*, that receives even more media attention than *PowerBase 10*. At this moment, you rationalize how much more vulnerable CyTech would have been had it not separated administrative activities from the operating core. Had it not done so, you tell yourself, the company would not have been able to maintain its product development focus, nor would it have sufficiently standardized operations for the mass market.

Sales of the old *PowerBases* fall off quickly, but *PowerBase 10* sales more than take up the slack as CyTech fights for market share. Unfortunately, Motorola's *Image Maker* proves a formidable competitor. Not only does the Motorola product dominate the market, but the company's organizational structure appears far more vibrant and forward looking than any competitor's. While your organizational decisions have carried the day until now, you realize that CyTech's organization seems lackluster compared to everything you hear about Motorola's.

Worn out and wondering what you could have done differently, you tender your resignation as CEO but offer to remain a member of the board of directors. The board reluctantly accepts your resignation and offer, but the development, coupled with market conditions, sends CyTech's stock down to $44 on January 1st, five years to the day after you took the helm. That problem, however, will soon be somebody else's worry.

At year end you turn the reins over to Jack Stallings, a bright young superstar from Motorola. CyTech's fifth year of results under your leadership appear in the following table.

Selected Financial and Stock Information
(Dollars in millions, except stock price in actual dollars)

	Year ended March 31	
	5th Year	4th Year
Sales	$11,383	$10,125
Profits	569	608
Profits as a % of:		
Sales	5%	6%
Assets	9%	11%
Common Equity*	17%	20%
Market Value**	11,632	15,300
Stock Price	44 $\frac{1}{8}$	59 $\frac{3}{4}$

* Total stockholders' equity includes capital stock, surplus, and retained earnings at the company's year end. For purposes of determining profits as a percent of common stockholders' equity, all preferred stock is excluded.

** Calculated by multiplying the number of common shares outstanding by the price per common share as of March 31.

You have come to the end of this particular decision-making track, but you can review other alternatives you have not yet explored on this track, or you can pursue one of the other tracks.

- *If you want to compare how the results of your last five years of organizational decision making stack up against the other positive outcomes in The Organization Game, turn to Chapter 78.*

- *If you decide to explore other alternatives on this track, turn to:*

   Chapter 3, Moving Toward a Mass Market Organization;

   Chapter 4, Adopting a Horizontal Organization;

   Chapter 7, Separating Product Development from All Other Operations;

   Chapter 8, Increasing Ad Hocracy Throughout the Organization;

   Chapter 11, Hiring a Consultant; or

   Chapter 75, Following in Thermo Electron's Footsteps.

- *If you decide to pursue another decision-making track, turn to:*

   Chapter 14, Developing a Synthesis of Best Practices;

   Chapter 26, Imbuing the Culture with Empowerment and Accountability;

   Chapter 38, Pursuing a Work Team Approach;

   Chapter 50, Reengineering Work Processes; or

   Chapter 62, Embracing a Revolutionary New Perspective.

Your senior team worries openly about the implications of this move, but they do support it and work hard to implement the changes required to separate new product development from production, distribution, marketing, and sales. As you also separate administrative support services associated with product development from other administrative services, you end up creating two distinct divisions, CyTech New Products and CyTech Operations.

7

SEPARATING PRODUCT DEVELOPMENT FROM ALL OTHER OPERATIONS

As the price war continues, CyTech Operations works diligently to streamline the whole operation to turn CyTech into a mass-marketing machine. When sales increase a relatively modest 13 percent the board of directors gives you a half-hearted pat on the back. Your fourth year-end sales have crested over $9.6 billion, as shown in the table on page 44.

This performance causes you to worry about CyTech New Products' growing isolation from the market and customers. The latest thrust from New Products focuses on opto-electronics, a relatively insignificant issue compared to other developments sweeping the industry. While *PowerBase 6*, scheduled for release later this year, will feature improved display-screen quality and handwriting recognition capability, such developments mean much less to the market than the multimedia and voice-operated applications rumored to be coming soon from competitors.

Augmenting your concerns, Bob Kiechel gives Karen Walsh a free hand at directing most new product activities, while he himself

Selected Financial and Stock Information
(Dollars in millions, except stock price in actual dollars)

	Year ended March 31	
	4th Year	3rd Year
Sales	$9,613	$8,526
Profits	481	426
Profits as a % of:		
Sales	5%	5%
Assets	9%	10%
Common Equity*	17%	18%
Market Value**	11,682	10,971
Stock Price	45 $\frac{7}{8}$	43 $\frac{1}{4}$

* Total stockholders' equity includes capital stock, surplus, and retained earnings at the company's year end. For purposes of determining profits as a percent of common stockholders' equity, all preferred stock is excluded.

** Calculated by multiplying the number of common shares outstanding by the price per common share as of March 31.

takes charge of developing the best working environment possible for CyTech New Products. Kiechel's preoccupation with culture and Walsh's detachment from the needs of the market turn into major liabilities as competitors introduce new multimedia and voice-activated phone-fax-computers near the end of your fifth year as CEO.

Initially, you believe that CyTech can respond in time to maintain its market position, but your beliefs prove false as the hoped-for strong sales of *PowerBase 6* fail to materialize in the wake of more exciting rival product breakthroughs.

Lackluster sales of *PowerBase 6*, combined with sales discounts on the other *PowerBase* products, produce mediocre results for the year, as shown in the table on page 45. A "no confidence" evaluation from Wall Street analysts drives CyTech stock down by 13 points, decreasing market value by over $3 billion.

Early in your sixth year as CEO, the board of directors communicates its feeling that the time has come for you to step aside and allow fresh blood to run CyTech. While the board offers you a seat on the board, it relieves you of all operating responsibilities. As you pass the baton to the next CEO, Bill Champy, an executive recruited

Selected Financial and Stock Information
(Dollars in millions, except stock price in actual dollars)

	Year ended March 31	
	5th Year	4th Year
Sales	$10,341	$9,613
Profits	414	481
Profits as a % of:		
Sales	4%	5%
Assets	7%	9%
Common Equity*	14%	17%
Market Value**	8,250	11,682
Stock Price	32 ½	45 ⅞

* Total stockholders' equity includes capital stock, surplus, and retained earnings at the company's year end. For purposes of determining profits as a percent of common stockholders' equity, all preferred stock is excluded.
** Calculated by multiplying the number of common shares outstanding by the price per common share as of March 31.

from Motorola, CyTech's stock jumps to $40 in anticipation of a strong new leadership direction.

All in all, you feel good about your accomplishments at CyTech, especially your organizational decisions, with the exception of your most recent move to separate product development from the rest of the operation. If you could do it over, you would not have undertaken such a separation. While this marks the end of a decision-making track, you can remake certain past decisions.

- *If you want to compare how the results of your last five years of organizational decision making stack up against the other positive outcomes in The Organization Game, turn to Chapter 78.*

- *If you decide to explore other alternatives on this track, turn to:*
  Chapter 3, Moving Toward a Mass Market Organization;
  Chapter 4, Adopting a Horizontal Organization;

Chapter 6, Dividing Administrative Activities from the Operating Core;
Chapter 8, Increasing Ad Hocracy Throughout the Organization;
Chapter 11, Hiring a Consultant; or
Chapter 75, Following in Thermo Electron's Footsteps.

- *If you decide to follow another decision-making track, turn to:*
  Chapter 14, Developing a Synthesis of Best Practices;
  Chapter 26, Imbuing the Culture with Empowerment and Accountability;
  Chapter 38, Pursuing a Work Team Approach;
  Chapter 50, Reengineering Work Processes; or
  Chapter 62, Embracing a Revolutionary New Perspective.

You do not surprise your management team with this decision because it coincides with your earlier decisions, but within a few short months each of them becomes increasingly overloaded with the demands of ad hocracy throughout the organization. In frustration, they begin urging a major reengineering of the CyTech organization.

8

INCREASING AD HOCRACY THROUGHOUT THE ORGANIZATION

John Solo sums up their feelings when he says, "CyTech is getting too big to continue the kind of ad hocracy that worked when we were smaller. We can't continue without a major redesign of work processes and structures throughout the company. We lost over 20 of our best managers last year because they just wouldn't put up with the 16- to 18-hour days any longer. Ad hocracy has worked for CyTech, but it's built on a foundation of old managerial and organizational assumptions. We've been able to remove a lot of that old junk, but we certainly haven't gotten rid of it all. It's time to shake up this place."

For the next two hours you listen to variations on this theme from your direct reports, but you decide not to take any precipitous action. After all, you still suspect that the continuing hoopla over reengineering amounts to little more than the latest corporate fad. However, you agree to take your senior team's consensus into consideration.

Unfortunately, as the price wars continue, stress and strain on the CyTech organization and its people becomes more and more apparent. The need for standardization and efficiency increases as customer demand grows, while the need for flexibility and ad hocracy expands as the organization mushrooms and prepares to launch an array of technological advancements. However, the words "overloaded," "overworked," and "overstressed" begin to supplant "ad hocracy" and "flexibility" as key descriptors of CyTech's culture, until you find yourself battling to maintain your emphasis on ad hocracy.

In a quickly, but carefully, prepared 12-minute video presentation, you talk directly to every CyTech employee, unveiling a new and improved productivity-sharing compensation program that will benefit everyone. Although you don't supply all the details of the new program, you do stress that the new plan will enable every CyTech employee to increase his or her compensation by as much as 25 percent through productivity gains in the coming year. You also reaffirm your conviction that "ad hocracy" in an innovation-conscious organizational structure remains the key to these gains.

At the conclusion of the presentation you call for renewed commitment on the part of every CyTech employee: "I know each of you has worked long and hard during the past year. We all have. But it's paying off. We've held our market position throughout the price war, and we've remained profitable. However, we face new demands in the coming year—further cost cutting, new-product launches, higher levels of productivity. I know it's not going to be easy, but we simply must find ways to accomplish more in less time and at less cost. I know we can do it and that this new compensation plan will reward every individual who makes it happen. Thank you."

At a cost of over $200,000 you send a copy of the video and a pamphlet on the new compensation program to the home of each employee. The initial response gratifies you as people throughout the company exhibit new life and commitment.

By year end sales reach $1.1 billion, with CyTech stock soaring to $75 per share (p. 49).

However, in the first few months of your fifth year as CEO, the crisis you had temporarily forestalled mounts when Motorola introduces a new voice-operated phone-fax-computer that captures the interest of millions almost overnight. When the additional pressure causes even you to feel overloaded and overworked, it finally dawns on you that you have been mercilessly turning up the pressure on CyTech employees for the last three years by asking

Selected Financial and Stock Information
(Dollars in millions, except stock price in actual dollars)

	Year ended March 31	
	4th Year	3rd Year
Sales	$11,289	$8,526
Profits	790	426
Profits as a % of:		
Sales	7%	5%
Assets	12%	10%
Common Equity*	21%	18%
Market Value**	19,105	10,971
Stock Price	75 $\frac{3}{8}$	43 $\frac{1}{4}$

* Total stockholders' equity includes capital stock, surplus, and retained earnings at the company's year end. For purposes of determining profits as a percent of common stockholders' equity, all preferred stock is excluded.

** Calculated by multiplying the number of common shares outstanding by the price per common share as of March 31.

them constantly to do more and more with less and less. Now, you understand the consequences. Ad hocracy has done nothing but pile pressure on your people. Can CyTech respond to Motorola's challenge by introducing its own voice-operated phone-fax-computer within the next few months? Will CyTech people revolt under the new pressures? Can you continue squeezing your people for more productivity and still live with yourself? Answers to these and similar questions, won't come easy.

As you wrestle with this dilemma you wonder whether it's time for you to step down as CEO, to let someone else grapple with CyTech's new challenges. Maybe you have finally run out of ideas and energy. Your only recourse will mean doing exactly what you have asked every CyTech employee to do this past year: respond to the pressure for more results. While you're mulling over this hard decision, news leaks to the press about your apparent ambivalence over CyTech's future, causing analysts and stockbrokers to panic. Sell orders push CyTech's stock down 25 points to $50. You must decide quickly whether to stay or leave.

- *If you decide to stick it out and meet CyTech's new challenges, turn to Chapter 9.*

- *If you decide to step down as CEO, turn to Chapter 10.*

"I've never quit in my life," you remind yourself as you attempt to light a new fire under your senior team to meet Motorola's challenge with a CyTech version of the voice-operated phone-fax-computer within three months.

Bob Kiechel, senior VP of Product Development, laughs at your suggestion, saying, "You know we can't respond that quickly. Maybe in six months, but never in three."

"Not good enough!" you counter.

"People can't bear any more superhuman demands," says Nan Thurow, senior VP of worldwide operations. "They just don't have it to give. They're burned-out!"

Her anger hits you like a slap. "Look, if we fail to meet this challenge, we'll lose everything we've worked for. We must respond to Motorola's breakthrough within 90 days. If we don't, we'll all be on the street."

Karen Walsh, VP of the advanced technology lab, responds confidently and coolly, "You're out of touch with what's going on around here. Our people have been working on a voice-operated prototype for several months. It looks promising, but we're at least six months away from a product introduction."

9

STICKING IT OUT AS CEO

Now you feel angry. "I won't accept that!" you shout.

"Settle down, you're on overload too, just like the rest of us," John Solo, executive VP for worldwide sales and marketing, says as he stands up and buttons his jacket. "This is getting us nowhere. You're out of control."

With your emotions boiling, you too rise, and while you try to keep your voice steady, you realize you're losing your temper. "Don't talk to me like that. This meeting is over." With that, you storm out of the room.

In the ensuing weeks, Motorola's new voice-operated phone-fax-computer cuts deeply into CyTech's sales, adding new pressures from the board of directors to boost short-term sales. You find yourself at your wits' end, and, to make matters worse, your senior team won't even talk to you.

One month later the board of directors votes to replace you as CEO.

- *In real life you may have been able to handle the pressures and meet the challenges facing CyTech, but the time has come in this game for you to pass the baton to someone else. If you would like to find out why the author considers the other alternative preferable, turn to Chapter 10.*

- *If you wish to explore other options on this track, turn to:*

    Chapter 3, Moving Toward a Mass Market Organization;

    Chapter 4, Adopting a Horizontal Organization;

    Chapter 6, Dividing Administrative Activities from the Operating Core;

    Chapter 7, Seperating Product Development from all other Operations;

    Chapter 11, Hiring a Consultant; or

    Chapter 75, Following in Thermo Electron's Footsteps.

- *If you want to start from scratch, select one of the following:*

    Chapter 14, Developing a Synthesis of Best Practices;

    Chapter 26, Imbuing the Culture with Empowerment and Accountability;

    Chapter 38, Pursuing a Work Team Approach;

    Chapter 50, Reengineering of Work Processes; or

    Chapter 62, Embracing a Revolutionary New Perspective.

"Deciding when to quit is one of the most important decisions any CEO ever makes," you tell yourself. "And for me, the time has come. I've taken CyTech as far as I can. Now, I'd like to see Nan Thurow try her hand at CyTech's next phase of development." During a brief and emotional meeting with your senior team, you announce your decision that Nan Thurow will become president and chief operating officer effective immediately. You will remain chief executive officer until the end of the year, but Nan will make all important decisions from this point on. "I have full confidence in her ability to take CyTech to new heights," you conclude, and this is what you tell the press on June 1st, four years and four months after you assumed the same position. As for yourself, you look forward to doing something different in the years ahead.

10

STEPPING DOWN AS CEO

Since you have always wanted to teach at a business school, you entertain several offers to do so during the next few months. Eventually, you decide to accept an adjutant professor's position at Stanford, where you will begin teaching the fall semester.

At the same time Nan Thurow works miracles at CyTech, quickly entering into a strategic partnership with a Japanese firm that will manufacture voice-operated phone-fax-computers under the *PowerBase* label. The move averts disaster in the short term and affords her time to redesign CyTech's organization. You chose the right successor, as the year-end results prove. See table on page 54.

Selected Financial and Stock Information
(Dollars in millions, except stock price in actual dollars)

	Year ended March 31	
	5th Year	4th Year
Sales	$15,003	$11,289
Profits	1,050	790
Profits as a % of:		
Sales	7%	7%
Assets	13%	12%
Common Equity*	22%	21%
Market Value**	23,561	19,105
Stock Price	91 $^{13}\!/_{16}$	75 $^3\!/_8$

* Total stockholders' equity includes capital stock, surplus, and retained earnings at the company's year end. For purposes of determining profits as a percent of common stockholders' equity, all preferred stock is excluded.

** Calculated by multiplying the number of common shares outstanding by the price per common share as of March 31.

You leave CyTech with $75 million worth of company stock and the knowledge that you stepped down at the right time.

You begin the school year teaching a course on long-term career planning to MBA candidates.

This marks the end of a decision-making track, but you can continue playing the *Organization Game* by selecting one of the following options.

- *If you want to compare how the results of your last five years of organizational decision making stack up against the other positive outcomes in The Organization Game, turn to Chapter 78.*

- *If you decide to explore other alternatives on this track, turn to:*

  Chapter 3, Moving Toward a Mass Market Organization;

  Chapter 4, Adopting a Horizontal Organization;

  Chapter 6, Dividing Administrative Activities from the Operating Core;

  Chapter 7, Separating Product Development from All Other Operations;

  Chapter 11, Hiring a Consultant, or

  Chapter 75, Following in Thermo Electron's Footsteps

- *If you wish to embark on another decision-making track, turn to:*

  Chapter 14, Developing a Synthesis of Best Practices;

  Chapter 26, Imbuing the Culture with Empowerment and Accountability;

  Chapter 38, Pursuing a Work Team Approach;

  Chapter 50, Reengineering Work Processes; or

  Chapter 62, Embracing a Revolutionary New Perspective.

Given your senior team's ambivalence and your own hesitancy over the correct organizational direction CyTech should go, you decide to seek some outside expertise. You just can't risk making the wrong decision. After surveying a field of possibilities, from large international consulting firms such as McKinsey to smaller niche specialists, you decide to engage a medium-sized firm called Organizational Dynamics. Reese Stein, a senior vice president at Organizational Dynamics, will act as project leader during the consulting engagement. He's aggressive and supremely confident, and you feel comfortable with him. He brings impressive credentials and experience to the job. And, while he proposes a lot of time-consuming organizational data gathering as a first step, you feel the time, money, and effort will prove worthwhile. Besides, you've already reached the limits of your own capabilities by administering a huge *ad hoc* organization, and you hope that Reese Stein can come up with some answers that will restore your confidence in CyTech's future.

11

HIRING A CONSULTANT

As the consulting engagement begins, Organizational Dynamics brings in a team of six consultants to work closely with seven in-house people. The data-gathering phase moves so slowly members of your senior team begin complaining that nothing seems to be happening. However, with encouragement from Reese Stein, you convince them to relax and let the process run its course.

Six months later, with the data-gathering phase completed, Reese Stein begins holding a series of management retreats with you and your senior team. In the course of these retreats, Stein surprises you by acting as if he's the CEO, telling each of your senior executives exactly what he or she should do to make the organizational environment at CyTech more conducive to both innovation and mass marketing/production. He introduces a sophisticated matrix style of organization that strikes you as overly complicated, but having invested six months and $500,000 in this gambit, you decide to give Stein the benefit of the doubt and continue with the project. Eventually, however, Stein's confidence takes on tones of arrogance, which irritates both you and your senior team.

After the fifth retreat, John Solo, executive vice president of worldwide marketing and sales, pulls you aside and says, "Do you realize what's going on here?"

"What do you mean?"

"This guy Stein is on a major ego trip, making all of us feel like idiots. I don't trust him."

Though you have begun to share that feeling, you wait to hear what John thinks, so you ask, "What do you suggest?"

"I suggest you start leading this company again. Get rid of Reese Stein." With a disgusted bow of his head, John Solo stalks away, leaving you with a haunting suspicion that you've made a terrible mistake turning to an outsider for help.

After some reflection, you realize that you face a tough decision, dealing with Reese Stein and Organizational Dynamics. You could cut them off immediately, taking charge yourself of the implementation phase of Organizational Dynamics' recommendations. Or, you could sit down with Stein and work out an arrangement that would put you in charge again. Before you act, you informally survey your senior team to find out what they think.

One by one, you question each member of your senior team to obtain his or her candid views of Organizational Dynamics, Reese Stein, and the current reorganization plan. Every one of them tells you, some more pointedly than others, that you've lost control of CyTech's organizational development and have put it in the hands of an outsider. However, while you detect a lot of resentment and pent-up anger over what's been going on, in terms of the conceptual and practical process that Stein and his consulting firm have applied to CyTech's organizational situation, you also sense a certain amount of approval. Karen Walsh sums it up nicely: "We like what the guy says, we just don't like the way he says it. We'd rather hear it from you."

Now you must decide how to deal with the situation. If you fire Stein, bringing the engagement to an abrupt, and possibly premature halt, that move could raise eyebrows among the board of directors. On the other hand, if things continue as they have, you may never be able to move Stein into a more appropriate supportive role. As you consider the options, you review the impact of Stein's involvement to date. Some of his recommendations, such as the one to create permanent mass marketing/production teams, have already produced results as the teams have rapidly discovered new ways to standardize procedures and create efficiencies while avoiding unnecessary bureaucracy. This and other changes have helped CyTech cope with the price war, for which you feel deeply grateful.

Stock analysts report that CyTech "holds its own" in the industry, and year-end numbers bear out that opinion:

Selected Financial and Stock Information
(Dollars in millions, except stock price in actual dollars)

	Year ended March 31	
	4th Year	3rd Year
Sales	$9,516	$8,526
Profits	476	426
Profits as a % of:		
Sales	5%	5%
Assets	11%	10%
Common Equity*	18%	18%
Market Value**	10,653	10,971
Stock Price	42 $\frac{7}{8}$	43 $\frac{1}{4}$

* Total stockholders' equity includes capital stock, surplus, and retained earnings at the company's year end. For purposes of determining profits as a percent of common stockholders' equity, all preferred stock is excluded.
** Calculated by multiplying the number of common shares outstanding by the price per common share as of March 31.

While you still feel apprehensive about pulling the plug on Reese Stein and Organizational Dynamics, the board of directors won't put up with another lackluster year like the one just ended. What should you do?

- *If you decide to terminate your relationship with Reese Stein and Organizational Dynamics, turn to Chapter 12.*

- *If you choose to redirect Reese Stein and his consulting firm into a supportive role, turn to Chapter 13.*

With the price war dragging on, the strain takes an ever increasing strain on your organization, and you fear that you have wasted too much time listening to outsiders and gathering data. Even though some of Organizational Dynamics' recommendations have worked well, Reese Stein has undermined your leadership and fueled a lot of internal anxiety and political maneuvering. In light of all this, you decide to terminate your relationship with Reese Stein and Organizational Dynamics. To your surprise, however, this turns out to be harder than you could possibly have imagined.

12

TERMINATING YOUR CONSULTING RELATIONSHIP WITH ORGANIZATIONAL DYNAMICS

Over the course of the last eight months, Reese Stein, without your knowledge or approval, has been providing updates to members of the board of directors, essentially handing them a report card on your work as CEO. You have not received high marks, a fact that has deeply disturbed the board of directors. Consequently, some members of the board view your decision to terminate the consulting relationship as an effort to "shoot the messenger" who has brought them news of your shortcomings.

You become absolutely infuriated when you find out what Stein's been doing, and you plan to reveal his sabotage at the next board meeting. Much to your surprise, however, the chairman of the board invites Reese Stein to the next board meeting, asking him to summarize his view of what's happening within CyTech and to protest the termination of his services. You rue the day that you sought the board's approval before hiring Stein. Little did you know then that you had set the stage for an ugly betrayal.

What ensues in the first half hour of the board meeting curdles your blood as Reese Stein eloquently articulates what he considers to be your "abdication of leadership." Though you desperately attempt to rebut Stein's claims, you see that your indifference cuts little ice with the board. "This can't happen," you tell yourself, but you soon find out that it indeed can.

Within two weeks of the board meeting, the chairman asks for your resignation and appoints Reese Stein as interim CEO. In retrospect, you realize that Reese Stein's ambitions ran far beyond a mere consulting engagement. How did you fall such easy prey to his manipulations? Did you, in fact, abdicate your leadership? Did you give up on your own ability to chart CyTech's future? What should you have done differently?

- *You might have been able to reclaim your leadership of CyTech in a just and fair world, but in the real world of senior management you don't get many second tries. If you want to discover why the author considers other alternatives better, return to Chapter 5 and then select Chapters 6, 7, 8, or 78.*

- *If you would like to try your hand at one of the other initial alternatives, move on to one of the following:*
    Chapter 14, Developing a Synthesis of Best Practices;
    Chapter 26, Imbuing the Culture with Empowerment and Accountability;
    Chapter 38, Pursuing a Work Team Approach;
    Chapter 50, Reengineering Work Processes; or
    Chapter 62, Embracing a Revolutionary New Perspective.

Convinced that you cannot continue the current consulting engagement as it stands, you decide to ask Reese Stein to spend a day with you away from the office during which you hope to redirect his efforts and reexert your own leadership. The day with Stein begins pleasantly enough but soon erupts into a battle of egos as Stein enumerates a list of reasons why you are incapable of implementing the full range of his organizational recommendations yourself.

When you threaten to terminate your relationship with him, he tells you that since you first introduced him to the board of directors, several members have requested and received periodic updates from him directly. "Most of them have expressed serious reservations about your leadership," he says.

This infuriates you, but you manage to keep your cool until Stein exults "Without me, Cytech will not survive the next two years."

A shouting match ensues in which you accuse Stein of trying to sabotage your position. Stein counters that Cytech's stock should be trading at $85 instead of $45. "Look," he says, "you may not like it, but I have the confidence of the board, and you need me to hold on to your job."

13

REDIRECTING YOUR CONSULTING RELATIONSHIP WITH ORGANIZATIONAL DYNAMICS

You quickly conclude the meeting by saying, "We'll see about that."

During the next few weeks, you discover that Reese Stein had indeed been communicating directly with the board for the past eight months and has given you low marks as CEO. When you confront the board with the information, they admit to encouraging Stein's communications and claim they want only the best for CyTech. When you ask why they did not tell you about their conversations with Stein, the chairman of the board says, "These are difficult times for Cytech, with significant challenges and opportunities. We felt this was a legitimate opportunity for us to assess your performance as CEO, exercising our fiduciary responsibilities as members of the board and keeping close tabs on Cytech's organizational development."

Stung by these words, you resign on the spot, telling the board: "I have better things to do. Good-bye."

- *You might have been able to salvage this situation in real life, but in this game you placed too much trust and hope in an outside consultant. If you want to discover why the author considers other alternatives more productive, return to Chapter 5 and then select Chapters 6, 7, 8, or 78.*

- *If you would like to try your hand at one of the other initial alternatives, turn to one of the following:*
    Chapter 14, Developing a Synthesis of Best Practices;
    Chapter 26, Imbuing the Culture with Empowerment and Accountability;
    Chapter 38, Pursuing a Work Team Approach;
    Chapter 50, Reengineering Work Processes; or
    Chapter 62, Embracing a Revolutionary New Perspective.

After announcing your decision to pursue a synthesis of the best contemporary practices in corporate America, you immediately ask your team of senior executives to identify the ones they believe will benefit CyTech the most. Over the next 90 days, each member of your senior team works diligently, scouring the literature and talking with consultants to identify the best management and organizational practices in the world.

For your part, you contact an executive editor at *Fortune* magazine who interviewed you recently for an article on the future of the telecommunications industry. She likes the idea of synthesizing best practices and agrees to open her files to you if you, in turn, will share the results with her. You agree, and she sends you a large bundle of articles and resource material that *Fortune* recently used as background for an extensive feature article on state-of-the-art organizational and management practices in the United States. This material pinpoints several companies you should learn more about.

As the synthesis project gathers momentum, it energizes employees throughout the company as they anticipate borrowing exciting practices from other companies. The very idea of doing something new seems to generate excitement. After all, CyTech has done the same thing with its products, blending the best technologies to create what many experts consider the best phone-fax-computer on the market. Now the company will blend the best organizational and management processes to create the best-managed company in America.

Ninety days later, after much discussion, you review a summary of the six best practices that will compose CyTech's initial

14

DEVELOPING A SYNTHESIS OF BEST PRACTICES

synthesis. From the beginning, you had encouraged each of your direct reports to champion a different "best in world" practice for inclusion in the mix. Now you take great pride in the results of their efforts. Everyone has gotten excited not only by his or her own recommendations but with all the others as well. You sense total alignment behind the program.

Hal McPhee, CyTech's chief financial officer, champions General Electric's workout process in which the company engages in what it calls "workout sessions" to resolve pesky problems and to ensure that the leaders do not impede the input, suggestions, and problem solving of other people within the department, group, or team.

Bob Kiechel, senior vice president of product development, nominates 3M's autonomy as a critical component of CyTech's synthesis. 3M has long adhered to autonomy, even though, initially, it did not prove that successful. In the last two decades, however, 3M's approach has established a pattern for many companies throughout the world. Autonomy, which often looks on the surface like disorganization and chaos, will in fact allow people throughout the CyTech organization to pursue a variety of experimental paths to keep the company on the leading edge.

Morris Strandmeyer, vice president of production, proposes CNN's energy as another key attribute for the CyTech organization. CNN has become a world-news powerhouse through sheer determination and unflagging energy. Strandmeyer believes that such energy will prove vital to CyTech's future success, particularly as competition intensifies.

Karen Walsh, vice president of the advanced technology lab, offers up Merck's R&D as a guideline for all of CyTech's own R&D activities. She argues that Merck's approach to new-product development, based on a deep commitment to basic research, can provide continuing innovations for CyTech. "No matter what we do," Karen concludes "we must remain a leader in basic technological research and development."

John Solo, executive vice president of worldwide sales and marketing, promotes WalMart's superior service. He believes that WalMart's ability to serve customers better than other retailers, especially other discounters, stems from its closeness to customers and its constant questioning of its own policies. CyTech will need such a focus on service to remain tuned into changing customer needs in the coming years.

Finally, Nan Thurow, senior vice president of worldwide operations, pushes McKinsey & Company's on-the-job training as the best way to build CyTech's corporate culture. McKinsey & Company, probably the most respected international consulting firm in the world, follows no formal written policy and procedure manual, but, rather, employs a powerful and effective on-the-job training philosophy that maximizes communication among employees, stresses teamwork and, above all, demands critical thinking. According to Nan, "Building McKinsey's style of on-the-job training into the CyTech culture will keep our people learning and growing faster than our competition."

The mix represents an impressive array of practices, but you can't help wondering to yourself whether CyTech can really synthesize all of them into its organization. Theoretically, it can, but practically, how long will it actually take to make these six practices an integral part of your organization and culture? As you mull over this question, you keep reminding yourself, "There's no turning back now."

With the help of your senior team, you make arrangements with each of the six "best in world" companies for executives and managers from CyTech to attend various in-house training and development classes or spend time with key executives to discuss their companies' practices. Over the next several months, a frenzy of activity erupts as your scouts learn about and begin to apply the six new practices within CyTech. Employees throughout the organization bubble with enthusiasm as the practices begin taking hold throughout the organization, and their efforts help CyTech advance as the market heats up and competition intensifies.

While competitors introduce new phone-fax-computers with new computer chips, better designs, and other novel features, CyTech counters all those moves with its own product updating: a new generation of *PowerBases* with a new chip, new design, and enhanced capability to operate wireless or connected to telephone lines or fiber optic cable.

The synthesis of best practices increases productivity as people strive to be the best. Sales reach $5 billion by the end of your first year as CEO, and CyTech's stock price rises to $30 per share as shown in the table on page 68.

Unfortunately, all the initial excitement and enthusiasm proves short-lived. After the first wave of learning and implementation,

Selected Financial and Stock Information
(Dollars in millions, except stock price in actual dollars)

	Year ended March 31	
	1st Year	Previous Year
Sales	$5,136	$4,083
Profits	308	242
Profits as a % of:		
Sales	6%	6%
Assets	10%	9%
Common Equity*	17%	17%
Market Value**	7,867	6,123
Stock Price	30 $\frac{7}{8}$	23 $\frac{3}{4}$

* Total stockholders' equity includes capital stock, surplus, and retained earnings at the company's year end. For purposes of determining profits as a percent of common stockholders' equity, all preferred stock is excluded.

** Calculated by multiplying the number of common shares outstanding by the price per common share as of March 31.

people throughout the organization begin demanding clearer priorities among the six practices. In other words, if the WalMart-style service emphasis comes into conflict with the 3M autonomy strategy, which one takes precedence? Which one should be the more fundamental moving force within the CyTech organization? Case in point: A problem developed with the CD-ROM port that had been added to the latest *PowerBase*, but R&D, more interested in basic technological advances than in fixing the minor glitch in the CD-ROM port, responded slowly, compromising customer service. This sort of conflict and the resulting confusion grows as employees encounter similar problems every day. More and more people look to senior management for answers about the fundamental priorities that should guide their action.

Initially, you purposely avoid resolving the individual dilemmas, preferring instead to let employees in various company locations throughout the world struggle with them in order to hammer out the most workable compromises. To help them do so, you and your senior team launch a companywide training program entitled "Making the Synthesis Work," in which employees learn how to resolve dilemmas by modifying the mix of best practices to meet the needs of their particular situations. CyTech trainers stress flexibility and ad hocracy using case studies to help guide employees through the quagmire of day-to-day conflicts.

For the next six months, this effort seems to resolve most dilemmas as employees and work groups figure out their own synthesizing plans, but, before long, an even more serious problem emerges as different approaches to synthesizing the best practices create warring subcultures throughout the company. In one instance, for example, a production facility in Texas that values workout sessions and autonomy more highly than other practices refused to modify its product-distribution patterns to meet the sales force's new on-the-job training requirements aimed at improving technical service. Under the new "Making Synthesis Work" guidelines, there's no way to resolve such a conflict without intervention from above which took precious time and resources.

By the end of your second year as CEO, sales begin to stagnate and the enthusiasm that marked the passage of your first year almost completely disappears in your second.

At year end, CyTech's mediocre performance causes the stock price to fall 5 points as the following table reveals.

Selected Financial and Stock Information
(Dollars in millions, except stock price in actual dollars)

	Year ended March 31	
	2nd Year	1st Year
Sales	$5,883	$5,136
Profits	294	308
Profits as a % of:		
Sales	5%	6%
Assets	8%	10%
Common Equity*	15%	17%
Market Value**	6,752	7,867
Stock Price	26 $\frac{1}{8}$	30 $\frac{7}{8}$

* Total stockholders' equity includes capital stock, surplus, and retained earnings at the company's year end. For purposes of determining profits as a percent of common stockholders' equity, all preferred stock is excluded.

** Calculated by multiplying the number of common shares outstanding by the price per common share as of March 31.

Reluctantly, you and your senior team conclude that you must assign priorities to the best practices. You begin the process by discussing with your team the company's driving force or core competence, a discussion that quickly underscores the extent of the problem. Your senior team simply can't agree on CyTech's driving force. Kiechel, Walsh, and Thurow champion new-product development, while McPhee, Strandmeyer, and Solo stand behind mass marketing. You think to yourself, "No wonder we've run into problems synthesizing the best practices. As Yogi Berra once said, 'If you don't know where you're going, that's where you'll end up.'" You also realize that some of the six best practices—3M's autonomy and Merck's R&D—favor a new-product development driving force, while some—WalMart's service and CNN's energy—sustain a mass-marketing driving force, and still others—GE's workout sessions and McKinsey's on-the-job training—could support either.

After weeks of debate, your senior team finally agrees on one thing: CyTech must maintain a dual focus in the years ahead to remain a technological leader and to exploit the emerging mass market. Regardless of how schizophrenic this may prove, you realize that no other path will satisfy your senior team. With the dual-driving force established, you turn everyone's attention to the best practices, asking the question: "Which one should become the dominant characteristic of CyTech's culture? Which one best matches our dual strategic focus?" Again, debate rages, this time worse than before. Soon you find yourself dumbfounded at the political maneuvering and behind-the-scenes lobbying of your senior team as they try to influence you and even members of the board.

Each member of your senior team continues championing the best practice he or she originally promoted, making strong cases for why each should assume the dominant role in CyTech's evolving culture. While some express more willingness to compromise than others, you cannot help but conclude that each executive's personal biases, beliefs, and experiences are so wrapped up in his or her preferred best practice that none of them will ever feel fully comfortable with another's preference. You have encouraged this diversity, but now it has made it nigh on impossible for you to achieve the perfect alignment you feel the top level of CyTech must exhibit to the culture.

Hal McPhee argues that a solid *workout* philosophy at the top of the hierarchy of best practices will allow CyTech to solve its immediate and long-range problems most effectively; Bob Kiechel insists that *autonomy* should take the dominant position because it captures the very essence of the organization, making each individual, team, project, department, and function a major contributor to the overall results of the company; Strandmeyer pushes for *energy* as the only dominant attribute and attitude that can allow CyTech to embrace its dual strategic focus and win; Walsh points to *R&D commitment* and technological leadership as the key to everything, reiterating the fact that no mass market opportunity would exist without technological advancement; John Solo makes the case that only *service* will keep CyTech employees close to customers and conscious of the growing needs and wants of the exploding personal communications market. Finally, Nan Thurow argues that an overarching *on-the-job training* program will help every employee develop the necessary personal accountability and competence to resolve any dilemma or issue in the future.

As each one persuasively argues his or her case, you sway first one way, then another. Rather than belabor the discussions and debate, you tell your senior team that you'll make this decision yourself and that you expect their unified support and commitment once you make it. They each agree, but you wonder about the commitment of Karen Walsh and Hal McPhee if you do not select either of their choices.

Now it's up to you to determine which of the six best practices will dominate and guide CyTech's synthesis of best practices.

- *If you choose GE's workout sessions as the preeminent practice, turn to Chapter 15.*

- *If you prefer 3M's autonomy as the umbrella philosophy, turn to Chapter 16.*

- *If you want to emphasize CNN's energy as the overriding attribute, turn to Chapter 17.*

- *If Merck's R&D focus makes the most sense to you, turn to Chapter 18.*

- *If you believe WalMart's service should inform every other practice at CyTech, turn to Chapter 19.*

- *If you favor McKinsey's on-the-job training as the chief CyTech practice, turn to Chapter 20.*

Just as you announce this decision, an unexpected crisis strikes the whole industry. No one in the CyTech organization, including yourself, could have predicted that three foreign competitors would initiate an aggressive price war that sends you and your competitors scrambling to keep up. When phone-fax-computer prices drop below $500, you find your company thrust into a mass market environment a good two to three years before you expected it.

15
EMPHASIZING GE-STYLE WORKOUTS

Having chosen GE's workout sessions as CyTech's dominant practice, you quickly employ it companywide in an effort to resolve the many issues erupting from the deadly price war. The workout sessions bring groups of people within and across functions together to resolve pesky problems and eliminate needless activities. Hal McPhee, CFO and champion of the GE workout process, makes sure everyone in the organization understands that "workout" means two things: (1) working out problems, and (2) removing unproductive work from the organization. Through a new set of guidelines for planning, budgeting, and management reporting, McPhee weaves the workout philosophy into CyTech's management processes. Not everyone will make it through the price war alive, but you're willing to exhaust your resources in the battle for market shares. Obviously, CyTech must quickly and effectively reduce costs while, at the same time, introducing new technological developments. It's a tall order to fill.

Several months and hundreds of workout sessions later, you discover a fatal flaw: trying to be two organizations at once—a technological leader and a mass marketer/producer—doesn't work. Cutting costs during a price war requires the full attention of every element of your organization, from R&D through distribution, yet, technological leadership also demands full attention and commitment. One workout session after another further reveals the basic dilemma, and you watch helplessly as CyTech literally tears itself apart. Project teams, sales offices, production facilities, and staff groups attempt to work out this dilemma, but the mandate from the top, a dual strategic focus, has created a paralyzing schizophrenia. In fact, the heavy emphasis on workout sessions exacerbates the problem because it keeps people wrestling with an unresolvable paradox. You summarize the situation as precisely as possible: "There's no way for CyTech to maintain its technological leadership position and become a low-cost producer in the short-term, particularly during a strenuous price war." Even in CyTech's flexible work environment, the workout sessions do nothing to remove the gridlock. Hal McPhee argues that the workout sessions show the wrong-headedness of a dual strategic focus, but you counter that CyTech has no choice.

It doesn't take long for the board of directors to conclude that workout sessions as an overarching practice cannot give CyTech the cultural strength and vision it needs to implement a dual strategic focus. And, you continue to believe that without a dual strategic focus CyTech cannot sustain its advantage in the industry. It has turned out that in this particular situation you cannot have your cake and eat it, too.

At the end of your third year as CEO, CyTech's languishing performance becomes all too visible. Sales fail to break $6 billion, and the stock price drops further, as shown in the accompanying table.

On a cool morning in April, the chairman of the board asks for your resignation and apologizes for not allowing you more time to solve CyTech's problems. Both of you know that, given more time, you probably could have resolved the gridlock associated with the dual strategic focus, but time has run out. The chairman feels he must act to protect CyTech for the benefit of its many shareholders. With the stock price falling to $18 per share, someone must accept the blame for CyTech's internal gridlock, and, unfortunately, that someone is you.

Selected Financial and Stock Information
(Dollars in millions, except stock price in actual dollars)

	Year ended March 31	
	3rd Year	2nd Year
Sales	$5,922	$5,883
Profits	237	294
Profits as a % of:		
Sales	4%	5%
Assets	6%	8%
Common Equity*	13%	15%
Market Value**	4,939	6,752
Stock Price	19 3/8	26 1/8

* Total stockholders' equity includes capital stock, surplus, and retained earnings at the company's year end. For purposes of determining profits as a percent of common stockholders' equity, all preferred stock is excluded.

** Calculated by multiplying the number of common shares outstanding by the price per common share as of March 31.

- *In real life you might have been able to make the workout sessions work as CyTech's dominant practice, but if you want to know why the author considers other alternatives better review Chapter 14, then turn to one of the following:*

  Chapter 16, Enshrining 3M's Autonomy;

  Chapter 17, Infusing CNN's Energy;

  Chapter 18, Emulating Merck's R&D Commitment;

  Chapter 19, Centering on WalMart's Superior Service; or

  Chapter 20, Highlighting McKinsey's On-the-Job Training;

- *If you want to pursue a different decision-making track, move on to one of the following:*

  Chapter 2, Building a Classic Innovative Organization

Chapter 26, Imbuing the Culture with Empowerment and Accountability;
Chapter 38, Pursuing a Work Team Approach;
Chapter 50, Reengineering Work Processes; or
Chapter 62, Embracing a Revolutionary New Perspective.

An industrywide crisis takes you by surprise just as you begin implementing 3M-style autonomy as CyTech's primary organizational orientation. When three foreign competitors initiate a price war that drops the price of phone-fax-computers below $500, you suddenly find yourself thrust into a mass market environment a full two to three years earlier than you, or any of your senior team, thought possible. Bob Kiechel assures you that CyTech's new emphasis on autonomy will give employees and teams the ability to meet the crisis of the price war. He urges, "You know that CyTech has been slowly moving toward bureaucracy, just like every other large company, but with 3M-style autonomy giving people more power and authority to solve problems and marshall resources we can reverse the bureaucratization and win this lousy price war." You agree, informally dubbing Bob Kiechel as CyTech's autonomy czar and charging him with the responsibility of making every function, department, team, and individual in the organization more autonomous, independent, and empowered.

16

ENSHRINING 3M's AUTONOMY

With autonomy enshrined as CyTech's premier organizational principle, the company's numerous operating units develop their own syntheses of best practices to meet the needs of the marketplace. However, the intense pressure and anxiety brought on by the price war throws the entire CyTech organization into a tailspin as autonomous organizational units devise diverse and ever conflicting measures to meet the challenge, exacerbating the communication problems inherent in an autonomy-driven organization. For example, marketing mixes CNN's energy and WalMart's service, while R&D emphasizes GE's workout sessions and McKinsey's on-the-job training, making the communication gap even larger between the two functions. At a time when CyTech desperately needs more coordination and collective efficiency, it produces a thousand different creative solutions, all working against one another.

CyTech descends into utter chaos. Plants ship products without communicating to marketing and sales, R&D chooses to ignore the mass production frenzy, and internal squabbles eat up precious time and resources. Administrative support teams throughout the company attempt to marshall forces behind product redesign and production efficiency initiatives, but no one in the operating groups pays much attention. You see the organization unraveling before your eyes, but your ability to get your hands around the problem and stop it seems inexorably constrained by your prior organizational choices. You're convinced that many creative solutions will eventually emerge from the chaos, but will they come fast enough to reduce costs, meet enormous customer demand, and avoid major losses?

At the end of your third year as CEO, CyTech reports its first sales decline ever. The stock price drops to $17 a share, as shown in the accompanying table.

Selected Financial and Stock Information
(Dollars in millions, except stock price in actual dollars)

	Year ended March 31	
	3rd Year	2nd Year
Sales	$5,789	$5,883
Profits	174	294
Profits as a % of:		
Sales	3%	5%
Assets	5%	8%
Common Equity*	10%	15%
Market Value**	4,399	6,752
Stock Price	17 ¼	26 ⅛

* Total stockholders' equity includes capital stock, surplus, and retained earnings at the company's year end. For purposes of determining profits as a percent of common stockholders' equity, all preferred stock is excluded.
** Calculated by multiplying the number of common shares outstanding by the price per common share as of March 31.

At a special management meeting of the top five hundred executives and managers throughout the CyTech organization convened to deal with the crisis, you discover that your weakened credibility prevents you from pulling all the factions together. The business press reports CyTech's tailspin, extensively causing the stock price to fall even further. Within three weeks, the board of directors asks for your resignation.

- *In real life, you might have been able to avoid this disaster, but in an industry-rattling price war such as this one, you don't enjoy the luxury of lots of time to correct your mistakes. However, if you would like to find out why the author considers other alternatives preferable, review Chapter 14, then turn to one of the following:*

    Chapter 15, Emphasizing GE-Style Workouts;

    Chapter 17, Infusing CNN's Energy;

    Chapter 18, Emulating Merck's R&D Commitment;

    Chapter 19, Centering on WalMart's Superior Service; or

    Chapter 20, Highlighting McKinsey's On-the-Job Training.

- *If you want to put yourself on an entirely different decision-making track, select one of the following:*

    Chapter 2, Building a Classic Innovative Organization

    Chapter 26, Imbuing the Culture with Empowerment and Accountability;

    Chapter 38, Pursuing a Work Team Approach;

    Chapter 50, Reengineering Work Processes; or

    Chapter 62, Embracing a Revolutionary New Perspective.

Bowled over by the news that three foreign companies have just launched an aggressive price war, you wait anxiously to see how others in the industry will respond. Unfortunately, it doesn't take long for you to realize that everyone's entering the fray—just when you were making clear progress infusing CNN-style energy throughout your organization by adding third shifts to manufacturing, distributing cellular phones to all managers, promoting flex-hours with a 24-hour open-office policy, and asking everyone to make the necessary personal sacrifices to win the price war. Fortunately, however, your energy infusion program proves providential because it helps CyTech marshall the quickest response in the industry.

17

INFUSING CNN'S ENERGY

Working around the clock, everyone at CyTech embraces the challenge to win the price war, astonishing you with 24-hour work days. They display more energy than you dreamed possible, catching a few hours of sleep in their offices, morning, afternoon, and night, or waking up at home to answer middle-of-the-night E-mail and faxes. Employees tell their spouses and families, "Things will return to normal after the war." You sense, however, that things will never return to normal again. Morris Strandmeyer exults over the immediate success and transformation at CyTech, saying, "I know our people had the capacity for much more productivity than they were achieving. They're more satisfied too!" Showing your appreciation for his guiding influence in this decision, you promote Strandmeyer to senior vice president of production.

Armed with the motto "respond with energy," people throughout the organization find ways to cut costs, build new efficiencies into production, and ship more phone-fax-computers than any other competitor. Not only does CyTech gain market share, it posts huge profits, as the people in the organization, through sheer willpower, meet and beat the $500 price tag.

Looking back over the last several months, you congratulate yourself for selecting the focus on energy as CyTech's governing principle. The CNN model, it turns out, has provided the best possible focal point for CyTech's culture. It prepared the organization mentally and emotionally to rise to the challenge of the mass marketing/producing game. Stories about CNN's frenzy and ability to respond at a moment's notice helped sustain your people until, within a few short months, they developed their own war stories about mustering the energy to overcome any obstacle. Feature stories in newspapers, periodicals, and on television and radio throughout the world cite CyTech's energy and responsiveness as a model of "the new American competitiveness." A *Fortune* magazine cover story labels CyTech "the sleepless company." At the end of your third year as CEO, sales reach $8 billion, with the stock price soaring to $50 per share, as shown in the following table.

Selected Financial and Stock Information
(Dollars in millions, except stock price in actual dollars)

	Year ended March 31	
	3rd Year	2nd Year
Sales	$7,988	$5,883
Profits	559	294
Profits as a % of:		
Sales	7%	5%
Assets	12%	8%
Common Equity*	20%	15%
Market Value**	12,686	6,752
Stock Price	49 ¾	26 ⅛

* Total stockholders' equity includes capital stock, surplus, and retained earnings at the company's year end. For purposes of determining profits as a percent of common stockholders' equity, all preferred stock is excluded.
** Calculated by multiplying the number of common shares outstanding by the price per common share as of March 31.

During the fourth year of your leadership, however, an interesting dilemma arises when you and your senior team realize that CyTech has become so adept at directing its energy to the crisis of the moment that the organization has let longer-term technological development and strategic positioning go largely unattended. You have discovered the singular negative aspect of the energy attribute:

a company that thrives on *ad hoc* responsiveness to the moment tends to ignore the future. Even long-term thinkers like Karen Walsh, VP of the advanced technology lab, and Bob Kiechel, senior VP of product development, have become addicted to moment-by-moment reactions that have enabled CyTech to win the phone-fax-computer price war and deliver low-price technology to millions of people throughout the world, but they almost never talk about challenges that may lie five or ten years down the road. In one of your management meetings, Karen Walsh admits, "Energy is like a narcotic—once it gets into your system, you start to depend on it."

In all your business experience you've never experienced a situation quite like this. The energy level of the people at CyTech has completely transformed the organization's culture in a matter of 18 months, but you know in your heart that they can't maintain the pace forever. Now you must invent CyTech's future, helping it take maximum advantage of its high-energy culture, not just to meet today's challenges, but to create a healthier tomorrow. Can you maintain CyTech's dual strategic focus with the current culture? You worry that it's too biased toward mass marketing and production in a price war. However, the energy response just might do the trick in a technological war, too, if you can only fine-tune it properly.

Three alternative courses interest you. First, you could keep the company in its high-energy response mode, hoping that, no matter what happens in the marketplace, CyTech's organization can respond or react faster than anyone else. This posture's disadvantage lies in the possibility that a more future-oriented competitor will introduce technological advancements or other changes to which CyTech cannot respond overnight. In addition, the *reactor* posture has always represented the riskiest and least viable long-range position in any industry, because those who react to change but never invent change end up letting someone else control their future. However, in an age of chaos, an energy culture could provide the very ticket for CyTech's ongoing success.

A second alternative could turn CyTech's energy toward becoming the technological leader in the industry. Pursuing this path would require CyTech to spend more of its time and attention on technological developments during the next five to ten years, and it would mean moving most of its product-development efforts out of the *reactor* mode and into a long-term *inventor* mode. With CyTech winning the price war and achieving greater profitability at low prices than any of its competitors, you may well have time to shift the company's longer-term strategic focus away from reaction to, and toward initiation of, technological advancements.

The third alternative represents a combination of technological leadership and market followership in an effort to utilize the keen responsiveness of the CyTech organization most effectively. In this mode the company would initiate leadership in some circumstances, while following a competitor's lead in others. Avoiding the extremes of always leading the technological edge or constantly reacting to others' initiatives, this alternative would allow CyTech to analyze what's going on in the marketplace and then initiate or react selectively, with more efficiency, more profitability, and more power than any other competitor.

Most of your management team, including Strandmeyer, prefers the current reactor mode because it's working. They argue that the high-energy response posture will become the most viable organizational form in the twenty-first century. However, you're not convinced. You keep pondering the possibilities. For better or worse, your reputation and track record at CyTech prompt your senior team to pledge allegiance to whatever you ultimately decide. Even in the best of times, loneliness attends leadership. Now only you can decide.

While on vacation in Santa Fe, New Mexico, you leisurely pick up Monday's *Wall Street Journal* to see what's going on. As chance would have it, you read about a company called Thermo Electron, a $1.2 billion diversified technology company, which started out as a small laboratory instrument manufacturer but has used an innovative organizational approach to turn itself into a highly diversified technology factory. Relaxed and reflective, you see a bright possibility in the Thermo Electron story. According to the article, "What fuels Thermo's fertile hothouse for new businesses is its novel equity structure. It is designed like a solar system with planets orbiting a core. When a manager or engineer invents something or finds a new market for technology, Thermo often creates a whole new company in a strategy it calls a 'spin-out.' This strategy differs from the widely-used 'spin-off' in two ways: Thermo always retains a majority of the equity in the new company, and, in contrast to a spin-off distribution of stock to existing shareholders, it offers new stock to the public."

Thermo Electron seems to have perfected the art of fueling the entrepreneurial engine to motivate employees, maintain very high levels of productivity, and grow new businesses like crazy. This may be a perfect complement to the high-energy culture at work in CyTech's organization.

With Thermo Electron in mind, you review, once again, the three earlier alternatives for advancing CyTech's current organizational thrust. Now, you have found another option, the spin-out strategy. Though frustrated by the fact that none of the earlier alternatives has fully captured your imagination, you try to contain your impulsive excitement over Thermo Electron's approach. Sleep on it, you tell yourself. But, in the morning, you must decide.

- *If you decide to assume technological leadership, turn to Chapter 21.*

- *If you prefer remaining in the current reactor mode that has brought such great success in the past, turn to Chapter 22.*

- *If you want to combine the two alternatives, selectively choosing when to lead and when to follow, turn to Chapter 23.*

- *If you want to follow the Thermo Electron "best practice" of spinning out companies, turn to Chapter 75.*

Having chosen to emphasize commitment to R&D as the overriding organizational practice at CyTech, you encourage a continuing synthesis of the best practices implemented earlier, but with technological leadership as a beacon for every facet of the CyTech organization. You ask Karen Walsh, VP of CyTech's advanced technology lab, to spearhead a shift in focus to R&D commitment, which means making technological leadership the single driving force at CyTech. Walsh designs a conceptual map that relates all CyTech functions and activities to the R&D process, making every employee more R&D conscious and aware. Sales people focus more on selling CyTech's technological leadership, marketing people advertise R&D commitment, manufacturing people work more closely with R&D to improve product precision performance, and R&D people gain new status throughout the organization.

18

EMULATING MERCK'S R&D COMMITMENT

What occurs next blindsides you and makes your decision to place R&D at the top of CyTech's practices look extremely ill-advised. Three foreign competitors initiate a price war that forces the whole industry into a mass marketing/production frenzy two to three years earlier than anyone anticipated. Your decision to emphasize Merck's commitment to R&D collides with the demands of mass production and mass marketing, which thrive on efficiencies, rather than innovations. Your production people, encouraged by VP of production Morris Strandmeyer, begin screaming for R&D support to bring about efficiencies in production processes and product designs, but R&D, supported by senior VP of product development Bob Kiechel, holds true to its technological leadership commitment.

You quickly reverse your decision, calling for dual priority practices: Merck's commitment to R&D and WalMart's superior service. Your decision divides the company, creating conflict and gridlock that prevents the company from meeting the challenges brought on by the price war. News of CyTech's apparent paralysis reaches the marketplace overnight. Dealers everywhere begin promoting competitors' products over CyTech's, arguing that CyTech will probably not remain the dominant player for long.

Sales stall as your third year at the helm comes to an end. Not surprisingly, CyTech's stock price drops below $20 per share, as shown in the accompanying table.

Selected Financial and Stock Information
(Dollars in millions, except stock price in actual dollars)

	Year ended March 31	
	3rd Year	2nd Year
Sales	$6,001	$5,883
Profits	240	294
Profits as a % of:		
Sales	4%	5%
Assets	6%	8%
Common Equity*	11%	15%
Market Value**	4,814	6,752
Stock Price	18 $\frac{7}{8}$	26 $\frac{1}{8}$

* Total stockholders' equity includes capital stock, surplus, and retained earnings at the company's year end. For purposes of determining profits as a percent of common stockholders' equity, all preferred stock is excluded.

** Calculated by multiplying the number of common shares outstanding by the price per common share as of March 31.

You feel the situation remaining utterly out of control as the organizational forces you set in motion keep CyTech spinning in circles. The press calls it "Corporate Schizophrenia." *The Wall Street Journal* blames you for indecisiveness. CyTech's stock plummets further to $12 per share.

When the chairman of the board asks if you will consider resigning to allow CyTech to move forward, you accept his suggestion.

- *In real life, you might have prevented this outcome, but pursuing an R&D commitment while fighting a price war didn't work in this particular situation. To discover the author's rationale for choosing a different alternative, review Chapter 14, then turn to one of the following:*

    Chapter 15, Emphasizing GE-Style Workouts;

    Chapter 16, Enshrining 3M's Autonomy;

    Chapter 17, Infusing CNN's Energy;

    Chapter 19, Centering on WalMart's Superior Service; or

    Chapter 20, Highlighting McKinsey's On-the-Job Training.

- *If you care to pick another decision-making track altogether, select one of the following:*

    Chapter 2, Building a Classic Innovative Organization

    Chapter 26, Imbuing the Culture with Empowerment and Accountability;

    Chapter 38, Pursuing a Work Team Approach;

    Chapter 50, Reengineering Work Processes; or

    Chapter 62, Embracing a Revolutionary New Perspective.

At three o'clock one afternoon, you're relaxing in your office, going over the week's schedule with your executive assistant when John Solo, executive VP of worldwide sales, calls to inform you that three foreign competitors have just initiated a price war dropping phone-fax-computer prices to $499. You quickly call a meeting of your senior team to assess the situation, and by midnight you conclude that every competitor must drop its prices or lose market share to the foreign competition. The mass marketing/mass production game you thought you would be playing two to three years down the road has begun already. Since the last few months' emphasis on service has combined CyTech's best practices to promote service to customers, first and foremost, CyTech easily moves into a mass marketing mode to meet the escalating demand for low-priced phone-fax-computers. You're particularly heartened by Advanced Technology Lab VP Karen Walsh's response as she actually shifts gears at the lab to make sure CyTech customers get the best low-priced phone-fax-computer possible. That means redesigning the *PowerBase* product line to make it better and cheaper, a task to which Karen and her people rise with great relish.

19

CENTERING ON WALMART'S SUPERIOR SERVICE

Within six months, you've achieved a 33 percent decrease in costs, you're making solid profits on every phone-fax-computer you sell, even at $459. Sales reach $7 billion at year end, and CyTech's stock price shoots to $42 per share, as shown in the table on page 92.

The board praises you for these results, as does *Business Week,* which identifies CyTech as one of the sure winners in the phone-fax-computer price war. As a reward for his influence in guiding CyTech to this decision, you promote John Solo to president and

Selected Financial and Stock Information
(Dollars in millions, except stock price in actual dollars)

	Year ended March 31	
	3rd Year	2nd Year
Sales	$6,896	$5,883
Profits	414	294
Profits as a % of:		
Sales	6%	5%
Assets	12%	8%
Common Equity*	18%	15%
Market Value**	10,773	6,752
Stock Price	42 $\frac{1}{4}$	26 $\frac{1}{8}$

* Total stockholders' equity includes capital stock, surplus, and retained earnings at the company's year end. For purposes of determining profits as a percent of common stockholders' equity, all preferred stock is excluded.

** Calculated by multiplying the number of common shares outstanding by the price per common share as of March 31.

COO of CyTech. You are convinced he should succeed you as CEO in three to five years.

The service culture grows even stronger during your fourth year as CEO. CyTech ships more phone-fax-computers than any other competitor and achieves what most consider the market's predominant position. Stock analysts anticipate the stock price hitting $70 by year end.

However, just before the end of the year, disaster strikes. A Japanese competitor, Sansui, introduces a voice-operated phone-fax-computer that allows the user to enter all data by voice, eliminating the need for a key pad or writing wand. The technological breakthrough propels the industry back into a new technology war. In the United States, Motorola quickly responds with its own voice-operated machine. Unfortunately, CyTech's heavy service emphasis has neglected basic R&D projects, and both Karen Walsh and Bob Kiechel tell you that it will take at least two years for CyTech to produce anything similar. As customers flock to the new machines, CyTech's sales fall off by 50 percent, and while year-end sales results show a modest increase over last year, the stock price plummets to $14 per share as investors anticipate a tough year ahead for your company.

Selected Financial and Stock Information
(Dollars in millions, except stock price in actual dollars)

	Year ended March 31	
	4th Year	3rd Year
Sales	$7,035	$6,896
Profits	352	414
Profits as a % of:		
Sales	5%	6%
Assets	11%	12%
Common Equity*	17%	18%
Market Value**	3,602	10,773
Stock Price	14 $\frac{1}{8}$	42 $\frac{1}{4}$

* Total stockholders' equity includes capital stock, surplus, and retained earnings at the company's year end. For purposes of determining profits as a percent of common stockholders' equity, all preferred stock is excluded.

** Calculated by multiplying the number of common shares outstanding by the price per common share as of March 31.

You quickly find out that no past success compensates for current failure. Since someone must pay the price for CyTech's inability to adapt to this latest change in the market, the board asks for your resignation one month after the year end. However, in a surprise move, the board picks Morris Strandmeyer, VP of production, to succeed you. John Solo is fired.

- *Although you might have been able to produce a voice-operated machine faster than this outcome allows, in this scenario CyTech did ignore the technological development path too long for it to recover its expertise promptly. If you want to see why the author considers other alternatives preferable, review Chapter 14, then turn to one of the following:*

     Chapter 15, Emphasizing GE-Style Workouts;

     Chapter 16, Enshrining 3M's Autonomy;

     Chapter 17, Infusing CNN's Energy;

     Chapter 18, Emulating Merck's R&D Commitment; or

     Chapter 20, Highlighting McKinsey's On-the-Job Training.

- *If you want to switch to another decision-making track, select one of the following:*

     Chapter 2, Building a Classic Innovative Organization

     Chapter 26, Imbuing the Culture with Empowerment and Accountability;

     Chapter 38, Pursuing a Work Team Approach;

     Chapter 50, Reengineering Work Processes; or

     Chapter 62, Embracing a Revolutionary New Perspective.

Comfortable with McKinsey's on-the-job training philosophy as the overarching organizational practice at CyTech, you begin focusing on people development as the most important element of the company's synthesis of best practices. You increase the number of required training days for every employee within the company from five to twenty-five and ask your senior team to modify the on-the-job training process top to bottom, positioning it as the capstone of the CyTech culture. Nan Thurow, senior VP of worldwide operations, takes firm hold on this new training emphasis, weaving it into every aspect of the company's operations. Highly impressed with her clear vision and insight in this area, you recommend her to the board as your successor.

However, just as you're positioning this new philosophy at the top of CyTech's priorities, three foreign competitors launch a price war that turns the whole industry upside down. All of your competitors begin selling phone-fax-computers for under $500 two to three years earlier than anyone at CyTech expected it. The mass marketing/producing game has begun.

20
HIGHLIGHTING MCKINSEY'S ON-THE-JOB TRAINING

Can on-the-job training provide the necessary strength for meeting such a challenge? As you converse with your senior team, you discover that they think it can. While you still harbor doubts yourself, you decide to stick to your decision and hope it will provide the organizational strength necessary to implement CyTech's dual strategic focus.

In the next few weeks, however, you realize that bringing about a major change in the on-the-job training process and making it the capstone of CyTech's culture will take months, maybe years, requiring extensive education about how on-the-job training can best facilitate an ongoing synthesis of best practices. CyTech may not survive the current threat in such a time frame. You receive more and more pressure from the board of directors as competitors make inroads, stealing market share from CyTech with quicker, more aggressive responses to the price war. You finally conclude that CyTech has run out of time. The company simply does not have the time to develop on-the-job training as its cultural capstone, while, at the same time, trying to turn itself into a successful mass marketer and a mass producer. You switch gears in midstream, asking every employee in the organization to focus on the current challenge: winning the price war.

It doesn't take long for the business press to report that CyTech is panicking. You attempt to squelch the rumors, but even members of the board needle you with countless questions about CyTech's sluggishness. Members of your senior team begin losing faith in your ability to meet the challenge as rumors continue spreading inside and outside the organization about your inability to lead the charge in this time of crisis. At the end of your third year as CEO, sales increase modestly to $6.2 billion, attaining only 25 percent of the sales growth most competitors have achieved in the last six months. The stock price falls to $15 per share, as shown in the following table.

Selected Financial and Stock Information
(Dollars in millions, except stock price in actual dollars)

	Year ended March 31	
	3rd Year	**2nd Year**
Sales	$6,209	$5,883
Profits	310	294
Profits as a % of:		
Sales	5%	5%
Assets	8%	8%
Common Equity*	14%	15%
Market Value**	3,794	6,752
Stock Price	14 $\frac{7}{8}$	26 $\frac{1}{8}$

* Total stockholders' equity includes capital stock, surplus, and retained earnings at the company's year end. For purposes of determining profits as a percent of common stockholders' equity, all preferred stock is excluded.

** Calculated by multiplying the number of common shares outstanding by the price per common share as of March 31.

Within one month after the year end, CyTech's stock drops another five points to $10 per share. In an overnight takeover bid, Motorola purchases 60 percent of CyTech's stock at an average price of $15 per share, and within weeks of the takeover, Motorola management asks you to resign.

- *Well, this is only a game. In real life you might have pulled CyTech out of its sluggish development. However, if you want to know why the author considers other choices preferable, revisit Chapter 14, then select one of the following:*

    Chapter 15, Emphasizing GE-Style Workouts;

    Chapter 16, Enshrining 3M's Autonomy;

    Chapter 17, Infusing CNN's Energy;

    Chapter 18, Emulating Merck's R&D Commitment; or

    Chapter 19, Centering on WalMart's Superior Service.

- *If you would prefer striking out on a new decision-making track, proceed to one of the following:*

    Chapter 2, Building a Classic Innovative Organization

    Chapter 26, Imbuing the Culture with Empowerment and Accountability;

    Chapter 38, Pursuing a Work Team Approach;

    Chapter 50, Reengineering Work Processes; or

    Chapter 62, Embracing a Revolutionary New Perspective.

Against the advice of your senior team and, in particular, against the pleadings of your newest senior VP, Morris Strandmeyer, you move CyTech into a technological leadership posture, calling for a substantial redirecting of energy to longer-term planning and product development. You fail to anticipate the emotional division your decision creates and the way it saps the organization's high-energy culture and stalls the company's momentum in the price war while everyone redirects energy to technological leadership. The shift to longer-term concerns actually demotivates CyTech employees, who have become accustomed to living and working in the moment. Most of them just can't adjust. Strandmeyer begs you to reconsider this course of action, but you ignore his whining.

You realize, too late, that the energy focus had so cemented and unified CyTech's culture that everyone in the organization held the same overriding commitment to helping CyTech meet immediate market challenges. It captured the imagination, enthusiasm, and the best talents of every individual within the organization. Now you are asking them to play a totally different long-range planning-and-development game, which lacks the immediacy and urgency that fueled the success of the energy focus in the first place. Not only do your attempts to move into a technological leadership mode fail, responsiveness in the marketplace declines, affording competitors the time they need to match CyTech's strength and position. CyTech stock drops to $20 per share as reports of declining market share cause brokers to recommend selling CyTech stock. Even though sales increased 15 percent for the year, anticipation of an organizational unraveling in the coming year combined with declining profits spooks Wall

21

LEADING THE MARKET IN TECHNOLOGY

Street. The accompanying table shows your fourth-year's performance as CEO.

Selected Financial and Stock Information
(Dollars in millions, except stock price in actual dollars)

	Year ended March 31	
	4th Year	3rd Year
Sales	$9,186	$7,988
Profits	552	559
Profits as a % of:		
Sales	6%	7%
Assets	10%	12%
Common Equity*	17%	20%
Market Value**	5,164	12,686
Stock Price	20 $\frac{1}{4}$	49 $\frac{3}{4}$

* Total stockholders' equity includes capital stock, surplus, and retained earnings at
the company's year end. For purposes of determining profits as a percent of
common stockholders' equity, all preferred stock is excluded.
** Calculated by multiplying the number of common shares outstanding by the price
per common share as of March 31.

At the beginning of your fifth year as CEO of CyTech, you
resign on the advice of your doctor, who tells you, "You've aged
twenty years in the last five."

As you leave the company, all the glory you reaped for
introducing CNN-style energy to CyTech evaporates in light of
CyTech's failing performance in recent months.

- *In real life you might have handled the personal stress and recovered from the recent setback. However, if you want to know why the author questions your last decision, turn to Chapter 22 or 23.*

- *If you'd rather move to another decision-making track, move forward to one of the following:*

  Chapter 2, Building a Classic Innovative Organization

  Chapter 26, Imbuing the Culture with Empowerment and Accountability;

  Chapter 38, Pursuing a Work Team Approach;

  Chapter 50, Reengineering Work Processes; or

  Chapter 62, Embracing a Revolutionary New Perspective

When you decide to follow the advice of your senior team, especially Strandmeyer, setting aside your misgivings about continuing a *reactor* posture, your senior team reacts enthusiastically. Each executive assures you that you won't be sorry for perpetuating what Karen Walsh calls "the only kind of organizational culture that will bring American competitiveness back from the defeat."

22

MAINTAINING A HIGH-ENERGY REACTOR POSTURE

Over the next several months CyTech's energy grows even more robust as the price war continues. You institute a new vacation policy—which adds two weeks to everyone's vacation time and requires that individuals take at least one week of vacation quarterly—in order to reduce the high stress among the work force. You also introduce a sabbatical program that encourages employees to take off three months at a time every three years, and, you urge every manager and supervisor to figure out how to let every employee work at home at least one day a week.

The results astonish you. Employment applications quadruple, commitment among current employees deepens, sales reach $10 billion, and CyTech's stock soars to $69 per share, as shown in the table on page 104.

During your fifth year as CEO, another major change occurs in the marketplace as Motorola introduces a voice-operated phone-fax-computer, rendering writing instruments and key pads obsolete. Now users can operate their devices by voice, and they seem to love that.

The CyTech organization springs into action with lightning speed, rallying behind the banner of high-energy responsiveness and outshining every other competitor's reaction. CyTech offers its

Selected Financial and Stock Information
(Dollars in millions, except stock price in actual dollars)

	Year ended March 31	
	4th Year	3rd Year
Sales	$10,111	$7,988
Profits	809	559
Profits as a % of:		
Sales	8%	7%
Assets	15%	12%
Common Equity*	24%	20%
Market Value**	17,626	12,686
Stock Price	69 $\frac{1}{8}$	49 $\frac{3}{4}$

* Total stockholders' equity includes capital stock, surplus, and retained earnings at the company's year end. For purposes of determining profits as a percent of common stockholders' equity, all preferred stock is excluded.

** Calculated by multiplying the number of common shares outstanding by the price per common share as of March 31.

own voice-operated machine within three months, beating all other competitors after Motorola. You quickly gain market share parity with Motorola and demonstrate to the world just how nimbly a high-energy culture can shift gears.

Sales reach $13 billion at the end of your fifth year as CEO, sending the stock price to $86 per share. See table on page 105. Your own stock options, acquired over the last five years, are worth $280 million. However, a down side to all of this emerges when your 20-hour work days over the last three years takes a toll on your health. You suffer from high blood pressure, severe headaches, and unexplained heart palpitations. You've failed to follow the requirements of your own vacation policy, taking only two weeks in the last two years, and that has all but burned you out.

The board of directors wants you to remain CEO and become chairman of the board for the next five years. The next decision you face strikes at the very heart of whether such an energy-intensive culture can really sustain itself over time. Should you stay on as CEO? Will your health survive another five years of round-the-clock pressure? What has CyTech's energy-intensive culture done to the

Selected Financial and Stock Information
(Dollars in millions, except stock price in actual dollars)

	Year ended March 31	
	5th Year	4th Year
Sales	$13,286	$10,111
Profits	930	809
Profits as a % of:		
Sales	7%	8%
Assets	13%	15%
Common Equity*	21%	24%
Market Value**	21,882	17,626
Stock Price	85 $^{13}/_{16}$	69 $^{1}/_{8}$

* Total stockholders' equity includes capital stock, surplus, and retained earnings at the company's year end. For purposes of determining profits as a percent of common stockholders' equity, all preferred stock is excluded.

** Calculated by multiplying the number of common shares outstanding by the price per common share as of March 31.

overall well-being of employees and their families? Morris Strandmeyer divorced his second wife. Nan Thurow underwent surgery to remove a chronic ulcer. John Solo announced his early retirement. Karen Walsh suffered a miscarriage. Others express concern over burnout and stress overload.

You wonder about your ethical and moral responsibility for setting the tone for CyTech's future. Should you retire as CEO, sending the message to individuals within the CyTech organization that they should carefully manage their own careers and their own personal lives in a way that will allow for success but not crowd out everything else that's important in their lives? If you retire, you would be retiring earlier than most every other CEO in corporate America, but maybe that, too, could send an important message to the people at CyTech, as well as to people in other organizations.

On the other hand, if you stay another five years as chairman of the board and CEO, you could take an active hand in fine-tuning the company's high-energy culture, balancing it to meet the needs of the whole individual. You consider increasing sabbaticals, providing "whole person" training that goes well beyond the standard five days for every employee in the company, and integrating family and spouses into work at CyTech so that the high-energy culture does not cause employees to burn out, destroy their health, or lose touch with important relationships.

Now you must make this very personal, yet organizationally significant decision.

- *If you decide to retire as CEO of CyTech, turn to Chapter 24.*

- *If you decide to stay on as chairman of the board and CEO of CyTech for another five years, turn to Chapter 25.*

Your decision to adopt a combination position does not please your senior team. They argue that it runs totally against the grain of CyTech's corporate culture because it requires analysis of when to lead or follow rather than high-energy responsiveness. Even Hal McPhee argues intensely for maintaining the high-energy culture and not dampening it by adopting an "analyzer" posture.

You try to convince your senior executives that pursuing the combination of leadership and followership does not need to remove high-energy responsiveness; it just means redirecting the energy in a more analytical and less frenzied way. You can't believe McPhee's response: "Frenzy is exactly what works best around here!"

Strandmeyer, the major proponent of CNN-style energy, says, "This new high-energy attitude has affected CyTech's culture and, in particular, every member of this senior team, cutting across the deep psychological differences and personalities to create a oneness and alignment that I've never experienced before."

Finally, you decide to change your mind. You agree to maintain a high-energy-response culture.

23

LEADING AND FOLLOWING THE MARKET

- *Turn to Chapter 22.*

After a lot of soul searching, you decide to retire. However, you want to send a strong message to your coworkers as you depart because your departure can greatly influence the company and its future organizational development. Stories of the beginning of CyTech's high-energy responsiveness will shape the organization's pattern of development for years to come, and those stories must include the real reasons you left at such a relatively early age.

24

MAKING A STATEMENT WITH YOUR RETIREMENT

You decide to do it with quiet, yet unusual fanfare, tapping the company's video production capabilities to create a 30-minute presentation about your five years at CyTech, the future you envision for the company, and your own personal goals for retirement. In it, you talk about how you plan to spend the rest of your life pursuing knowledge and growth in new arenas, spending time with your family, your children and grandchildren, giving time to the arts, and contributing to causes that will improve the quality of life for others. Stressing your belief in the value of the whole person, you draw from Carl Jung's book, *Modern Man in Search of a Soul,* in which the renowned psychologist suggests that the second half of life, after age forty, should be devoted to exploring new dimensions of one's personality in order to become a whole person. You express your hope that all the employees at CyTech will embrace wholeness and balance in their lives, making sure the high-energy culture at CyTech does not create one-dimensional or deeply dissatisfied people. You encourage every employee at CyTech to find time in his or her high-energy life for more contemplation and personal growth. You also announce the establishment of a whole-person educational center within CyTech University to help employees, especially those over forty, explore the dimensions of their personalities they may have neglected or underdeveloped over the course of their first 40 years, implementing what Carl Jung envisioned as the second stage of human development.

You also announce a broad expansion of stock option and stock bonus programs to all people within the CyTech organization, making it possible for every employee who works hard to retire early, if he or she so chooses. Your farewell videotape reaches the people at CyTech just about the time you enroll at Yale University to begin a doctoral program in ancient history.

Following your lead, Nan Thurow, Bob Kiechel, and Hal McPhee decide to retire within the next year. You're pleased with their decisions and know that the high-energy culture at CyTech has groomed appropriate replacements.

Morris Strandmeyer takes over at CyTech, vowing to keep his tenure short and to help CyTech's high-energy people find faster paths out of the company to pursue other dimensions of their lives. You're pleased with what you've left behind.

This marks the end of a decision-making track, but you can continue playing *The Organization Game* by selecting one of the following options.

- *If you want to compare how the results of your last five years of organizational decision making stack up against the other positive outcomes in The Organization Game, turn to Chapter 78.*

- *If you decide to explore other alternatives on this track, review Chapter 14, then move to one of the following:*

  Chapter 15, Emphasizing GE-Style Workouts;

  Chapter 16, Enshrining 3M's Autonomy;

  Chapter 18, Emulating Merck's R&D Commitment;

  Chapter 19, Centering on WalMart's Superior Service;

  Chapter 20, Highlighting McKinsey's On-the-Job Training;

  Chapter 21, Leading the Market in Technology;

  Chapter 23, Leading and Following the Market; or

  Chapter 25, Signing Aboard for Five More Years.

- *If you want to embark on another decision-making track, go to one of the following:*

  Chapter 2, Building a Classic Innovative Organization

  Chapter 26, Imbuing the Culture with Empowerment and Accountability;

  Chapter 38, Pursuing a Work Team Approach;

  Chapter 50, Reengineering the Work Processes; or

  Chapter 62, Embracing a Revolutionary New Perspective

Since you believe you can help the organization achieve the necessary balance and integration to temper—without dampening—the high-energy culture, you choose to remain at CyTech. However, the marketplace continues exploding with new developments as computer monitors replace television sets and communications networks develop as never before imagined. Developments in multimedia production allow people everywhere to create programming, communicate with one another at will, and learn from the best minds, the greatest artists, and the finest performers from all over the world. CyTech remains at the very center of all this activity, creating new generations of *PowerBases* with all the latest communication's gadgetry. New hand-held devices will soon enter the market, allowing users to videotape, compose music, draw upon an infinite number of databases for resource material, and create multimedia programs for transmission around the world. Much of your agenda for achieving balance and integration and focusing on the whole person gets set aside early in your sixth year as the marketplace consumes every ounce of your energy.

25

STAYING ABOARD FOR FIVE MORE YEARS

CyTech's high-energy culture demands more of you than ever before. According to your doctor, the accumulated stress in your body has made you particularly vulnerable to a stroke or heart attack.

Before the end of your sixth year as CEO of CyTech, you suffer a massive stroke that almost completely disables you. You're forced to resign. This marks the end of a decision-making track, but you can continue playing *The Organization Game* by selecting one of the following options.

- *If you want to compare how the results of your last five years of organizational decision making stack up against the other positive outcomes in The Organization Game, turn to Chapter 78.*

- *If you decide to explore other alternatives on this track, revisit Chapter 14, then move to one of the following:*

  Chapter 15, Emphasizing GE-Style Workouts;

  Chapter 16, Enshrining 3M's Autonomy;

  Chapter 18, Emulating Merck's R&D Commitment;

  Chapter 19, Centering on WalMart's Superior Service;

  Chapter 20, Highlighting McKinsey's On-the-Job Training;

  Chapter 21, Leading the Market in Technology;

  Chapter 23, Leading and Following the Market; or

  Chapter 24, Making a Statement with Your Retirement.

- *If you would like to begin a new decision-making track, turn to one of the following:*

  Chapter 2, Building a Classic Innovative Organization

  Chapter 26, Imbuing the Culture with Empowerment and Accountability;

  Chapter 38, Pursuing a Work Team Approach;

  Chapter 50, Reengineering the Work Processes; or

  Chapter 62, Embracing a Revolutionary New Perspective.

Convinced that a greater sense of empowerment and accountability among workers and managers alike will make the most difference in CyTech's future, you move forward aggressively with the idea. You begin driving home two crucial precepts: that every employee always asks, "What else can I do to achieve desired results?" and

26

IMBUING THE CULTURE WITH EMPOWERMENT AND ACCOUNTABILITY

that every manager gives people the freedom and authority to do what they must to get those results. You know that it will take a massive companywide effort to imbue these precepts into every individual and manager within the company, but you strongly believe the effort will pay off.

As you discuss your program with your senior team, consultants, and the people in corporate training and development, you emphasize the long-term nature of this commitment to accountability and empowerment. Changing peoples' attitudes not only takes time, but results from those altered attitudes will take time as well. Meanwhile, the market continues to change rapidly. CyTech introduces a freshly redesigned *PowerBase 3* with a new chip and the capacity to function in both wireless and wired modes. At the same time, competitors upgrade their own product offerings in a number of ways, making the phone-fax-computer market even more fiercely competitive than before.

In your reflective moments, you wonder what other CEOs in the industry are doing to address the organizational issues that arise in a quickly evolving mass production and marketing environment that continues to demand innovation and new-product development. Those who resolve the issues most wisely will surely determine the winners in the years ahead. The right organizational approach will propel the most successful strategy, while the wrong one could court disaster. You've got to make the right choices for CyTech's organizational culture and work environment. As you mull over the situation, you grow more concerned than ever that the right choice hinges on attitudes and philosophy, not structure, *per se.* However, as you lie in bed at night, you still worry that your chosen focus lacks a certain hard-edged and structured component to make the necessary changes happen.

On the one hand you believe Jack Welch, CEO of General Electric, who spoke his mind in the highly insightful book by Noel Tichy and Stratford Sherman, *Control Your Destiny or Someone Else Will: How Jack Welch Is Making General Electric the World's Most Competitive Company.* When asked by authors Tichy and Sherman, who both have worked at or written about GE for years, whether his fuzzy and soft-sounding concepts about empowerment and accountability could really produce results, Welch concludes the book with these words:

"If you're not thinking all the time about making every person more valuable, you don't have a chance. What's the alternative? Wasted minds? Uninvolved people? A labor force that's angry or bored? That doesn't make sense!"

As you ponder Welch's words, you puzzle over some statements he made earlier in the book, such as, "You've got to be hard to be soft....If you've got a fat organization, soft values won't get you very far....Before you can get into stuff like that [empowerment and accountability], you've first got to do the hard structural work. Take out the layers. Pull up the weeds. Scrape off the rust. Every organization needs values, but a lean organization needs them even more. When you strip away the support systems of staffs and layers, people have to change their habits and expectations, or else the stress will just overwhelm them." Have you done enough of the hard structural reworking at CyTech? You wonder. Is the company lean enough to shift its focus to empowerment and accountability? Implementation of accountability and empowerment could prove more difficult than the more formal structure or process-oriented changes you've undertaken in the past, and you can't be sure your people will respond quickly enough, given the rapid changes in the marketplace and among your competitors, to maintain CyTech's leadership position. You feel lonely in your role as CEO and wish the ambiguity inherent in your job would magically disappear.

As you consider the various alternatives for implementing your new focus, you spend time with each of your senior team, asking them to share their insights and worries about making empowerment and accountability work at CyTech. John Solo, executive vice president for worldwide sales and marketing, advises you just to start implementing the program by stressing empowerment and accountability everywhere you go, asking the senior team, as well as every other manager in the company to do likewise. He suggests you identify a simple six-point program for making empowerment and accountability work and then, "just do it." Given John's personality, his response doesn't surprise you.

As you expected, Bob Kiechel, senior vice president of product development, offers inventive advice, suggesting that you adopt a totally new performance appraisal system based on accountability. Believing that empowerment will naturally follow accountability, he urges you to develop a new set of management skills and tools based on accountability.

Your chief financial officer, Hal McPhee, prefers a more elaborate program that includes guidelines, planning meetings, review sessions, reports, and milestone evaluation points. True to McPhee's nature, his recommendations reflect a hierarchical and tightly organized approach.

Your senior vice president of worldwide operations, Nan Thurow, tells you, "We'll have to work hard to make people at CyTech aware of *accountable* and *victim* behavior, helping them to understand the difference between the two." She emphasizes the fact that people will have to "become" different before they can truly accept more accountability for results. Of course, Nan's ideas about "becoming" spring from her own personal biases.

Karen Walsh, vice president of CyTech's advanced technology lab, argues that unless every employee understands the full picture of where CyTech is going and how it fits into the industry, it won't matter whether people feel accountable and empowered or not. She argues for sharing a comprehensive vision of where CyTech stands in the industry, relative to competitors, and what technologies will drive the future. You thank Karen for her input, expressing admiration for her logical and holistic view.

When Morris Strandmeyer, vice president of production, warns you that you must control the implementation process very carefully, you detect his strong suspicion that this whole empowerment and accountability gambit will not really work. He says, "You cannot give up all of the structural and hierarchical aspects of the organization while you're focusing on making people more accountable and more empowered. If you do, you'll just create confusion."

Having gathered the ideas of your senior team and after a great deal of further consideration of the issues involved, you decide that you can't focus on both empowerment and accountability at the same time but must choose one as the primary focus in the short run. It boils down to a "chicken or egg" dilemma: does accountability follow empowerment, or *vice versa?* As you wrestle with this question for several weeks, you eventually conclude that it's always easier to empower accountable people, which supports a primary focus on accountability. However, just as you're about to announce your decision, you can't rid yourself of the thought that when people feel empowered they more easily behave in an accountable fashion, which suggests empowerment as a primary focus. You toy with the idea of discussing this dilemma with your senior team, but given the biases of each member, you decide that will only fuel more debate and further cloud your decision. What should you do?

- *If you decide to emphasize accountability, turn to Chapter 27.*

- *If you prefer an empowerment focus, turn to Chapter 28.*

Your senior team welcomes your decision to stress accountability first and foremost, and you immediately begin employing the concepts laid out in the books *Control Your Destiny or Someone Else Will,* by Noel Tichy and Stratford Sherman, and *The Oz Principle,* by Roger Connors and Tom Smith. From *The Oz Principle* you adapt a diagram called "Achieving Accountability," which identifies a thin line separating accountable and victim behavior, as shown on page 120.

27

STRESSING ACCOUNTABILITY FIRST AND FOREMOST

As the authors described it, "Below the line lies excuse making, blaming others, confusion, and an attitude of helplessness, while above the line lies a sense of reality, ownership, commitment, and solutions to problems, and determined action." According to to *The Oz Principle,* losers "languish below the line preparing stories that explain why past efforts went awry, and winners reside above the line powered by commitment and hard work."

In a meeting with your senior team, you unveil a poster depicting the accountability diagram. To help your team appreciate its message, you explain *The Oz Principle,* in your own words: "People and organizations get stuck below the line every time they avoid accountability for personal or organizational results. Then, they exhibit victim behavior and feel powerless. If they remain below the line, things always get worse. Only when people and organizations rise above the line, assuming accountable behavior, can they regain their lost power."

Then you quote GE CEO Jack Welch from *Control Your Destiny or Someone Else Will:* "The only way I see to get more productivity

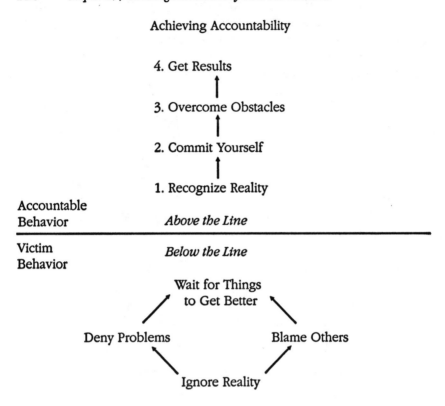

is by getting people involved and excited about their jobs. You can't afford to have anyone walk through a gate of a factory, or into an office, who's not giving 120 percent."

A good deal of spirited discussion ensues, and at the end of a rather lengthy meeting you ask your senior team to commit themselves body and soul to operating above the line, giving 120 percent. You also ask each of them to help one another avoid the victim cycle by speaking up whenever someone falls below the line or below 120 percent. This last request creates an interesting catalyst for discussion in the weeks ahead; phrases such as "you're dropping below the line" or "you're not giving 120 percent" get repeated again and again in senior staff meetings and in the hallways of CyTech's executive suite.

Within a couple of months you note that *The Oz Principle* language of accountability and victimization takes hold; however, some of your executive team tend to talk more about the victim cycle while others tend to talk more about the accountability ladder. As your senior team's awareness of the new attitude of accountability increases, you ponder exactly how you should roll out the message to the entire organization, asking yourself three questions in particular:

1. Should you primarily emphasize the rungs of the accountability ladder and how to climb each one?
2. Should you stress the victim cycle and how to avoid it?
3. Should you attempt to focus simultaneously on the steps to accountability and the victim cycle, never talking about one without including the other?

Much like your earlier dilemma, this one perplexes you, particularly when you recognize the enormous impact of such questions during a companywide roll out. Your decision here will determine how accountability grows throughout the organization for years to come.

Though John Solo tells you you're worrying too much about "minor issues," you continue to wrestle with the impact of the symbols. In a program built on principles of accountability, the right symbols can make all the difference when it comes to translating ideas into actions.

Emphasizing the steps to accountability offers the advantage of directing everyone's attention toward the positive side of the equation and the goal of greater accountability for everyone, while stressing the victim cycle addresses the reality that everybody gets trapped in the victim cycle from time to time, without even realizing it. Finally, focusing on both the steps to accountability and the victim cycle at the same time might help people keep the total picture in perspective, always helping the individual who's fallen into the victim cycle toward the steps to accountability and always cautioning the person who's taken the steps to accountability to beware of the possibility of again falling below the line.

The idealism embodied in the accountability ladder could alienate some people who desire a more realistic approach, while the realism embodied in the victim cycle could strike others as too negative. Though this argument seems to favor a simultaneous focus, your experience with the senior team suggests that people will wind up emphasizing one or the other, depending on their personalities. Trying to emphasize both could compromise either an acute understanding of the victim cycle or an accurate comprehension of the steps to accountability. Like it or not, such subtleties compose the very essence of successful organizational and cultural change, and since you're attempting to bring about a major attitudinal change, as opposed to a structural or even behavioral change, you must remain keenly sensitive to such issues.

While your senior team works hard at incorporating the ideas of accountability into their own behavior and you wrestle with the issues surrounding its more widespread implementation, CyTech records a respectable performance for its first year under your leadership, as shown below.

Selected Financial and Stock Information
(Dollars in millions, except stock price in actual dollars)

	Year ended March 31	
	1st Year	Previous Year
Sales	$5,285	$4,083
Profits	317	242
Profits as a % of:		
Sales	6%	6%
Assets	9%	9%
Common Equity*	18%	17%
Market Value**	7,621	6,123
Stock Price	29 $\frac{7}{8}$	23 $\frac{3}{4}$

*   Total stockholders' equity includes capital stock, surplus, and retained earnings at the company's year end. For purposes of determining profits as a percent of common stockholders' equity, all preferred stock is excluded.
** Calculated by multiplying the number of common shares outstanding by the price per common share as of March 31.

Now, with the beginning of a new fiscal year, you must keep things moving, and make your next move decisively.

- *If you decide to stress the victim cycle as the beginning point for companywide implementation, turn to Chapter 29.*

- *If you want to emphasize the steps to accountability as the initial step in your roll-out throughout the organization, turn to Chapter 30.*

- *If you prefer a simultaneous focus on the steps to accountability and the victim cycle, never applying one without discussing the other, turn to Chapter 31.*

Your decision to concentrate on empowerment first, then accountability, receives mixed reviews from your senior team. Kiechel and Thurow feel comfortable with this approach, while McPhee and Strandmeyer remain skeptical. Walsh and Solo appear ambivalent. Nevertheless, you forge ahead, applying the concepts from Tichy and Sherman's book *Control Your Destiny or Someone Else Will* and Peter Block's books *The Empowered Manager* and *Stewardship*. In a meeting with your senior team you argue, as Peter Block does, that all organizations tend to follow the bureaucratic cycle. See chart on page 126.

28

PUTTING EMPOWERMENT FIRST

You explain the cycle to your senior team: "As organization's grow they become more structured and controlled. Roles and responsibilities get clearly defined. Workers demand consistency and uniformity. Slowly, but surely, professional managers sow the seeds of bureaucracy." You point out to your team, "The self-reinforcing nature of the bureaucratic cycle promotes patriarchal contracts, myopic self-interests, manipulative tactics, and, ultimately, dependency as shown in the chart." (See next page.)

You then remind your senior team that you have all worked hard to avoid bureaucracy and the dependency it creates, but you admit that it has, nonetheless, in incremental, ever increasing ways, gained a foothold at CyTech. "This is what we're fighting against by focusing on empowerment," you insist, as you present Peter Block's entrepreneurial cycle. You read from *The Empowered Manager* again, "The alternative to the bureaucratic cycle is the entrepreneurial cycle,...to act as if the whole organization we are a part of is in fact our own."

Again, you point out, "The self-reinforcing nature of the

The Bureaucratic Cycle

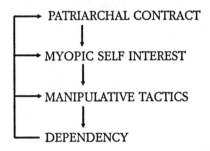

PATRIARCHAL CONTRACT

MYOPIC SELF INTEREST

MANIPULATIVE TACTICS

DEPENDENCY

The Entrepreneurial Cycle

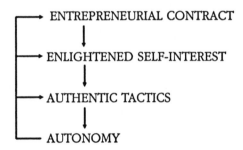

ENTREPRENEURIAL CONTRACT

ENLIGHTENED SELF-INTEREST

AUTHENTIC TACTICS

AUTONOMY

entrepreneurial cycle promotes entrepreneurial contracts between employers and employees, the pursuit of enlightened self interests, authentic tactics, and, ultimately, autonomy." You conclude, "I want this sort of empowerment cycle to create entrepreneurial autonomy and accountability at CyTech." However, you can still see skepticism on the faces of McPhee and Strandmeyer.

In the months that follow, you decide that McPhee's and Strandmeyer's skepticism points to the very reason why empowerment has proved so illusive to many organizations. You discover, too late, that the ideas it embodies do not translate easily into action. Feedback from people throughout the company shows they perceive empowerment as a fuzzy, soft, and idealistic notion. Most people complain they don't know how to make it work. When they try, nothing happens. People just keep operating the same old way. You pull out *Control Your Destiny or Someone Else Will* to reread

Jack Welch's words, which leave a big pit in your stomach: "You've got to be hard to be soft. You have to demonstrate the ability to make the hard, tough decisions—closing plants, divesting, delayering—if you want to have any credibility when you try to promote soft values."

You continue to believe empowerment offers tremendous benefits, but you also realize it lacks hard, practical teeth. As this realization sinks in, you conclude that you made the wrong choice between accountability and empowerment. CyTech completes a rather mediocre year under your leadership, as shown below.

Selected Financial and Stock Information
(Dollars in millions, except stock price in actual dollars)

	Year ended March 31	
	1st Year	Previous Year
Sales	$4,703	$4,083
Profits	235	242
Profits as a % of:		
Sales	5%	6%
Assets	7%	9%
Common Equity*	14%	17%
Market Value**	5,929	6,123
Stock Price	23 ¼	23 ¾

* Total stockholders' equity includes capital stock, surplus, and retained earnings at the company's year end. For purposes of determining profits as a percent of common stockholders' equity, all preferred stock is excluded.
** Calculated by multiplying the number of common shares outstanding by the price per common share as of March 31.

Soon after the beginning of your second year as CEO, disaster strikes. Three foreign competitors in the industry launch a price war that engulfs you and your competitors two to three years earlier than anyone expected. As the price of phone-fax-computers drops below $500, CyTech suddenly finds itself thrust into a mass production/mass marketing gambit for which it has not prepared itself. The conceptual idealism and confusion surrounding empowerment only exacerbates the growing anxiety as people throughout the CyTech organization scramble to respond to the challenge.

For the rest of your life, you will never forget the ensuing nightmare. Sensing your own anxiety and confusion, members of the board of directors approach each member of your senior team to find out what's happening. The majority of your senior team, especially *McPhee* and *Strandmeyer,* describe your pursuit of empowerment as idealistic, suggesting that you've lost touch with reality at a time when CyTech's success and survival depend on tough, practical measures. The board, under pressure from shareholders and increasingly concerned about their own reputations, unanimously vote for your replacement, appointing Hal McPhee as CyTech's new CEO.

You made a poor choice you'll probably regret for years to come. However, in this game, you can try your hand again.

- *In real life you may have been savvy enough to make empowerment a concrete reality, but if you want to find out why the author considers the other option preferable, review Chapter 26, then turn to Chapter 27, "Stressing Accountability First and Foremost."*

- *If you'd prefer embarking on a new decision-making track, turn to:*
    Chapter 2, Building a Classic Innovative Organization;
    Chapter 14, Developing a Synthesis of Best Practices;
    Chapter 38, Pursuing a Work Team Approach;
    Chapter 50, Reengineering Work Processes; or
    Chapter 62, Embracing a Revolutionary New Perspective.

You conclude that only by focusing on the victim cycle can you shock the entire organization into acknowledging its accountability. Predictably, Nan Thurow, your senior vice president of worldwide operations, thinks you're taking the wrong track. She argues, "Focusing on the victim cycle causes people to look at the negative side. It's like looking at the glass half empty instead of half full." You respond to Nan during a conference with your senior team that you believe that the coming competitive pressures on CyTech will demand rooting out all forms of victim behavior, saying, "In a dynamic organizational operation like CyTech's, it's easy for people to fall back on finger pointing, confusion, or waiting and hoping. Only by recognizing the exact moment an individual or a group falls below the line into the victim cycle can we expect to correct that tendency. It's the fastest and best way to make people in this organization accountable for superior results."

29

STRESSING THE VICTIM CYCLE

After much discussion, your senior team accepts your plan, with Nan Thurow finally allowing you the benefit of the doubt. Rumors of a price war floating around the industry make it imperative that CyTech do something, anything, immediately. When three foreign competitors do indeed launch a price war that changes the face of the entire industry, two to three years before you expected it, CyTech, along with other competitors, finds itself thrust into a mass production/mass marketing game. Phone-fax-computer prices quickly fall below $500.

With new overnight pressure to reduce costs, maintain quality, and develop continuing innovations, CyTech's organization finds itself thrust into the midst of chaos. All the old rules have changed. CyTech must not only maintain its technological thrust, it must become a mass marketer and mass producer of phone-fax-computers as well. Your first task: reduce manufacturing costs with lightning speed.

Avoiding the victim cycle under this extreme pressure takes effort, but it quickly provides a strong motivational tool that production VP Morris Strandmeyer uses to cut manufacturing costs and that senior operations VP Nan Thurow employs to bring new efficiencies to CyTech's worldwide operations. It appears that focusing on the victim cycle has indeed made people accept more accountability, even in these chaotic and trying circumstances.

Admonitions to avoid getting trapped in the victim cycle provide the reality shock necessary to keep everyone in the CyTech organization on their toes with "make it happen" attitudes. Even when members of your senior team, such as technology lab VP Karen Walsh, complain that resources are getting diverted from product innovations to improve production processes, other members tell that person he or she has fallen below the line into the victim cycle. Just like everyone else, Karen must figure out some way to help CyTech reduce costs while staying abreast of technological developments. To your delight, consistent efforts to avoid the victim cycle inspires every employee within CyTech to accept responsibility to help the company emerge victorious from the price war.

In the months that follow, you discover that the focus on avoiding victimization builds a strong survival culture throughout CyTech, something even you could not have predicted. Upon reflection, you realize there's nothing altruistic or idealistic about focusing on the victim cycle; doing so attacks the very real negative attitudes that afflict people and organizations when they don't assume responsibility for results. In fact, the harsh message of deadly victim attitudes and behavior elicits the survival mentality among CyTech employees and allows the company to emerge from the price war in better shape than any of its competitors.

At the end of your second year as CEO, sales reach $7 billion, and the price of CyTech stock jumps to $45 per share, as shown in the table on the next page.

As some competitors raise prices on their phone-fax-computers, CyTech is able to introduce a line of *PowerBases* for under $400, which continues to build market share and customer loyalty throughout the world. Organizationally, you feel that CyTech employees have developed a clear understanding of the victim cycle, able to identify when they're falling below the line and thus able to

Selected Financial and Stock Information
(Dollars in millions, except stock price in actual dollars)

	Year ended March 31	
	2nd Year	1st Year
Sales	$7,136	$5,285
Profits	428	317
Profits as a % of:		
Sales	6%	6%
Assets	10%	9%
Common Equity*	19%	18%
Market Value**	11,422	7,621
Stock Price	44 ¾	29 ⅞

* Total stockholders' equity includes capital stock, surplus, and retained earnings at the company's year end. For purposes of determining profits as a percent of common stockholders' equity, all preferred stock is excluded.

** Calculated by multiplying the number of common shares outstanding by the price per common share as of March 31.

get back above the line quickly. Now you must move the culture into the next phase of organizational development by focusing on accountability to ensure longer-term progress.

A crucial question arises: How do you shift emphasis to accountability so that it will build on the widespread understanding of the victim cycle and produce ever greater results? Should you start with your senior team, helping them understand all the subtleties surrounding accountability and the best ways to nurture, develop, and refine a sense of it throughout the organization? Or should you immediately launch a companywide accountability program designed to educate, train, and develop everyone in the organization? On the other hand, if your senior team already understands accountability and a companywide launch would be too ambitious, perhaps you should address middle management first, because these people represent a potent day-to-day force within the organization. As you consider this option, yet a fourth possibility emerges: developing individualized, customized accountability-improvement programs tailored to the needs of specific groups in the organization.

Each of these alternatives offers certain advantages. Starting with the senior team will ensure that you "walk the talk" from the top before rolling it out to the rest of the organization; the company-wide roll-out would expose everyone in the organization to the same accountability learning and training process, which worked well with the earlier focus on the victim cycle; addressing middle management could train the company's core people, turning them into highly accountable managers who could aid in developing accountability in all their people; and individualized programs could meet the needs of a diverse work force.

However, each alternative also poses certain disadvantages. Starting with the senior team delays the roll-out to the rest of the company; the companywide option doesn't allow management to learn and internalize the steps to accountability so they can help subordinates; the middle management approach assumes that the senior team, as well as the next layer of senior executives, has already mastered the art of accountability; and individualized programs would cost more and take longer to implement.

After several weeks and much consideration, you identify two additional alternatives that you must work into the mix of possibilities: find some way to combine the four alternatives into one comprehensive, simultaneous approach, or scrap all of the alternatives and figure out some new initiatives with the help of an outside consultant.

Feeling some ambivalence about the six alternatives, you decide to maintain CyTech's current course until after the end of the fiscal year. Fortunately, CyTech's victimization-conscious, survival-driven culture produces another banner year, as shown in the table on the next page.

The board praises your foresight and you breath a little easier as the price war cools down. However, with the year-end machinations over, you must now decide on CyTech's next organizational development step. Which of the six alternatives will you pursue?

Selected Financial and Stock Information
(Dollars in millions, except stock price in actual dollars)

	Year ended March 31	
	3rd Year	2nd Year
Sales	$9,211	$7,136
Profits	645	428
Profits as a % of:		
Sales	7%	6%
Assets	13%	10%
Common Equity*	21%	19%
Market Value**	15,076	11,422
Stock Price	59 $\frac{1}{8}$	44 $\frac{3}{4}$

* Total stockholders' equity includes capital stock, surplus, and retained earnings at the company's year end. For purposes of determining profits as a percent of common stockholders' equity, all preferred stock is excluded.
** Calculated by multiplying the number of common shares outstanding by the price per common share as of March 31.

- *If you choose to start with your senior team, turn to Chapter 32.*

- *If you want to launch a companywide roll-out, turn to Chapter 33.*

- *If you decide to address middle management first, turn to Chapter 34.*

- *If you prefer individualized and customized programs for specific groups, turn to Chapter 35.*

- *If you wish to combine the above alternatives into one integrated program, turn to Chapter 36.*

- *If you believe none of these options provide the best solution and desire the advice of an outside consultant, turn to Chapter 37.*

Everyone on your senior team, except CFO Hal McPhee, agrees that focusing on accountability will cause employees throughout the organization to feel positive about reaching higher for results. McPhee argues that this approach lacks the bite to make people really behave more accountably: "I think we could be headed for tough times in this industry, and I'm not sure that a focus on accountability, without stressing the victim cycle, will give us enough muscle to meet the challenge."

Unfortunately, what ensues in the weeks that follow takes everyone, except Hal McPhee, by surprise. Three foreign competitors launch a price war that engulfs everyone in the industry, driving prices below $500. In the heat of battle, your emphasis on accountability gets pushed aside quickly as people find it a distraction to accomplishing the task at

30

EMPHASIZING THE STEPS TO ACCOUNTABILITY

---

hand. While you keep trying to call attention to the steps to accountability because you sincerely believe that will help CyTech's people meet the price war challenge, you encounter stiff resistance. One second-level executive says, "To spend a lot of time preaching about 'how to see it, how to own it, how to solve it, how to do it,' seems redundant at this point." A middle manager complains, "We need no-nonsense management, not a lot of time-wasting theoretical discussions about four steps to accountability."

You continue working hard to counter such comments and feelings throughout the organization by visiting facilities, holding employee meetings, and directing your training and development department to communicate the importance of the steps to accountability in all employee communications. What occurs, however, pierces you like a knife. Everywhere you go you see people operating below the line in the victim cycle, pointing fingers, acting confused, and waiting for someone to solve their problems. While your emphasis on the need to "see it, own it, solve it, and do it" helps some people, it does nothing to check the chaos that's enveloping the organization. You discover, too late, that the organization cannot thrive on or overcome the present chaos with the idealism of the accountability ladder. It appears that the only way people can thrive on chaos is by keeping out of the victim cycle. It's all so clear to you now. Is it too late to shift gears?

Immediately, you ask your senior team to help you shift the company's focus to combatting the victim cycle, but as soon as you do, word gets back to the board of directors that you've wasted six months pursuing a program that Hal McPhee told you would never work. To make matters worse, CyTech can't push manufacturing costs below the new price war levels. Conflicts, confusion, finger pointing, a lot of waiting and hoping for the price war to go away permeate every corner of the organization. The board's confidence in you disappears.

At the end of your second year as CEO, profits drop and the stock price plummets, as shown in the following table.

Selected Financial and Stock Information
(Dollars in millions, except stock price in actual dollars)

| | Year ended March 31 | |
	2nd Year	1st Year
Sales	$5,589	$5,285
Profits	112	317
Profits as a % of:		
Sales	2%	6%
Assets	6%	9%
Common Equity*	9%	18%
Market Value**	3,010	7,621
Stock Price	12 $\frac{1}{8}$	29 $\frac{7}{8}$

* Total stockholders' equity includes capital stock, surplus, and retained earnings at the company's year end. For purposes of determining profits as a percent of common stockholders' equity, all preferred stock is excluded.

** Calculated by multiplying the number of common shares outstanding by the price per common share as of March 31.

Two weeks after the year-end closing, the board asks you to step aside and appoints Hal McPhee president and CEO at CyTech. Though the board invites you to join it, you refuse, deciding to look elsewhere for employment.

- *You may have been able to shift gears to meet the challenge of the price war in real life, but if you want to find out why the author considers another alternative preferable, review Chapter 27, then turn to Chapter 29, Stressing the Victim Cycle, or Chapter 31, Focusing on Both Accountability and Victimization Simultaneously.*

- *If you would like to start fresh on a new decision-making track, move on to:*

    Chapter 2, Building a Classic Innovative Organization;

    Chapter 14, Developing a Synthesis of Best Practices;

    Chapter 38, Pursuing a Work Team Approach, or Chapter 50, Reengineering Work Processes;

    Chapter 62, Embracing a Revolutionary New Perspective.

Deciding to balance emphasis on the victim cycle with stress on the accountability ladder, urging people never to discuss one without bringing the other into the picture, makes good sense to everyone on your senior team, and you feel confident that this will provide the right thrust for CyTech's further organizational development.

One team member, CFO Hal McPhee, goes so far as to say, "If CyTech doesn't run into any major surprises that completely changes the ball game in this industry, this strategy should work beautifully!" That sentiment seems to capture everyone's feelings as you begin designing a plan to launch your program throughout the organization.

31

FOCUSING ON ACCOUNTABILITY AND VICTIMIZATION SIMULTANEOUSLY

Just two months later, however, disaster strikes when three foreign competitors launch a price war that drags CyTech and every other competitor into a life-or-death battle for the future. However, your tempered, balanced program fails to muster the strength necessary to meet this crisis. Hal McPhee reminds you of his cautionary advice that a simultaneous emphasis on accountability and victimization would work only if there were no surprises. "The price war has changed everything," he says.

"What do you recommend?"

"It may be too late!"

"What do you mean?"

"Rumor has it Motorola's already licking its chops."

"We can beat this price war. I know we can."

"Not with our current culture we can't."

"Why so negative, Hal? Do you want a Motorola takeover?"

"No, but you've forgotten what your hero Jack Welch said, 'people have to change their habits and expectations, or else the stress will just overwhelm them.' Our people are overwhelmed. We haven't prepared them for this price war. Most of them are currently stuck below the line in the victim cycle."

Having gotten caught off guard and now taking too much time to respond to the price war initiatives, you watch in alarm as CyTech stock drops precipitously to $15 per share. Motorola seizes the opportunity, tendering an offer of $25 per share to CyTech stockholders, a move your board of directors supports. When Motorola acquires over 51 percent of the company, one consequence of the takeover stings you: You're out of a job. Motorola gives you six months and an attractive severance package, but your opportunities to further shape the CyTech organization have come to an end. Your decision may have worked in normal times, but an extreme crisis required an extreme response, which you failed to produce.

- *You might have been able to make this course of action work in real life, but if you want to know what the author considers a better approach, review Chapter 27, then turn to:*

  Chapter 29, Stressing the Victim Cycle or

  Chapter 30, Emphasizing the Steps to Accountability.

- *If you want to start a new decision-making track, begin with:*

  Chapter 2, Building a Classic Innovative Organization;

  Chapter 14, Developing a Synthesis of Best Practices;

  Chapter 38, Pursuing a Work Team Approach;

  Chapter 50, Reengineering Work Processes; or

  Chapter 62, Embracing a Revolutionary New Perspective.

Believing it necessary that an example of accountability flow from the top, you engage your senior team in extensive personal assessments aimed at helping each of them weave the steps to accountability into all their management-related activities. In a series of retreats away from the office, both with and without spouses, you bring in several facilitators to help develop an accountability mind set at the top, so that a "see it, own it, solve it, and do it" attitude will permeate everything your senior executives say and do.

You gain many insights over the following weeks and months as each member of your senior team deals with accountability in a slightly different way. Morris Strandmeyer, for example, vice president of production, whose strong take-charge orientation makes him wonder why everyone else doesn't act the same way, finds it hard to assume responsibility for the larger picture, the longer-term strategic vision of CyTech. Accustomed to confining his thoughts to his own sphere of influence, he cannot easily expand his thinking to other spheres. Strandmeyer worries so much about the here and now, trying to control everything in his own bailiwick, he must work extra hard to accept accountability for what his control orientation does to other people, and he must struggle to think about the future.

For Karen Walsh, the issues play themselves out differently. Highly accountable for the long-term view and CyTech's position in the larger scheme of things, she struggles to face problems in bringing great ideas or breakthroughs to the marketplace. A perfect case in point currently preoccupies Karen: Rumors regarding voice-operated phone-fax-computers as the next wave of product intro-

32

STARTING WITH THE SENIOR TEAM

ductions have failed to shift her from long-term basic R&D to short-term product development. Learning to accept more accountability for short-term results represents an important goal for her as she works her way up the accountability ladder.

Nan Thurow, a deeply feeling and passionate person, assumes great accountability for people development throughout the CyTech organization, making her uniquely effective in her role as senior vice president of worldwide operations. While her attentiveness to the corporate culture at CyTech has always been a great strength, she learns quickly that she lacks a sense of accountability, at times, for the economic exigencies associated with the growth of an individual, a team, or an organization. She must learn how to assume accountability in this arena as she embarks on her own personal journey to "see it, own it, solve it, and do it."

CFO Hal McPhee, characterized by some as a "control-freak" and quick decision maker who lives largely within himself, assumes broad accountability for ensuring organizational efficiency and effectiveness. However, he now struggles to assume accountability for his effect on other people who sometimes view his behavior as abrasive and confrontational. Slowly, he accepts feedback from his peers and begins valuing management styles different from his own.

Senior vice president of product development, Bob Kiechel, stands high above the line in his inventiveness, ability to gain new insights, and creative problem solving, all of which guide CyTech's product development thrust, but Bob so anxiously strives to discover new ways of doing things that he sometimes overlooks the details one must control when launching a new product. The steps to accountability help Bob see and own this weakness, making it possible for him to ensure, through other people, more careful and detailed product launches.

Finally, action-oriented John Solo, executive vice president for worldwide sales and marketing, displays high accountability in terms of sizing up current situations and responding to them quickly, but such impulsive, precipitous action often causes problems in the organization. The steps to accountability help him assume responsibility for communicating with others, letting them know what he's thinking and what he's planning to do. In fact, his new attitude has already helped him avoid mistakes his impulsiveness might otherwise have caused.

Your decision to deepen accountability in each one of your direct reports makes a strong impact on the company as people throughout the organization begin taking notice of how the senior executives, you included, "walk the talk" when it comes to assuming accountability for results. You realize how profoundly the concepts of victimization and accountability have changed your own perspective and approach to leadership. Now, you rarely look at any situation or person without consciously or unconsciously discerning evidence of victim or accountable attitudes and behavior.

The work with your senior team pays off for CyTech as the company introduces the first voice-operated phone-fax-computer to the market near the end of your fourth year as CEO. The new product beats your nearest competitor by three months, pushing CyTech's sales to $12 billion and the stock price to $75 per share, as shown in the table.

Selected Financial and Stock Information
(Dollars in millions, except stock price in actual dollars)

	Year ended March 31	
	4th Year	3rd Year
Sales	$12,147	$9,211
Profits	850	645
Profits as a % of:		
Sales	7%	7%
Assets	14%	13%
Common Equity*	22%	21%
Market Value**	19,074	15,076
Stock Price	74 $^{13}/_{16}$	59 $^{1}/_{8}$

* Total stockholders' equity includes capital stock, surplus, and retained earnings at the company's year end. For purposes of determining profits as a percent of common stockholders' equity, all preferred stock is excluded.

** Calculated by multiplying the number of common shares outstanding by the price per common share as of March 31.

As you review the year just completed, you believe that your focus on the steps to accountability with your key executives made the difference in speeding up and streamlining the product-development and product-introduction processes, allowing CyTech to take the market by storm with its new voice-operated machine.

During the next twelve months, you work hard to spread the accountability word throughout the organization, but you find the task easier than expected because your senior executives continue walking their talk. CyTech holds on to its market leadership position and introduces two upgraded versions of the voice-operated phone-fax-computer with a variety of multimedia enhancements.

At the end of your fifth year as CEO, CyTech's sales reach $14 billion, and the stock price climbs to $96 a share.

Selected Financial and Stock Information
(Dollars in millions, except stock price in actual dollars)

	Year ended March 31	
	5th Year	4th Year
Sales	$13,989	$12,147
Profits	979	850
Profits as a % of:		
Sales	7%	7%
Assets	13%	14%
Common Equity*	21%	22%
Market Value**	24,704	19,074
Stock Price	96 $\frac{7}{8}$	74 $\frac{13}{16}$

* Total stockholders' equity includes capital stock, surplus, and retained earnings at the company's year end. For purposes of determining profits as a percent of common stockholders' equity, all preferred stock is excluded.
** Calculated by multiplying the number of common shares outstanding by the price per common share as of March 31.

When you accept the title of chairman of the board, you begin grooming your replacement. With such a successful business career at its peak, you decide to retire within three years to explore other avenues of life and to enjoy your family. Congratulations! You have made it to the end of a decision-making track. If you would like to continue playing, however, you can pick one of the following options.

- *If you want to compare how the results of your last five years of organizational decision making stack up against the other positive outcomes in The Organization Game, turn to Chapter 78.*

- *If you want to peruse the other alternatives on this track, review Chapter 26, then turn to one of the following:*

  Chapter 28, Putting Empowerment First;

  Chapter 30, Emphasizing the Steps to Accountability;

  Chapter 31, Focusing on Both Accountability and Victimization Simultaneously;

  Chapter 33, Launching a Companywide Roll-Out;

  Chapter 34, Moving Middle Management Above the Line;

  Chapter 35, Customizing Individualized Accountability Programs;

  Chapter 36, Installing an Integrated Accountability Program; or

  Chapter 37, Hiring an Outside Consultant.

- *If you choose to begin another decision-making track, start anew with:*

  Chapter 2, Building a Classic Innovative Organization;

  Chapter 14, Developing a Synthesis of Best Practices;

  Chapter 38, Pursuing a Work Team Approach;

  Chapter 50, Reengineering Work Processes; or

  Chapter 62, Embracing a Revolutionary New Perspective.

Though this route represents an ambitious undertaking, you decide that CyTech cannot afford to wait for the slower-moving options for pushing people up the accountability ladder. The sooner you move, the better.

CyTech's training and development group gears up for the roll-out and launches an eight-month program that takes every individual in the organization through a five-day account-ability course that builds upon CyTech's victim cycle foundation. To support the effort, you and your senior team work full time helping groups and individuals throughout the organization understand how to get above the line and stay there. In many instances, however, the organization's sensitivity to any "below the line" victim behavior or attitudes slows the progress of the program. Perhaps, you think, there is not a short-cut to implementing the steps to accountability. Whenever those at the upper levels in the organization make a misstep themselves, subordinates mock their failure to practice what they preach.

In one instance, Nan Thurow, senior VP of worldwide operations, grilled Dave

33

LAUNCHING A COMPANYWIDE ROLL-OUT

Crosby, one of her direct reports, during a staff meeting for falling below the line on a project completion deadline. Embarrassed and offended, Crosby vowed revenge. Within two weeks, at another staff meeting, he caught Thurow justifying and excusing her own failure to meet an important deadline. Without reservation or remorse, Crosby mercilessly attacked Thurow for failing to walk her talk.

"You demand accountability from us, but excuse yourself. How can you expect us to stay above the line if you can't?"

"We'll talk about this later, Dave."

"Hold it! You can't brush this under the rug. You criticized me a week ago for doing the same thing you're doing now. Why is victim behavior acceptable for you?"

"It's not. Can we please discuss your concerns later?"

"I'm sorry. I think you owe me an apology and explanation now. Right here, in front of everyone."

"This staff meeting is adjourned until Dave and I work through this issue. We'll reconvene after lunch."

After a heated discussion in Thurow's office, Crosby settled down when Thurow reluctantly agreed to apologize for her grilling and admit her own below the line behavior. However, when the staff meeting resumed, Thurow downplayed her apology and lectured the group about loyalty and resolving conflicts in private. Within a few weeks Dave Crosby left the company to take a job at Apple Computer.

It doesn't take long for cynical stories about instances of senior-level or middle management lapses into below the line behavior to rumble around the organization. It seems you failed to anticipate the reality that a companywide roll-out would expose everyone, including senior management, to harsh scrutiny and that you didn't give your senior executives and managers enough chance to model the new attitudes and behavior. Their miscues and missteps have become laughing jokes to too many people.

At the end of your fourth year as CEO, a major competitor, Motorola, introduces a voice-operated phone-fax-computer. Unfortunately, according to Bob Kiechel and Karen Walsh, CyTech cannot possibly introduce its own version for another six months. Sales reach $10 billion before the end of the year, with the stock price hovering at $62 per share, as shown in the table on the next page.

Determined to solve the stalemate that plagues the organization, you initiate a second wave of development focused on your senior executives and the next level of management, a total of 44 people.

You put them on a "walk the talk" program directed by a team of corporate culture consultants from Ernst & Young. Each of the 44 executives embarks on an intense personal and managerial devel-

Selected Financial and Stock Information
(Dollars in millions, except stock price in actual dollars)

	Year ended March 31	
	4th Year	3rd Year
Sales	$10,382	$9,211
Profits	623	645
Profits as a % of:		
Sales	6%	7%
Assets	11%	13%
Common Equity*	17%	21%
Market Value**	15,841	15,076
Stock Price	62 ⅛	59 ⅛

* Total stockholders' equity includes capital stock, surplus, and retained earnings at the company's year end. For purposes of determining profits as a percent of common stockholders' equity, all preferred stock is excluded.
** Calculated by multiplying the number of common shares outstanding by the price per common share as of March 31.

opment regimen that focuses on modeling accountable attitudes and behavior in all aspects of their lives. A "360°-review" that collects feedback from the full range of business and personal associates surrounding each executive fuels rapid development and growth among the key executives. Within a few short months the accountability of the 44 executives proves more and more exemplar, quelling much of the cynicism that had been building within CyTech.

With the company operating in a crises mode, you attempt to eliminate any remaining ridicule of accountability in the organization. Motorola's success with the voice-operated machine pushes it past CyTech in the marketplace, robbing CyTech and other competitors of market share. You work hard and fast along with your senior executives to continue building accountability among CyTech's 44 key executives and managers, demanding that they get even better at modeling the appropriate behavior for everyone in the organization.

After nine months you finally introduce CyTech's voice-operated phone-fax-computer, but the tardiness of the introduction places CyTech at third position in the marketplace. However, by the end of your fifth year as CEO, you turn the tide with accountable behavior modeled from the top, and the cynical stories and jokes finally disappear completely. At year end sales reach $11 billion, and stock increases to $66 per share.

Selected Financial and Stock Information
(Dollars in millions, except stock price in actual dollars).

	Year ended March 31	
	5th Year	4th Year
Sales	$11,474	$10,382
Profits	688	623
Profits as a % of:		
Sales	6%	6%
Assets	12%	11%
Common Equity*	18%	17%
Market Value**	16,766	15,841
Stock Price	65 ¾	62 ⅛

* Total stockholders' equity includes capital stock, surplus, and retained earnings at the company's year end. For purposes of determining profits as a percent of common stockholders' equity, all preferred stock is excluded.
** Calculated by multiplying the number of common shares outstanding by the price per common share as of March 31.

You renew your contract with the board of directors for another five years as CEO and vow to yourself that you'll not make the same mistakes again. This represents the end of a decision-making track, but you can try your hand again by choosing one of the following options.

- *If you want to compare how the results of your last five years of organizational decision making stack up against the other positive outcomes in The Organization Game, turn to Chapter 78.*

- *If you choose to review other alternatives on this decision-making track, review Chapter 26, then turn to:*

    Chapter 28, Putting Empowerment First;

    Chapter 30, Emphasizing the Steps to Accountability;

    Chapter 31, Focusing on Both Accountability and Victimization Simultaneously;

    Chapter 32, Starting with the Senior Team;

    Chapter 34, Moving Middle Management Above the Line;

    Chapter 35, Customizing Individualized Accountability Programs;

    Chapter 36, Installing an Integrated Accountability Program; or

    Chapter 37, Hiring an Outside Consultant.

- *If you prefer embarking on a new decision-making track, start again at:*

    Chapter 2, Building a Classic Innovative Organization;

    Chapter 14, Developing a Synthesis of Best Practices;

    Chapter 38, Pursuing a Work Team Approach;

    Chapter 50, Reengineering Work Processes; or

    Chapter 62, Embracing a Revolutionary New Perspective.

Your decision to address the accountability of middle managers assumes that your team of senior executives has already internalized accountable behavior and attitudes. Unfortunately, this assumption proves false.

As you roll out an accountability program that emphasizes personalized training for almost five hundred middle managers throughout CyTech, it becomes evident within three months that your middle managers more readily grasp the implications of accountability than your senior executives do. You realize, too late, that your senior executives recognize the destructive nature of the victim cycle, but have not developed a strong understanding of accountability habits. Nan Thurow grills subordinates for falling below the line but excuses her own missed deadlines. John Solo refuses to take the accountability training seriously, claiming immunity from victim cycle problems. Hal McPhee goes to the other extreme, zealously holding direct reports accountable for things that are obviously outside their sphere of influence or control.

At midyear, this problem comes to a head as numerous middle managers throughout the organization cry for more support

34

MOVING MIDDLE MANAGEMENT ABOVE THE LINE

and commitment from senior executives regarding their own "see it, own it, solve it, do it" plans and activities. For example, one middle manager in product development had incorporated the accountability steps into his group's management process for new projects, which required a substantial investment in the first step, "seeing it," to overcome the group's inherent difficulty in placing a new product project in the larger context of corporate goals and on a realistic implementation path. Ironically, the middle manager runs into opposition from his boss, one of Bob Kiechel's direct reports, for spending too much time trying to get his group to see reality. His boss simply does not appreciate what he was trying to accomplish or understand why it's a critical step to laying the foundation for accountability for results. This kind of miscuing occurs again and again over several months as you play catch-up with your senior team.

Things grow worse as almost 25 percent of your middle managers leave CyTech for competing organizations. Armed with new accountability skills, they can no longer work for executives who don't understand or aren't committed to their program. Their departures deal a decimating blow to CyTech.

At the end of your fourth year, sales inch up to $9.5 billion, while the stock price drops to $51 per share, as shown in the following table.

Selected Financial and Stock Information
(Dollars in millions, except stock price in actual dollars)

| | Year ended March 31 | |
	4th Year	3rd Year
Sales	$9,548	$9,211
Profits	573	645
Profits as a % of:		
Sales	6%	7%
Assets	11%	13%
Common Equity*	17%	21%
Market Value**	13,069	15,076
Stock Price	51 $\frac{1}{4}$	59 $\frac{1}{8}$

* Total stockholders' equity includes capital stock, surplus, and retained earnings at the company's year end. For purposes of determining profits as a percent of common stockholders' equity, all preferred stock is excluded.

** Calculated by multiplying the number of common shares outstanding by the price per common share as of March 31.

Shortly after the year-end closing, Motorola introduces a new voice-operated phone-fax-computer six months before you can even begin testing a CyTech prototype.

Not surprisingly, the losses of key personnel and market leadership prompts the board of directors to suggest that you resign as CEO and become a member of the board for a term of three years. You reluctantly agree to resign as CEO but wrestle with whether you should look for another CEO job or simply let your business career as a line manager come to an end.

- *In real life you might have been able to turn this situation around, avoiding the loss of personnel and market decline. However, if you want to know why the author considers other alternatives better, turn to:*

    Chapter 32, Starting with the Senior Team;

    Chapter 33, Launching a Companywide Roll-Out;

    Chapter 35, Customizing Individualized Accountability Programs;

    Chapter 36, Installing an Integrated Accountability Program; or

    Chapter 37, Hiring an Outside Consultant.

- *If you choose to embark on a different decision-making track, turn to:*

    Chapter 2, Building a Classic Innovative Organization;

    Chapter 14, Developing a Synthesis of Best Practices;

    Chapter 38, Pursuing a Work Team Approach;

    Chapter 50, Reengineering Work Processes; or

    Chapter 62, Embracing a Revolutionary New Perspective.

As you announce your decision to customize learning systems that will allow each individual and group to develop a self-directed twelve-month accountability course, your senior team responds with strongly mixed emotions.

Nan Thurow, senior vice president of worldwide operations,

35

CUSTOMIZING INDIVIDUALIZED ACCOUNTABILITY PROGRAMS

thinks it's a good idea and believes it might work. Hal McPhee, chief financial officer, thinks it's ridiculous and says, "The board will string us up if we do this." The rest of your senior team range in between these two extreme views, but no one agrees wholeheartedly that you've chosen the ideal solution.

When you eventually find yourself in a showdown with your senior executives, you ask yourself, "Should I stand my ground, requiring alignment behind this decision, or should I listen to my senior executives and reconsider it?" Before you make this decision, you meet with each of your senior people individually and talk with them about their views, their feelings, and their recommendations regarding the next stage of organizational development. At the end of two weeks, you feel immobilized by the continuing disagreement among your team. Too many questions about exactly how to implement the steps to accountability remain. One comment from John Solo captures the dilemma, "Trying to implement an individualized and customized learning process in this organization at this time does not take into account the tremendous pressures we face in the marketplace. This approach might work for an educational institution, but it won't work here. I think the first thing we have to do is 'see' the reality that CyTech currently faces."

After a lot of soul searching, you decide you can't implement this course of action without the complete support of your senior executives. You conclude to follow their advice. It's time to go back to the drawing board and choose one of the other options.

- *If you choose to focus on your senior team's accountability, turn to Chapter 32.*

- *If you want to launch a companywide roll-out of the accountability ladder, turn to Chapter 33.*

- *If you decide to focus on middle management as the best way to build accountability attitudes and behavior, turn to Chapter 34.*

- *If you want to combine all of these alternatives in an integrated program, turn to Chapter 36.*

- *If you believe none of these options provides the best solution and want the advice of an outside consultant to help you develop new initiatives, turn to Chapter 37.*

Your senior team, including Solo and Walsh, who are often prone to ambivalence, responds favorably to this alternative because they think it will result in the quickest and most thorough implementation of the accountability steps. With their help, you work out a series of programs for the organization, beginning at the top.

You immediately develop a customized accountability-training program for the 38 executives who report directly to your senior team. Kiechel, Walsh, Solo, Thurow, Strandmeyer, and McPhee are each asked to create the same kind of accountability-oriented environment they're experiencing with you at the top in their respective management teams. Personally, you work hard to exemplify above-the-line leadership in all your words, deeds, and thoughts.

Then, you move to the middle-management level, where you establish through CyTech's training and development organization a comprehensive ac-

36

INSTALLING AN INTEGRATED ACCOUNTABILITY PROGRAM

countability awareness and effectiveness system that includes subordinate-peer-supervisor reviews, intensive week-long training sessions, high-frequency accountability performance reviews, and an "Above the Line" leadership recognition award for those exemplifying highly accountable behavior and leadership.

Finally, you roll it out companywide, all the while allowing for longer-term customized and individualized programs specially designed for certain individuals and groups. While you promote a standardized training program for all employees, you also allow for flexibility to accommodate the needs of individuals, teams, organizational units, and major groups throughout the company.

Your initial efforts with the senior team prove extremely important as you and your senior executives discover the difference between an awareness of victim behavior and an understanding of exactly how to apply the tenets of "see it, own it, solve it, do it" again and again in every situation throughout CyTech. This recognition proves invaluable as your senior executives learn to walk their talk and then focus on helping more than five hundred managers do the same thing before the program rolls out companywide.

Events move quickly in the ensuing months. Having learned to apply the steps to accountability, CyTech introduces a new voice-operated phone-fax-computer early, two months before the end of your fourth year as CEO. Sales jump to $12 billion, and the stock price reaches $70 per share, as shown here.

Selected Financial and Stock Information
(Dollars in millions, except stock price in actual dollars)

| | Year ended March 31 | |
	4th Year	3rd Year
Sales	$11,935	$9,211
Profits	835	645
Profits as a % of:		
Sales	7%	7%
Assets	14%	13%
Common Equity*	21%	21%
Market Value**	17,835	15,076
Stock Price	69 $^{15}/_{16}$	59 $^{1}/_{8}$

* Total stockholders' equity includes capital stock, surplus, and retained earnings at the company's year end. For purposes of determining profits as a percent of common stockholders' equity, all preferred stock is excluded.
** Calculated by multiplying the number of common shares outstanding by the price per common share as of March 31.

With this success occurring in the midst of your roll-out of the accountability steps to the entire organization, the combination punch magnificently stimulates the organization as the culture habitually avoids victimization and accepts full accountability for results. The timing is near perfect. Everyone now grasps the full picture of the victim cycle and the steps to accountability, and that enables people in every function, team, and organizational unit to work tirelessly for their own and CyTech's benefit.

The organization grows ever more responsive in the next year as the company launches three upgraded versions of the voice-operated phone-fax-computer and several other innovations, including multimedia applications. The marketplace responds enthusiastically, and sales reach $13.5 billion by the end of your fifth year as CEO. The stock price rises to $92 a share, as shown in the following table.

Selected Financial and Stock information
(Dollars in millions, except stock price in actual dollars)

	Year ended March 31	
	5th Year	4th Year
Sales	$13,561	$11,935
Profits	949	835
Profits as a % of:		
Sales	7%	7%
Assets	14%	14%
Common Equity*	22%	21%
Market Value**	23,651	17,835
Stock Price	92 ¾	69 ¹⁵⁄₁₆

* Total stockholders' equity includes capital stock, surplus, and retained earnings at the company's year end. For purposes of determining profits as a percent of common stockholders' equity, all preferred stock is excluded.
** Calculated by multiplying the number of common shares outstanding by the price per common share as of March 31.

These results propel you to chairman of the board of CyTech, and *Forbes* magazine features you and the company in a cover story. Organizations throughout the world seek to understand your management philosophy and your organizational approach, sending teams of executives to meet with people throughout your organization to learn more about what you've accomplished. To accommodate this demand as well as fuel the continued development of CyTech's culture, you acquire a large piece of property just outside Savannah, Georgia, as a site for CyTech University, an institution where your employees as well as executives from other companies can continue to learn, grow, and develop.

CyTech maintains its leadership position in the market. CyTech University quickly becomes a premiere corporation-based training and development center, even eclipsing Bob Galvin's Motorola University. Your decision making on this track has come to a bright conclusion. However, you can try your hand again if you'd like.

- *If you want to explore the other alternatives on this same decision-making track, review Chapter 26, then turn to:*

  Chapter 28, Putting Empowerment First;

  Chapter 30, Emphasizing the Steps to Accountability;

  Chapter 31, Focusing on Both Accountability and Victimization Simultaneously;

  Chapter 32, Starting with the Senior Team;

  Chapter 33, Launching a Companywide Roll-Out;

  Chapter 34, Moving Middle Management Above the Line;

  Chapter 35, Customizing Individualized Accountability Programs;

  Chapter 37, Hiring an Outside Consultant.

- *If you choose to pursue another decision-making track, start fresh in:*

  Chapter 2, Building a Classic Innovative Organization;

  Chapter 14, Developing a Synthesis of Best Practices;

  Chapter 38, Pursuing a Work Team Approach;

  Chapter 50, Reengineering Work Processes; or

  Chapter 62, Embracing a Revolutionary New Perspective.

Unable to decide on the right course of action, you hire an outside expert to help you develop a program that can build upon CyTech's heightened awareness of below the line behavior and attitudes. If you don't build upon that strength, you could find yourself worrying that a wrong move could destroy what you have already achieved.

Your decision to turn to an outsider for help communicates hesitancy to your senior team, however, and while they understand and sympathize, they believe you've fallen below the line. Perhaps you have, but that doesn't deter you from searching for the right consultant to help the company move forward.

37

HIRING AN OUTSIDE CONSULTANT

Not surprisingly, Hal McPhee, your chief financial officer, confronts you in an early morning management meeting saying, "I've talked to everyone, and we believe that you have fallen below the line on this decision. You're acting confused and seem to be waiting and hoping that some consulting firm will figure out the best approach for us to take in the months ahead." McPhee's comments cut to your core as you confront your own weakness. With all your commitment to remain aware of any below the line behavior, you had ignored your own inability to see the reality of your current indecision. You really shouldn't have let your senior team see that weakness.

In a move that ends up hurting your business career, you violate the very cultural attributes you are working so hard to instill by ignoring feedback and justifying your decision to hire outside help. For the next hour, you go to great lengths dissecting the complexities of this situation and why you need specialists trained in organizational development and psychological behavior to help CyTech implement the next phase of its growth.

You stand by your decision, and you ask your people to stand by you. Saddened and disheartened, your senior executives criticize you among themselves over the next several weeks. Hal McPhee even goes to the board of directors with his and others' concerns.

In the meantime, you privately wonder whether you have mortally wounded yourself and damaged CyTech's culture, but you finally decide to hire Senn-Delaney Leadership Consulting Group to help you design the next phase of organizational development. Unfortunately, by the time you bring Senn-Delaney aboard to begin their first wave of interviews and data gathering, Motorola introduces a voice-operated phone-fax machine that takes the market by storm. This turn of events catches CyTech by surprise, with the company unprepared to introduce a rival product for at least six months.

By the end of your fourth year as CEO, sales fall to $8 billion and the company's stock price drops to $32 per share.

Selected Financial and Stock Information
(Dollars in millions, except stock price in actual dollars)

	Year ended March 31	
	4th Year	3rd Year
Sales	$8,324	$9,211
Profits	416	645
Profits as a % of:		
Sales	5%	7%
Assets	9%	13%
Common Equity*	15%	21%
Market Value**	8,129	15,076
Stock Price	31 $\frac{7}{8}$	59 $\frac{1}{8}$

* Total stockholders' equity includes capital stock, surplus, and retained earnings at the company's year end. For purposes of determining profits as a percent of common stockholders' equity, all preferred stock is excluded.

** Calculated by multiplying the number of common shares outstanding by the price per common share as of March 31.

The chairman of the board of CyTech asks you to come to his office for a long visit in which he tells you that you have lost the confidence of your senior executives and very possibly mismanaged CyTech's position in light of Motorola's recent competitive move. He offers you the job of vice chairman, but tells you that Hal McPhee will replace you as chief executive officer at the end of the month. McPhee immediately fires Senn-Delaney, which hadn't really been on board long enough to make any worthwhile recommendations, and focuses on improving accountability among members of his new senior team. In an interview with *The Wall Street Journal,* McPhee decries your indecision, hesitance, and dependence on outside input as subtle, yet deadly, signs of below the line patterns. "We will not tolerate such victim attitudes at CyTech," he exclaims, which becomes the subtitle of a front page *Wall Street Journal* article.

Embarrassed and humiliated, you decide to leave the company to figure out what you're going to do with the rest of your life.

- *In the real world you might have been able to accept the input from your senior team and overcome your pride at that fateful moment, but in this game it spelled disaster. If you want to see why the author considers other alternatives better, review Chapter 26, then turn to:*

    Chapter 28, Putting Empowerment First;

    Chapter 30, Emphasizing the Steps to Accountability;

    Chapter 31, Focusing on Both Accountability and Victimization Simultaneously;

    Chapter 32, Starting with the Senior Team;

    Chapter 33, Launching a Companywide Roll-Out;

    Chapter 34, Moving Middle Management Above the Line;

    Chapter 35, Customizing Individualized Accountability Programs; or

    Chapter 36, Installing an Integrated Accountability Program.

- *If you want to start anew on a different decision-making track, go on to:*
    Chapter 2, Building a Classic Innovative Organization;
    Chapter 14, Developing a Synthesis of Best Practices;
    Chapter 38, Pursuing a Work-Team Approach;
    Chapter 50, Reengineering Work Processes; or
    Chapter 62, Embracing a Revolutionary New Perspective.

After reading more than a dozen books on teams and attending several team-development seminars, you decide that teams really could provide the key to improving performance in organizations, particularly flexible organizations like CyTech. All the literature, your own thinking, and discussions with experts in the field convince you that today's business organizations have overlooked the tremendous opportunities for exploiting the potential of teams at every level of an organization. In fact, Motorola, one of your chief competitors, has relied heavily on teams to surpass the Japanese in producing the lightest, smallest, and highest quality cellular phones on the market. In addition to Motorola, a number of companies, such as 3M, Hewlett Packard, and other organizations that face demands similar to CyTech's have made teams work, so if you're going to deploy them, you've got to do it even better than the competition.

38

PURSUING A WORK TEAM APPROACH

You firmly believe that state-of-the-art team performance will benefit not only individual team members but overall company performance in ways that no other approach can. While CyTech must maintain a solid organizational structure and reporting hierarchy, the organization can not become rigid. It should, rather, afford guidance while stimulating the initiative and the drive teams need to accomplish their goals.

When you present the decision to your senior executives, you lead off by reading a paragraph from Chapter One of *The Wisdom of Teams: Creating the High Performance Organization,* written by John Katzenbach and Douglas Smith, two veteran McKinsey & Company consultants: "Teams have existed for hundreds of years, are the subject of countless books, and have been celebrated throughout many countries and cultures. Most people believe they know how teams work as well as the benefits teams offer. Many

167

have had firsthand team experiences themselves, some of which were rewarding and others a waste of time. Yet, as we explored the use of teams, it became increasingly clear that the potential impact of single teams, as well as the collective impact of many teams, on the performance of large organizations is woefully under-exploited—despite the rapidly growing recognition of the need for what teams have to offer. Understanding this paradox and the discipline required to deal with it are central to the basic lessons we have learned about team performance."

After letting the quote sink in for a few moments, you draw upon another book *Leading Teams: Mastering the New Role,* by Zenger, Musselwhite, Hurson, and Perrin to make a cautionary point, "Even though many managers feel that teams will eliminate their role in the organization...managers can [and must, you add] carve an enduring and vital position for themselves in a team environment."

You then discuss with your senior executives your own feelings about teams and what you have learned over the past several weeks from your research and various seminars, giving each team member a chance to express his or her own feelings. John Solo, executive vice president for worldwide sales and marketing, along with Bob Kiechel, senior vice president of product development, and Nan Thurow, senior vice president of worldwide operations, seem most enthusiastic about teams as the next wave of organizational development at CyTech. John Solo comments, "I have always been able to accomplish more when I've been part of a team, and I know we have some good ones at CyTech, but I also know that we're just scratching the surface of what's possible at all levels in the company." Nan Thurow and Bob Kiechel confirm John Solo's view and lend their full support to an all-out team effort.

On the other side, Hal McPhee, chief financial officer, Karen Walsh, vice president of CyTech's advanced technology lab, and Morris Strandmeyer, vice president of production, voice concerns that range from Karen's skepticism to Hal's fairly firm opposition. As a lively discussion ensues, Morris Strandmeyer sums up the opposition by saying, "Yeah, I think teams can be important in an organization, but the bottom line is still getting the job done and meeting performance goals. I hope this team business doesn't divert us from our clear focus on results."

You assure Morris and his less enthusiastic cohorts that your belief in pursing a team approach springs solely from a desire to improve performance throughout the organization. Although they remain skeptical, you convince them to give you the benefit of the doubt. Now, you must show them exactly how teams and team performance can inspire the next phase of development in the company.

To conclude the meeting, you draw again from Katzenbach and Smith, putting their philosophy in your own words: "Groups don't automatically become teams and teams don't necessarily produce high performance. However, I do believe teams represent an untapped potential at CyTech that's begging for our attention. We must learn and apply the wisdom of teams."

You recommend several books your senior team should review over the next few weeks and encourage them to attend any relevant seminars, including one offered internally by CyTech Training & Development. Now that you've thrown your lot with teams, you must develop the right approach for getting the greatest results as quickly as possible.

Meanwhile, a lot of upgrading occurs in the industry as CyTech and its competitors improve their phone-fax-computers with new chips, wireless upgrades, redesigned packages, and a host of other product improvements. CyTech itself introduces *PowerBase 3* and *4* versions and holds its position as one of the lead players in the marketplace. You know, however, that the industry will undergo some major changes that could push the price of phone-fax-computers below $500 within the next two to three years, turning the market into a mass marketing and production game. To prepare for that inevitability, you must make the team approach succeed within the next 12 months.

As the first year of your tenure as CEO comes to an end, CyTech's sales reach $5.5 billion, and the stock price climbs to $32 per share, as shown in the table on page 170.

The board seems pleased with these results and endorses your focus on teams. You keep them updated on your latest thinking and your continuing discussions with your senior executives. You encourage your senior executives to read the latest books on the subject and provide their own input over the next 60 to 90 days.

As you gather feedback from your senior executives and

Selected Financial and Stock Information
(Dollars in millions, except stock price in actual dollars)

	Year ended March 31	
	1st Year	Previous Year
Sales	$5,498	$4,083
Profits	330	242
Profits as a % of:		
Sales	6%	6%
Assets	9%	9%
Common Equity*	16%	17%
Market Value**	8,129	6,123
Stock Price	31 $\frac{7}{8}$	23 $\frac{3}{4}$

* Total stockholders' equity includes capital stock, surplus, and retained earnings at the company's year end. For purposes of determining profits as a percent of common stockholders' equity, all preferred stock is excluded.

** Calculated by multiplying the number of common shares outstanding by the price per common share as of March 31.

members of the board you synthesize the various team approaches into five distinct alternatives. The first stresses the performance challenge facing everyone at CyTech and uses that performance challenge to drive the development of teams at all levels of the company. This alternative assumes that the performance challenge always sits at the heart of any strong team. As part of this alternative, you would make sure that every individual and group within CyTech internalizes the performance challenge in such a way that it energizes all teams, regardless of where they operate in the organization. Of course, while you expect this alternative to result in a powerful response to current challenges, the primary thrust during the first stage of its implementation would emphasize defining and establishing the performance challenge at CyTech.

The second alternative would first try to eliminate all pseudo-team behavior throughout CyTech. Adopting this alternative, you would totally redefine what the team really means, eliminating many old beliefs about teams and team building. This alternative assumes that many misconceptions and misinterpretations about teams plague most organizations. To build the right kind of team environment at CyTech, you must replace many traditional views with new ones. With all of the new talk about teams, a proliferation of different approaches and ideas about team development has occurred, and you must cut through all the nonsense that surrounds any new fad.

The third alternative would teach team basics first. Without spending a lot of time worrying about the old habits and traditions and wrong views, this alternative begins teaching the fundamentals of team power at all levels throughout the company. Addressing such key issues as team size, purpose, goals, skills, approach, and accountability would drive this education-oriented alternative throughout the organization. The idea here rests on getting everyone thinking the same way about what makes a team successful.

The fourth alternative would begin at the top with your own group of senior executives. You know that building a strong team at the top would prove difficult because, according to some consultants, that's the hardest place to develop team performance, but this alternative would provide a top-down example other teams throughout the organization could follow. You anticipate the difficulty of making this alternative work. The entire American business system fosters individualism at the top, stresses heavy travel schedules, and reinforces performance pressures, making it difficult for any senior group to function smoothly as a team. However, this alternative could make the most sense, given the need for role models at the top.

The fifth alternative changes the role of senior management as it relates to teams, team development, and team performance throughout the organization. Since top management in most organizations has left the development of teams to other people, this alternative would stress the need for making team development and team performance the primary role of your senior executives. Certainly the senior executives would continue focusing on strategy and on the overall performance of CyTech, but from an organizational perspective they would place teams at the forefront of all their thinking and activities. Bringing such a change would certainly take time and effort, but it could pay off handsomely.

Before you discuss these alternatives with your senior executives, you develop a summary of the pros and cons for each one. (See chart on page 172.) After you present the pros and cons of these five alternatives to your senior team, lengthy discussions take

Alternative	Pros	Cons
1. Stressing the Performance Challenge.	Gets to the heart of what makes real teams.	Doesn't focus directly on team development.
2. Eliminating Pseudo Teams.	Gets rid of wrong thinking.	Focuses on the negative.
3. Teaching Team Basics.	Educates team members in what makes a real team.	Places too much emphasis on education as the key to developing strong teams.
4. Developing a Strong Team at the Top.	Provides a model for the entire organization.	The most difficult place to develop strong teams, not as important as teams at other levels.
5. Changing the Role of Senior Management.	Makes team development and team performance a focal point for top management.	Too indirect and slow.

place over three consecutive management meetings. Morris Strand-meyer, vice president of production, and Hal McPhee, chief financial officer, favor Alternative 1: Stressing the Performance Challenge. Bob Kiechel, senior vice president of product development, and Nan Thurow, senior vice president of worldwide operations, favor Alternative 5: Changing the Role of Top Management. Karen Walsh, vice president of CyTech's advance technology lab, favors Alternative 2: Eliminating Pseudo Teams. John Solo, executive vice president for worldwide sales and marketing, prefers Alternative 4: Building a Strong Team at the Top.

Curiously, no one selected Alternative 3: Teaching Team Basics. When you ask why, the responses vary but reveal a consensus that merely teaching people about teams won't ensure their actual implementation. You wonder about this conclusion and decide you must still give it careful consideration.

You thank your senior executives for their helpful input, informing them that you will make a decision within the week. It's Thursday afternoon, and you decide to fly to Fort Walton Beach on the Gulf Coast with your spouse for a long weekend to ruminate on the options and finalize your own thinking. You know that what you decide will form a critical pivot point for CyTech's further development. Making a mistake here could cost your job, CyTech's market position, and employment for a lot of people.

- *If you decide to stress the performance challenge, turn to Chapter 39.*

- *If you want to eliminate all pseudo-team notions, turn to Chapter 40.*

- *If you choose to teach team basics, turn to Chapter 41.*

- *If you decide to build a strong team at the top, turn to Chapter 42.*

- *If you conclude that you must change the role of top management with respect to team development, turn to Chapter 43.*

According to the research of Katzenbach and Smith, the McKinsey & Company consultants who wrote *The Wisdom of Teams,* performance challenges build strong teams. You underline a particularly relevant passage in their book: "The hunger for performance is far more important to team success than team-building exercises, special incentives, or team leaders with ideal profiles." This idea that teams succeed or fail depending on the challenges they face reaffirms your own commitment to stressing the performance challenge as the guiding principle during the initial phase of CyTech's new team approach. Impressed by Katzenbach and Smith's work, you use it extensively as you present your choice to the senior team. In a morning meeting you paint the broad strokes of your vision: "We must present a performance challenge that really means something to our people. It goes beyond interpersonal chemistry or the basic desire to play on a winning team. I think real teamwork means more than just forming teams. It takes a compelling set of shared performance goals that the team really wants to accomplish. After all, teams are a means, not an end. Performance is the end."

39

STRESSING THE PERFORMANCE CHALLENGE

Your senior financial officer, Hal McPhee, and your vice president of production, Morris Strandmeyer, applaud your choice as the logical place to begin this team approach, and the other members of your team grow more enthusiastic as you talk. You consider yourself fortunate to have won over two of your more skeptical executives. Both McPhee and Strandmeyer had been lukewarm, even skeptical, when you originally selected the team path, but now they seem fully committed and excited about the idea of performance challenges. Even Karen Walsh, vice president of the advanced technology lab, slowly warms up to the concept because, as she puts it, "Actually, we've always been committed to performance at CyTech. Maybe this is the right way to begin our team focus."

In succeeding weeks, you work closely with your senior executives to establish compelling and challenging performance requirements throughout the organization, identifying performance challenges for each level of the organization that incorporate CyTech's dual strategic focus on maintaining technological leadership and preparing for a mass production and mass marketing game. Managers and employees throughout the organization respond to these challenges by developing specific performance criteria at each level. The overall challenges expressed from the top include: increasing market share; maintaining technological leadership in the industry; preparing for mass marketing and sales; gaining bold improvements in operating costs and efficiencies; and growing the market value of CyTech's stock by at least 20 percent annually. These performance challenges guide all levels of managers and employees, who quickly adopt specific supporting performance challenges, such as identifying new target customer groups, automating the product assembly line, reorganizing the marketing and sales interface, and expanding R&D to multimedia applications.

Over the next few months teams across the company flourish as they work tirelessly to meet the new challenges. Midway through the year three foreign competitors launch a price war that immediately affects CyTech and every other competitor in the industry. As a result, the mass market/mass production game explodes at least two years before you expected it. You wonder whether CyTech can incorporate this additional challenge, but to your delight, the organization responds brilliantly, using this new challenge to further stimulate the company's team culture.

As phone-fax-computer prices drop below $500, competitors scurry to lower their costs without going out of business, but CyTech responds more smoothly than anyone as teams throughout the organization band together behind a common purpose. The company introduces *PowerBase* versions 5, 6, and 7, the first two of which sell for under $500, the third for under $400. These enhanced products increase CyTech's market share over the next several months, verifying the correctness of your stress on team performance challenges.

As you come to the end of your second year as CEO, sales reach $7 billion, and CyTech's stock price climbs to $55 per share as shown here.

Selected Financial and Stock Information
(Dollars in millions, except stock price in actual dollars)

	Year ended March 31	
	2nd Year	**1st Year**
Sales	$7,201	$5,498
Profits	432	330
Profits as a % of:		
Sales	6%	6%
Assets	10%	9%
Common Equity[*]	17%	16%
Market Value[**]	14,089	8,129
Stock Price	55 ¼	31 ⅞

[*] Total stockholders' equity includes capital stock, surplus, and retained earnings at the company's year end. For purposes of determining profits as a percent of common stockholders' equity, all preferred stock is excluded.

[**] Calculated by multiplying the number of common shares outstanding by the price per common share as of March 31.

Not only do these numbers prompt rave reviews from your board of directors, they lead the business press to name CyTech "a model team organization." However, you know that progress to date represents only the first stage of team building, and that you must now take further steps to solidify and further enhance the role of teams throughout the organization.

After reviewing at least a dozen alternatives, you boil down your choices to two. The first would shift focus to team-building skills and activities throughout the organization, while the second would continue stressing team performance with an additional emphasis on helping teams assess their own performance and understand the different phases of the team performance curve, as outlined by Katzenbach and Smith in their book *The Wisdom of Teams*. (See diagram on next page.)

One alternative emphasizes team building as the important second phase, while the other reinforces team performance. Since

The Team Performance Curve

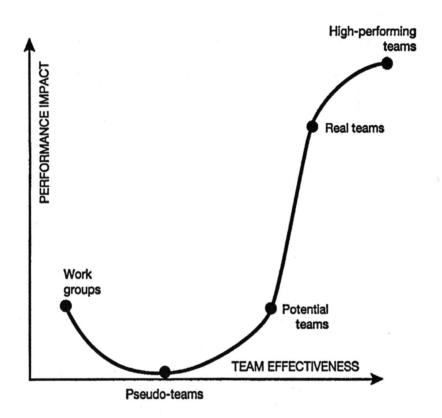

you've already established the performance challenge, the first option might add a new dimension to your team-building effort. On the other hand, it might weaken the power of the company's stress on performance.

Continuing to stress team performance while developing ways to assess and better understand team performance might further solidify the performance challenge culture at CyTech. However, people might also react to it as overkill at the very time you need more team development in order to win the price war.

Given the current pressures on CyTech, you know you must make this decision quickly and without a lot of discussion. Believing that your senior team will support either direction, you decide to make this decision yourself.

- *If you choose to focus on team building and team development, turn to Chapter 44.*

- *If you prefer continuing the stress on team performance and a greater understanding of the team performance curve, turn to Chapter 45.*

Not surprisingly, Karen Walsh, vice president of CyTech's advanced technology lab, agrees wholeheartedly with your choice to eliminate all erroneous team thinking, team behaving, team building, and team performing. In fact, as you announce your decision, Karen exclaims to your senior team, "I think it's so smart to start off eliminating all wrong-headed illusions and misguided thinking about teams."

Hearing that comment, Nan Thurow, senior vice president of worldwide operations, responds, "I don't think we're so misguided."

"Oh, yes, we are," Karen insists.

With such strong emotions clouding the issues, you assume leadership of the group, agreeing with Karen that the many false assumptions about what makes a team work can only cause problems with CyTech's team approach, while at the same time continuing your belief that CyTech's people have already made some gratifying progress toward forming teams that surpass performance goals.

40

ELIMINATING PSEUDO TEAMS

You continue by saying, "Exceptional teams are rare in any organization, especially those with confused and wrong-headed ideas about what propels a group of people from merely functioning as a work group to a whole new level of performance. Our people can get there, but they need our help."

The rest of your senior executives seem somewhat uneasy with your choice of alternatives, but you remain firm in your decision, asking for their unflinching support. They greet it grudgingly, and over the next several days you hear a lot of questioning about your chosen course of action.

Drawing on the work of Katzenbach and Smith in *The Wisdom of Teams*, you identify a list of characteristics for the pseudo team and the real team.

Pseudo Team	*Real Team*
One strong leader	Shared leadership
Individual accountability	Joint accountability
Broad organization mission	Specific team purpose
Efficient meetings	Open-ended discussions and problem solving meetings
Measures effectiveness indirectly	Measures performance directly
Delegates work	Does real work together

When you share this chart with your senior team, you ask them to pass it along to their directors and managers throughout the organization. You also encourage your training and development group to develop a list of "dos and don'ts" designed to hammer home the difference between pseudo teams and real teams. This promotes a lot of discussion throughout the organization as people argue about what differentiates a real team from a pseudo team. Some people twist the "dos and don'ts" for their own personal agendas, making Katzenbach and Smith's approach to listing the characteristics of pseudo and real teams an inordinate source of contention throughout the organization.

Initially, you think the discussion and debate will eventually promote understanding of real teams throughout the organization. However, when three foreign competitors begin a vicious price war within the industry, your concern about CyTech's internal strife deepens. The world of mass market, mass production arrives two to three years earlier than you expected, and CyTech must respond quickly to that development with lower prices, production efficiencies, and more aggressive marketing and sales.

Unfortunately for you and the rest of the CyTech organization, you fail to gain any benefit from your months of discussing and planning CyTech's team approach. In fact, the recent debate about pseudo teams versus real teams confuses, rather than enlightens, people, sparking unproductive debates across departments and teams about just how the company should meet this latest challenge. As in most crises, the CyTech organization naturally returns to its known habits and patterns of doing business.

Over the next several months, CyTech fails to sufficiently lower production costs and introduces only one new version of the *PowerBase* priced at $499. Frustrated with your own decision making and feeling mounting pressure for better performance, you scrap all focus on teams in favor of turning CyTech into a short-term mass producer and mass marketer.

This move requires some drastic steps, including the replacement of executive vice president John Solo and vice president of production Morris Strandmeyer with executives from Frito Lay and Proctor & Gamble who can immediately improve operational efficiency, get costs down and fuel stronger marketing and sales efforts.

The board of directors interprets your precipitous firing of two senior executives and your scraping of all work on CyTech's team approach as signs of personal instability. To them, the company looks out of control.

Their fears prove true when year-end results show sagging sales and declining profits, as shown in the accompanying table.

Selected Financial and Stock Information
(Dollars in millions, except stock price in actual dollars)

	Year ended March 31	
	2nd Year	1st Year
Sales	$5,638	$5,498
Profits	113	330
Profits as a % of:		
Sales	2%	6%
Assets	5%	9%
Common Equity*	9%	16%
Market Value**	4,909	8,129
Stock Price	19 $\frac{1}{4}$	31 $\frac{7}{8}$

* Total stockholders' equity includes capital stock, surplus, and retained earnings at the company's year end. For purposes of determining profits as a percent of common stockholders' equity, all preferred stock is excluded.

** Calculated by multiplying the number of common shares outstanding by the price per common share as of March 31.

Within four weeks, they ask for your resignation, and your opportunity to shape the CyTech organization comes to an abrupt end.

- *In real life you might have been able to eliminate wrong-headed ideas about teams more productively, but if you want to see why the author considers other alternatives more effective, review Chapter 38, then select:*

  Chapter 39, Stressing the Performance Challenge;

  Chapter 41, Teaching Team Basics;

  Chapter 42, Developing a Strong Team at the Top;

  Chapter 43, Changing the Role of Top Management.

- *If you'd rather start fresh on a new decision-making track, turn to:*

  Chapter 2, Building a Classic Innovative Organization;

  Chapter 14, Developing a Synthesis of Best Practices;

  Chapter 26, Imbuing the Culture with Empowerment and Accountability;

  Chapter 50, Reengineering Work Processes;

  Chapter 62, Embracing a Revolutionary New Perspective.

Using *The Wisdom of Team*'s outline of team basics and *Leading Team*'s description of team principles as starting points, you ask your director of corporate training and development to adapt it to CyTech's needs. The outline covers six major team guidelines.

Team Basics	**Team Principles**
1. Small enough in number;	1. Focus on the issue, behavior, or problem, not on the person;
2. Adequate levels of complementary skills;	2. Maintain the self-confidence and self-esteem of others;
3. Truly meaningful purpose;	
4. Specific goal or goals;	3. Maintain constructive relationships;
5. Clear working approach; and	4. Take initiative to make things better; and
6. Sense of mutual accountability.	5. Lead by example.

These two lists form the framework for CyTech's basic team-learning course that every employee throughout the CyTech organization will take over the next 12 months.

In order to drive home your decision with maximum force, you do all of this before informing your senior team. Since none of them saw this was the right direction for CyTech's first phase of team implementation, you have chosen to push this decision through without the usual discussion and debate. You've grown impatient with the senior team's reluctance and feel in your heart that you must strike while the iron is hot. Otherwise, you could end up wasting valuable time. However, the violent reaction with which they greet your decision takes you aback.

After a lot of heated discussion, Hal McPhee finally says, "This is nonsense!" He stalks out of the room.

41
TEACHING TEAM BASICS

Nan Thurow watches the door slam, then looks hard, "Don't overreact to Hal," she says. "The truth is, we all feel the same way."

"I don't," you snap. "This is what CyTech really needs."

"No, it doesn't," responds Nan in a gentle, but firm manner.

You stare long and hard at the remaining members of your senior team, wondering whether you should fire them or listen to them. They have rejected your authority. You've lost their respect. Can you salvage anything out of this impasse? Finally, you decide to listen to your senior executives and go back to one of the other alternatives.

- *If you decide to stress the performance challenge, turn to Chapter 39.*

- *If you want to eliminate all pseudo-team notions, turn to Chapter 40.*

- *If you decide to build a strong team at the top, turn to Chapter 42.*

- *If you wish to change the role of top management relative to team development and performance, turn to Chapter 43.*

When you announce this decision, John Solo's energetic approval proves infective with your whole senior team. The groups accepts his challenge: "If we can't play team ball, how can we expect anyone else to?" However, in the weeks and months that follow, the senior group finds it is not so easy to practice what John preached. No specific purpose binds them together, other than the general mission of the company. As a result, each team member remains mostly dedicated to his or her own function in the organization, which automatically keeps the team members apart from one another. No one seems willing to invest the extra time to communicate and work together, and that breakdown hardly serves as a proper role model for others in the organization. In the end, the senior executives grow fractious and frustrated.

42

DEVELOPING A STRONG TEAM AT THE TOP

You go back to Katzenbach and Smith's book, *The Wisdom of Teams*, rereading their cautionary suggestion that forming a team at the top requires careful questioning concerning their ability to function smoothly as a team. Given their distinct and strong personalities and their accustomed habit of focusing on their respective functions, they probably wouldn't have responded well to any amount of coaching on your part. At the very best, it would have taxed your leadership to the fullest.

To make matters worse, three foreign competitors launch a price war that engulfs CyTech and every other competitor in a price-slashing, cost-cutting frenzy that no one expected to occur this early in the game. The pressure of the price war, combined with the growing frustration of your senior team, ignites fierce arguments that spread throughout the entire organization and eventually reaches the board of directors.

Frustrated yourself by all the turmoil, you become more and

more autocratic and demanding in your effort to whip the organization into shape. Bob Kiechel asks for a meeting away from the office; you reluctantly agree. In a private dining room at a nearby country club, Kiechel tells you that you're destroying the company. After three intense hours you decide to change your course by going back to one of the other alternatives you had previously considered.

- *If you decide to stress the performance challenge, turn to Chapter 39.*

- *If you want to eliminate all pseudo-team notions, turn to Chapter 40.*

- *If you decide to build a strong team at the top, turn to Chapter 41.*

- *If you wish to change the role of top management relative to team development and performance, turn to Chapter 43.*

Your decision to change the role of senior management at CyTech, focusing it more toward developing and monitoring strong teams, meets with the approval of your senior executives. Even McPhee, Walsh, and Strandmeyer, who had expressed some skepticism when you originally decided to move in the team direction, come around to embrace a new definition of top management's role in developing and nurturing high-performance teams throughout the organization.

43
CHANGING THE ROLE OF TOP MANAGEMENT

In a management meeting, you review with your team both the common sense and the less obvious findings of Katzenbach and Smith, as outlined in their book *The Wisdom of Teams*. The ensuing discussion begins molding a new perspective for team development at CyTech. In the meeting, you paraphrase from *The Wisdom of Teams*: "Teams will be the key to company performance in the organization of the future because only teams can meet the challenges emerging from an increasingly complex and changing business environment. The best companies in the future will create a reinforcing cycle of performance challenges shaping teams and teams achieving high performance. Teams will help such companies build new strengths, develop needed skills, intensify focus, expand commitment, and make things happen. That's what we want at CyTech."

At this point, your senior executives see their own role in team formation as a critical factor. Without their constant coaching, they conclude, CyTech cannot meet the challenges it faces and adapt to the need for constant change in the years ahead.

As the meeting unfolds, everyone in the room becomes more and more committed to this course of action. They actually relish the opportunity to direct a momentous transformation at CyTech.

You tell them and they fully accept that they must provide the key to this transformation. Next, you draw on the work from the Zenger-Miller associates' *Leading Teams,* to help your senior team recognize the need to help managers and supervisors throughout the company "let go." Drawing on Zenger's and his associates' recommendations, you point out:

- When managers give up absolute power over their teams they gain the power to bring the best out of their teams.
- When managers respect the abilities of their teams they gain the respect of their teams.
- When managers learn to make others valuable they gain value in the eyes of the company.

As the meeting comes to a close, you're pleased that your team has captured the vision of their role in the team movement at CyTech. As homework, you encourage each member of the senior group to finish reading the two team books.

In the weeks that follow, your senior executives work individually and collectively to identify the key teams throughout the organization that must reach the high performance level if CyTech expects to reach its objectives and remain an industry leader.

Together, you map out a plan for emphasizing your senior team's new role directing and coaching groups and individuals throughout the company to move:

- *From* individual accountability *to* joint accountability;
- *From* dividing those who think and decide from those who work and do *to* expecting everyone to think, decide, work, and do;
- *From* building functional excellence *to* encouraging people to play multiple roles and work together throughout the organization for continuous improvement;
- *From* relying on managerial control *to* getting people to buy into meaningful purpose, shared direction, and learning; and
- *From* providing a fair day's pay for a fair day's work *to* aspiring to personal growth that expands as well as exploits each person's capabilities.

Senior management's attention to the development of teams and to team performance begins to affect the organization deeply and fundamentally by expanding team capabilities and individual productivity, which proves none too soon when three foreign competitors launch a price war, turning the industry upside down. The price war takes everyone by surprise, since most experts expected it to occur two to three years from now. The price of phone-fax-computers drops below $500.

As you and your senior team scramble to respond to this new challenge, you hold firmly to the changed role of top management that emphasizes team development and team performance. Together with your senior executives, you solemnly agree that you cannot allow the new focus to be sidetracked by the crisis of the moment.

In an off-site three-day strategy session with your six senior executives, you identify 62 different teams throughout the organization that you consider critical to CyTech's winning the current price war. More than half of these teams relate to production and operations, where costs must be reduced dramatically. The rest of the teams relate to marketing, sales, and product innovation.

Everyone recognizes the overriding challenge: becoming a mass marketer and mass producer overnight. Equally important, however, the company must maintain a long-term commitment to new-product development, an almost extinct idea amid the current crisis. However, Bob Kiechel, senior vice president of product development, and Karen Walsh, vice president of CyTech's advanced technology lab, respond to the challenge, forming teams charged with figuring out a way for CyTech to conquer the current circumstance and win long-term leadership as well.

As adrenalin rushes through the veins of every employee at CyTech, particularly among members of the key teams, CyTech emerges at the end of a very challenging year as a profitable market leader. By the end of your second year as CEO, sales reach $7 billion, and the stock price climbs to $49 per share, as shown in the table on page 192.

Early in the third year of your tenure as CEO, you begin looking to the next major challenges the company will face, and you conclude that it's time to embark on the second phase of team development. With senior management's role clearly directed to-

Selected Financial and Stock Information
(Dollars in millions, except stock price in actual dollars)

	Year ended March 31	
	2nd Year	1st Year
Sales	$6,899	$5,498
Profits	414	330
Profits as a % of:		
Sales	6%	6%
Assets	8%	9%
Common Equity*	15%	16%
Market Value**	12,559	8,129
Stock Price	49 $\frac{1}{4}$	31 $\frac{7}{8}$

* Total stockholders' equity includes capital stock, surplus, and retained earnings at the company's year end. For purposes of determining profits as a percent of common stockholders' equity, all preferred stock is excluded.

** Calculated by multiplying the number of common shares outstanding by the price per common share as of March 31.

ward teams, you could stress performance challenges, making them the focal point of all your communications, or you could emphasize process guidelines for building and developing teams.

The advantage of focusing on performance challenges lies in the fact that such challenges provide the very essence of what pulls teams together. Having witnessed the power of a new philosophy at the top, you have come to appreciate that performance challenges drive any team, be it at the top or the bottom of the organization. The disadvantage to this option lies in the fact that it potentially neglects team-development processes and techniques that could make a big difference in the continuing growth of CyTech's teams.

The obvious advantage to implementing process guidelines could come from providing structure and texture to the overall team-development approach now receiving emphasis from the top. The performance challenge of the recent price war may need support from education, structure, technique, and process aimed at developing strong teams throughout the organization. On the other hand, this alternative might direct attention from performance goals.

Too much technique and process could, in fact, hinder the creation of high performance teams.

As you struggle with these two options, you know that you must make the right decision.

- *If you decide to make performance challenges the focal point in Phase 2 of CyTech's team approach, turn to Chapter 46.*

- *If you choose to develop process guidelines for improving and enhancing team-development as the second step in CyTech's team approach, turn to Chapter 47.*

Believing that the "hard" side and the "soft" side of business go hand-in-glove, you conclude that this second phase of team development must emphasize the soft side. A successful organization, you believe, has a strong emphasis on performance with a focus on the softer side of team development and the value of building teams.

To guide CyTech toward such a balance, you rely on the work of a local consulting firm that has been providing seminars and workshops for some of CyTech's training courses. The firm, Human Dynamics, stresses the nonperformance reasons for people drawing together in a common bond: identifying a common set of values, understanding differences in personality and psychological type, and learning to complement each other's skills in a way that promotes more personal growth and higher human fulfillment in the work place. The HD philosophy preaches that living in teams will make up the natural order for people and organizations in the twenty-first century.

44

FOCUSING ON TEAM BUILDING

With the help of Human Dynamics, you direct the development of an intricate set of activities designed to move people from traditional leadership that directs people, to participative leadership that involves people, and ultimately to team leadership that builds trust and inspires teamwork, all the while balancing team building with the rather "hard" focus on performance that ruled Phase 1. In the months following, people really do get into the spirit of team building. Unfortunately, without your realizing it, the pendulum shifts too far to developing and building teams for their own sake rather than to promoting performance. For example, many teams throughout the company spend so much time attending workshops, sharing team-building exercises, and disseminating information about teamwork that they lose touch with the marketplace.

At year end, impressive numbers belie the underlying erosion of CyTech's culture.

Selected Financial and Stock Information
(Dollars in millions, except stock price in actual dollars)

	Year ended March 31	
	3rd Year	2nd Year
Sales	$8,531	$7,201
Profits	512	432
Profits as a % of:		
Sales	6%	6%
Assets	10%	10%
Common Equity*	18%	17%
Market Value**	15,841	14,089
Stock Price	62 $\frac{1}{8}$	55 $\frac{1}{4}$

* Total stockholders' equity includes capital stock, surplus, and retained earnings at the company's year end. For purposes of determining profits as a percent of common stockholders' equity, all preferred stock is excluded.

** Calculated by multiplying the number of common shares outstanding by the price per common share as of March 31.

Reality hits you hard, however, when a major competitor introduces a voice-operated phone-fax-computer that takes the market by storm in the first quarter of your fourth year as CEO. The shift from performance to team development catches CyTech by surprise. If you'd had more time before this bold competitor move, you might have been able to perfect the balance you were seeking when you introduced the team-building phase, but that balance now seems impossible. Team development has, to your chagrin, taken everyone's eyes off the challenge of the marketplace.

By the end of your fourth year as CEO, sales drops to $7 billion, and CyTech's stock plummets to $21 per share, as shown in the table on the next page. With CyTech still months away from introducing its own voice-operated phone-fax-computer, market analysts begin lamenting that CyTech may have lost the battle and its position in the fast-paced personal electronics/personal computing industry. Shareholders scream bloody murder. The board of directors votes to accept a $35 per share offer from Compaq Computer to gain control of CyTech, and Compaq executives inform you that your services will no longer be required.

Selected Financial and Stock Information
(Dollars in millions, except stock price in actual dollars)

	Year ended March 31	
	4th Year	3rd Year
Sales	$6,986	$8,531
Profits	279	512
Profits as a % of:		
Sales	4%	6%
Assets	6%	10%
Common Equity*	12%	18%
Market Value**	5,324	15,841
Stock Price	20 $\frac{7}{8}$	62 $\frac{1}{8}$

* Total stockholders' equity includes capital stock, surplus, and retained earnings at the company's year end. For purposes of determining profits as a percent of common stockholders' equity, all preferred stock is excluded.

** Calculated by multiplying the number of common shares outstanding by the price per common share as of March 31.

With time now to ponder your last organizational development decision, you realize, more than ever before, that the success of teams hinges on the performance challenge.

- *In real life you might have been able to avoid CyTech's loss of market value and remain at the helm, but if you want to know why the author considers the other alternative preferable, turn to Chapter 45.*

- *If you want to start fresh on a new decision-making track, turn to:*

    Chapter 2, Building a Classic Innovative Organization;

    Chapter 14, Developing a Synthesis of Best Practices;

    Chapter 26, Imbuing the Culture with Empowerment and Accountability;

    Chapter 50, Reengineering Work Processes; or

    Chapter 62, Embracing a Revolutionary New Perspective.

Your senior team greets your decision to continue focusing on team performance with enthusiasm. Only Nan Thurow, senior vice president of worldwide operations, objects, saying, "If we're not careful, all of this performance stuff could overload our people, stressing them out and ultimately causing more problems than it solves."

John Solo, executive vice president for worldwide sales and marketing, adds a minor concern of his own, suggesting that the company must find a way to stress performance without turning it into a club used to beat people over the head. You respond to these concerns by expressing your basic belief that performance challenges drive every strong team. "Nothing will ever change that," you insist. However, you agree to work diligently to avoid pressure overloads, though not at the expense of maintaining the challenges that will help strengthen all of CyTech's teams.

As more discussion ensues, you seize the opportunity to flesh out your own philosophy about performance challenges as the key to developing strong, high-performance teams. You say, "I want

45

CONTINUING TO STRESS TEAM PERFORMANCE

every employee at CyTech to understand that a performance challenge really does lie at the core of his or her success. Keeping such challenges ever present, moving from one challenge to the next with speed and clarity, must characterize our managerial culture."

Sensitive to Nan Thurow's concern, John Solo tries to convince her with a sports analogy, something he's well known for among the senior team: "Nan, I know you don't go to that many baseball games, but baseball provides a neat analogy here. Pitching is 75 percent, maybe 90 percent, of the game. If you have a good pitching staff, you win—if you don't, you lose. That's what we're talking about here. If a group of people embraces a performance challenge, setting clear performance goals to meet that challenge, that's 75 to 90 percent of what makes teams win."

Nan responds, "I understand what you're saying, and as long as we remain sensitive to the tendency of some organizations to overload their people with too much pressure, using the performance challenges as baseball bats to hammer them into line, then I feel fairly comfortable with going ahead. But I still want to hear more about how, precisely, we're going to implement this second phase of our team approach."

Responding to her invitation, you introduce the group to Katzenbach and Smith's team-performance curve, which charts the path from a working group to a high-performing team, as indicated in the following graph.

The Team Performance Curve

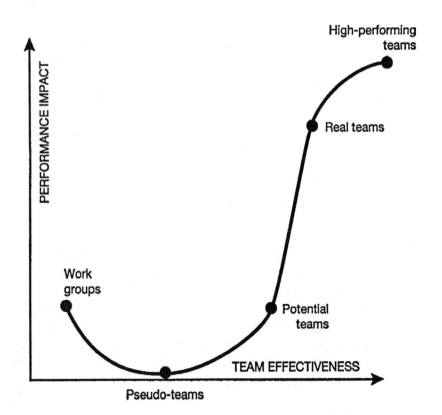

You spend a lot of time discussing each phase on the team-performance curve, suggesting that the second phase of CyTech's team approach must help teams throughout the organization to recognize that a continuing focus on challenges will improve their performance and effectiveness.

Drawing from Katzenbach and Smith's work, you explore each team-performance stage fully. The working group sees "no significant incremental performance need or opportunity that would require it to become a team." Your senior team acknowledges that some working groups at CyTech do not need to achieve higher levels of performance. Typically, these groups consist of loosely connected people who do not share common purposes. While some must continue, CyTech should strive to reduce the overall number of mere working groups throughout the organization.

The pseudo-team "has not focused on collective performance and is not really trying to achieve it." In other words, the pseudo-team lacks any definition of collective performance.

The potential team "is trying to improve its performance impact." Here, the team begins identifying how it must focus on performance and function differently.

The real team "is a small number of people with complementary skills who are equally committed to a common purpose, goals, and working approach for which they hold themselves mutually accountable." You spend an hour discussing the real team, emphasizing that common purpose, working together, and finding ways to complement one another in the application of capabilities, talents and skills drives the challenge to perform and creates the opportunity to excel.

Finally, you discuss high-performance teams: "A group that meets all the conditions of real teams and has members who are also deeply committed to one another's personal growth and success." If CyTech can achieve this level of teamwork, it will reap the ultimate payoff in terms of record results and deeply satisfied team players.

Over the next several weeks you continue discussions of high-performance teams, and slowly but surely your senior team comes to believe that the performance challenge determines a team's position on the team-performance curve and provides the key to reaching the high-performance level.

As this focus on team performance and an understanding of the team-performance curve spreads throughout the organization during the second stage of CyTech's team approach, increases in sales and profits reflect the performance challenge philosophy.

Selected Financial and Stock Information
(Dollars in millions, except stock price in actual dollars)

	Year ended March 31	
	3rd Year	2nd Year
Sales	$9,514	$7,201
Profits	666	432
Profits as a % of:		
Sales	7%	6%
Assets	12%	10%
Common Equity*	20%	17%
Market Value**	18,136	14,089
Stock Price	71 ⅛	55 ¼

* Total stockholders' equity includes capital stock, surplus, and retained earnings at the company's year end. For purposes of determining profits as a percent of common stockholders' equity, all preferred stock is excluded.

** Calculated by multiplying the number of common shares outstanding by the price per common share as of March 31.

Soon after the year end, you receive competitive intelligence that Motorola will introduce a voice-operated phone-fax-computer within the next three months. You adroitly use this challenge to spur the performance of several of CyTech's new product development and product introduction teams.

CyTech people perform beautifully as they introduce their own voice-operated phone-fax-computer at the same time Motorola introduces its version. The two products revolutionize the marketplace. CyTech and Motorola carve up most of the market share for phone-fax-computers, with both gaining in profitability, sales growth, and stock value.

At the end of your fourth year as CEO of CyTech, sales climb to $13 billion. CyTech stock rises to $87 per share. The shareholders have made millions of dollars in the last year, as shown in the following table.

Selected Financial and Stock Information
(Dollars in millions, except stock price in actual dollars)

	Year ended March 31	
	4th Year	3rd Year
Sales	$12,875	$9,514
Profits	901	666
Profits as a % of:		
Sales	7%	7%
Assets	13%	12%
Common Equity*	22%	20%
Market Value**	22,154	18,136
Stock Price	86 $\frac{7}{8}$	71 $\frac{1}{8}$

* Total stockholders' equity includes capital stock, surplus, and retained earnings at the company's year end. For purposes of determining profits as a percent of common stockholders' equity, all preferred stock is excluded.
** Calculated by multiplying the number of common shares outstanding by the price per common share as of March 31.

In addition to great praise from your board of directors, you reap kudos from the business press and employees throughout CyTech. Everyone feels you have kept your eye on the ball, and you work to deserve that reputation by launching the third phase of deepening CyTech's team approach. Once again, you boil your options down to two. On the one hand, you could focus on the discipline necessary to work in teams, as well as the team basics needed to shape-up and complete CyTech's team development. On the other hand, you could champion team building as a cheerleader, increasing and reinforcing enthusiasm for the team approach.

If you focus on team basics and discipline, that move might perpetuate the cultural and organizational values of teams. This alternative might allow you to cement a knowledge of exactly what drives teams, creates teams, and brings teams to a high-performing level in a disciplined fashion, keeping them functioning productively well into the future. This alternative's disadvantage lies in introducing techniques and processes that thus far you avoided in an effort to keep bureaucracy and policies from hampering team power.

Team building and cheerleading offers a clear advantage, too: It's fun, it's exciting, it appeals to people's emotions, and it's based on the belief that fun and enjoyment can keep teams fresh and alive. The disadvantage: It may prove to be fluff, without the power to perpetuate strong teams for years to come.

As you think about these two alternatives, you think the one may be too serious, too hard hitting, while the other may be too soft, too easygoing. However, you just can't bring yourself to consider some combination of these two, believing a combination would water down both, creating a wishy-washy third phase of implementation that could do more harm than good. What should you do?

- *If you decide to focus on team basics and discipline, turn to Chapter 48.*

- *If you choose a team-building and cheerleading approach, turn to Chapter 49.*

With the role of your senior team fundamentally changed, you now move to ensure that teams within the CyTech organization set performance challenges at the core of their efforts. You work closely with your senior executives to lay out the performance challenges for the entire organization—five or six key challenges that will stimulate the performance of all levels of the organization.

After weeks of discussion and analysis, input from consultants, and suggestions from task forces within CyTech, your senior executives, under your direction, come up with the following key performance challenges:

46

MAKING PERFORMANCE CHALLENGES THE NEXT FOCAL POINT

1. Keep making technological breakthroughs;
2. Maintain a mass marketing and mass production flexibility that stresses growth and profits;
3. Iron out any contradictions between technological leadership and mass marketing production;
4. Maximize the market value of CyTech's stock; and
5. Empower more and more customers throughout the world with *PowerBase* products.

With these five challenges as the driving force for the entire CyTech organization, you engage every manager in the task of designing performance challenges for both their management teams and all the teams under their supervision.

The results gratify you, as sales reach $8.5 billion and the stock price moves to $64 per share at the end of your third year as CEO. See table on page 206.

Selected Financial and Stock Information
(Dollars in millions, except stock price in actual dollars)

	Year ended March 31	
	3rd Year	2nd Year
Sales	$8,487	$6,899
Profits	509	414
Profits as a % of:		
Sales	6%	6%
Assets	9%	8%
Common Equity*	17%	15%
Market Value**	16,274	12,559
Stock Price	63 $^{13}/_{16}$	49 $^1/_4$

* Total stockholders' equity includes capital stock, surplus, and retained earnings at the company's year end. For purposes of determining profits as a percent of common stockholders' equity, all preferred stock is excluded.

** Calculated by multiplying the number of common shares outstanding by the price per common share as of March 31.

Rather than resting on your laurels, you immediately pinpoint the most significant challenge of the new year: developing a voice-operated phone-fax-computer, something that you know Motorola has been working on for a year and could introduce to the market any minute now. To meet this challenge, teams at CyTech work around the clock to introduce the company's own voice-operated *PowerBase,* and shortly after the beginning of your fourth year as CEO at CyTech, CyTech unveils *VoiceBase 1,* a mere four weeks after the Motorola introduction. Together, CyTech and Motorola storm the market, driving sales to dizzying levels. You rely heavily on Nan Thurow, senior VP of worldwide operations, because of her natural affinity for teams and her enthusiastic support for changing the role of the senior team.

The year rolls along without a hitch as CyTech's teams match the new demands of the marketplace. Not surprisingly, the new voice-operated machine not only expands the market, but opens new avenues of growth such as voice-operated desk-top publishing systems.

Your fourth year as CEO passes with lightning speed and with wonderful results as shown in the accompanying table.

Selected Financial and Stock Information
(Dollars in millions, except stock price in actual dollars)

	Year ended March 31	
	4th Year	3rd Year
Sales	$11,877	$8,487
Profits	831	509
Profits as a % of:		
Sales	7%	6%
Assets	11%	9%
Common Equity*	21%	17%
Market Value**	21,484	16,274
Stock Price	84 $\frac{1}{4}$	63 $^{13}\!\!/\!_{16}$

* Total stockholders' equity includes capital stock, surplus, and retained earnings at the company's year end. For purposes of determining profits as a percent of common stockholders' equity, all preferred stock is excluded.

** Calculated by multiplying the number of common shares outstanding by the price per common share as of March 31.

As CyTech's attention to performance challenges draws international praise and becomes an integral part of CyTech's team organizational culture, you still do not rest easy, but work tirelessly to identify a third phase of implementation. Two options present themselves: a program that promotes team basics and discipline, or one that relies on team building and cheerleading to further strengthen CyTech's team approach.

A program of team basics and discipline might allow people to duplicate team successes rather easily with proven techniques and a growing awareness of what drives, creates, and maintains top-performing teams. Even a wildly innovative organization needs some discipline to keep it functioning smoothly into the future. On the other hand, you have purposely avoided lockstep programs and the bureaucracy they engender because strict policies and red tape only hamper team creativity.

The team-building, cheerleading approach would be fun and exciting, and it would appeal to people's emotions. Nothing keeps teams fresh and alive like fun and enjoyment. However, people might perceive this as a superficial approach lacking the power to perpetuate teams well into the future.

As you think about these two alternatives, you worry that one may be too serious, too hard hitting, while the other may be too soft, too easygoing. However, you can't bring yourself to consider some combination of these two, because such a course would water down both, creating a rudderless third phase of team implementation. What should you do?

- *If you decide on a program of team basics and discipline, turn to Chapter 48.*

- *If you choose to rely on team building and cheerleading, turn to Chapter 49.*

To help your senior executives teach team development and team performance throughout the organization, you specifically enlist the help of John Solo, your training and development group, as well as a few outside consultants, who develop a unique CyTech process that follows a set of guidelines for achieving high-performance team results. The process builds on Zenger-Miller's four pillars of implementation—values, skills, alignment, and deployment—by adding principles at the beginning of the process and measurement at the end. You ask your senior executives to use this process throughout the CyTech organization in the second phase of implementation in CyTech's team approach.

As the process guidelines take hold throughout the organization, you worry about whether you've made the right choice. You do see benefits accruing as your senior executives and next level of executives effectively teach and train managers and team leaders throughout the organization, but by the end of the year you realize that your emphasis on process has reduced attention to performance. Sales begin to fall off quickly at the end of the year, rendering mediocre numbers for the year, shown on the following page.

47

DEVELOPING PROCESS GUIDELINES FOR CYTECH'S TEAMS

The full extent of CyTech's sluggishness doesn't hit you until Motorola introduces a voice-operated phone-fax-computer that takes the market by storm and keeps most of CyTech's products gathering dust in the warehouses. Still months away from introducing your own voice-operated *PowerBase,* your people feel demoralized by Motorola's competitive move. Your senior team turns against you, accus-

209

Selected Financial and Stock Information
(Dollars in millions, except stock price in actual dollars)

	Year ended March 31	
	3rd Year	2nd Year
Sales	$7,231	$6,899
Profits	362	414
Profits as a % of:		
Sales	5%	6%
Assets	7%	8%
Common Equity*	13%	15%
Market Value**	12,113	12,559
Stock Price	47 $\frac{1}{2}$	49 $\frac{1}{4}$

* Total stockholders' equity includes capital stock, surplus, and retained earnings at the company's year end. For purposes of determining profits as a percent of common stockholders' equity, all preferred stock is excluded.

** Calculated by multiplying the number of common shares outstanding by the price per common share as of March 31.

ing you of focusing too much on process to the detriment of performance. John Solo points out that "team process concerns assumed the top-of-the-mind position for most employees almost overnight, placing team performance in a distant second position." Hal McPhee and Morris Strandmeyer agree that you pushed the "process" focus too far.

You discover how *superficial* your relationship with your six direct reports has always been. You think to yourself, "Such relationships depend on the performance challenges a company faces. Why did I forget that?" You have clearly underestimated the importance of performance challenges in developing CyTech's teams. Too late, you realize that you made a poor choice for the second phase of CyTech's team approach.

Sales drop precipitously at the end of your fourth year, and CyTech's stock plummets to $24 per share, as shown in the accompanying table on the next page.

News of the chaos at the top and an apparent inability to meet the challenge of Motorola's new product introduction hits the business press. A front page *Wall Street Journal* article blasts you for mismanaging CyTech and reverting to a 1970s preoccupation with technique and process. No longer an effective CEO, you resign, deciding that it's time for you to do something else.

Selected Financial and Stock Information
(Dollars in millions, except stock price in actual dollars)

	Year ended March 31	
	4th Year	3rd Year
Sales	$5,311	$7,231
Profits	159	362
Profits as a % of:		
Sales	3%	5%
Assets	5%	7%
Common Equity*	7%	13%
Market Value**	6,151	12,113
Stock Price	24 $\frac{1}{8}$	47 $\frac{1}{2}$

* Total stockholders' equity includes capital stock, surplus, and retained earnings at the company's year end. For purposes of determining profits as a percent of common stockholders' equity, all preferred stock is excluded.
** Calculated by multiplying the number of common shares outstanding by the price per common share as of March 31.

- *You might have been able to make this last decision work in real life, even though the shift to process guidelines failed to recognize the importance of performance challenges. If you want to know why the author considers the other alternative preferable, turn to Chapter 46, Making Performance Challenges the Next Focal Point.*

- *If you'd like to start fresh on another decision-making track, go to:*

   Chapter 2, Building a Classic Innovative Organization;

   Chapter 14, Developing a Synthesis of Best Practices;

   Chapter 26, Imbuing the Culture with Empowerment and Accountability;

   Chapter 50, Reengineering Work Processes; or

   Chapter 62, Embracing a Revolutionary New Perspective.

Convinced of the importance of team basics and discipline in perpetuating the CyTech team approach, you begin by taking your senior executives through a session devoted to designing a reliable program. Drawing once again upon the work of Katzenbach and Smith, two McKinsey & Company consultants who wrote *The Wisdom of Teams,* you quote: "By focusing on performance and team basics—as opposed to trying 'to become a team'—most small groups can deliver the performance results that require and produce team behavior."

To strengthen CyTech's team basics and discipline, you also draw on the Zenger-Miller associates' *Leading Teams.* You tell your senior team, "By applying the team basics involved in moving from traditional leadership to team leadership, as shown in the accompanying chart (see following page), we can solidify CyTech's team approach and maintain superior performance."

With all this in mind, you suggest to your senior executives that CyTech hire Katzenbach and Smith to launch a team basics course at CyTech that can provide an annual training experience for everyone in the organization, especially new employees. You also suggest that you engage McKinsey & Company to help CyTech develop the disciplined follow-up necessary to keep the team philosophy and the team approach at CyTech ever renewed and revitalized. You anticipate McKinsey & Company developing an approach for continuously monitoring staffing levels, work processes, organizational change, team dynamics, and performance levels. Your senior executives like the suggestion, and within weeks Katzenbach and Smith are working with

48

INTRODUCING A PROGRAM OF TEAM BASICS AND DISCIPLINE

Attaining Team Leadership

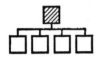

<u>Traditional Leadership:</u> Train individual employees in the tasks that comprise their jobs.

<u>Participative Leadership:</u> Improve individual performance by training people in the higher level skills required to make more innovative individual contributions.

<u>Team Leadership:</u> Expand team capabilities through training, coaching, monitoring performance, sharing leadership and assessing team readiness to take on new tasks.

other McKinsey & Company consultants to develop the necessary approach.

As the months unfold and your fifth year as CEO comes to an end, sales reach $16 billion as customers throughout the world flock to the voice-operated *PowerBases.* CyTech's stock reaches $101 per share as shown in the table on the next page.

CyTech still shares market leadership with Motorola, but all other competitors have dropped far behind. Both companies enjoy great profitability and tremendous increases in the market value of their stock. As you look back over the five years, you realize that your senior team has become a true high-performing team because it met the challenges and, in so doing, forged a deep devotion to the purposes of CyTech as well as a deep commitment to one another.

You decide to retire and pursue other interests, such as teaching and writing, and while the board and your team try valiantly to dissuade you from this decision, you maintain your own commitment to seeking new challenges for yourself. However, you find it so hard to leave the team behind that as a compromise you decide to enter into a three-year contractual arrangement with

Selected Financial and Stock Information
(Dollars in millions, except stock price in actual dollars)

	Year ended March 31	
	5th Year	4th Year
Sales	$15,676	See Chapter 45 or 46,
Profits	1,097	depending on which one
Profits as a % of:		you chose to get here.
Sales	7%	
Assets	14%	
Common Equity*	22%	
Market Value**	25,819	
Stock Price	101 ¼	

* Total stockholders' equity includes capital stock, surplus, and retained earnings at the company's year end. For purposes of determining profits as a percent of common stockholders' equity, all preferred stock is excluded.

** Calculated by multiplying the number of common shares outstanding by the price per common share as of March 31.

CyTech that will allow you to spend about a fourth of your time over the next three years working with the senior executive committee.

As your last act as CEO of CyTech, you make an unusual move, asking your six senior executives to decide who should take over as CyTech's new CEO. You tell them, "The board has asked me for my recommendation and has indicated that they will follow that recommendation, whomever I select. They do believe it should be one of you, and so do I, but I'm not going to make that decision; you are."

Astonished, yet sensitive to your feelings, the senior team express their feelings about one another and the growth that each has achieved over the last five years. John Solo gets praised for his team commitment and acute awareness of the company's current conditions, no matter what the situation. Bob Kiechel wins accolades for his inventive insightfulness and ability to immediately turn his attention to critical issues. Hal McPhee receives appreciation for his steadiness and quick, accurate judgment. Nan Thurow finds positive feedback about the breadth of her concern for the human side of CyTech and her ability to articulate CyTech's values. Karen

Walsh gains unanimous recognition as CyTech's best and brightest mind. Morris Strandmeyer discovers how much his consistent, organized approach is really valued by his peers. And you receive many praises for your sensitivity to the importance of teams and team leadership.

One by one your senior team acknowledge that they really have become a team and, as such, conclude that they must share the responsibility for leadership of CyTech. In the end they meet your unusual challenge with their own unusual plan for you to present to the board of directors. Their recommendation: a member of the team will function as CEO for two years and then pass the baton to another member of the team, moving from one senior team member to another, indefinitely. Affirming their desire to continue functioning as a team, they select Nan Thurow, senior vice president of worldwide operations, as the first in a series of future CEOs. They vow to select the right replacement for Nan and to bring that person fully into the team. You applaud their ingenuity, their commitment to CyTech, and their dedication to one another. You take the recommendation to the board of directors, who think you've lost your marbles, but eventually warm up to the idea as you explain the wisdom of teams.

During the next three years, as you spend about a quarter of your time consulting with the senior executives, the company continues to flourish and even outpaces Motorola in the fast-paced personal computing and communications arena. You take special delight in the interaction with the members of your senior team, something you intend to continue for the rest of your life.

Congratulations, you have successfully arrived at the end of a decision-making track. Now you can embark on another, if you wish.

- *If you want to compare how the results of your last five years of organizational decision making stack up against the other positive outcomes in The Organization Game, turn to Chapter 78.*

- *If you want to explore the other alternatives you could have selected on this track, turn to the chapters you didn't read the first time through:*
  Chapter 39, Stressing the Performance Challenge;
  Chapter 40, Eliminating Pseudo Teams;
  Chapter 41, Teaching Team Basics;
  Chapter 42, Developing a Strong Team at the Top;
  Chapter 43, Changing The Role of Top Management;
  Chapter 44, Focusing on Team Building;
  Chapter 45, Continuing to Stress Team Performance;
  Chapter 46, Making Performance Challenges the Focal Point;
  Chapter 47, Developing Process Guidelines for CyTech's Teams;
  Chapter 49, Relying on Team Building and Cheerleading.

- *If you want to embark on a new track, turn to:*
  Chapter 2, Building a Classic Innovative Organization;
  Chapter 14, Developing a Synthesis of Best Practices;
  Chapter 26, Imbuing the Culture with Empowerment and Accountability;
  Chapter 50, Reengineering Work Processes; or
  Chapter 62, Embracing a Revolutionary New Perspective.

Feeling yourself worn out by constant pressure of the performance challenges, you decide that Nan Thurow was right when she said, "Too much stress on performance can become a burden to our people." You hope your feelings do not stem from a bad month or a cynical mood, but you really do think that the third and final phase of CyTech's team approach must bring back the fun and enjoyment of an earlier time.

As you communicate your decision to your senior executives, they express some misgivings, but you assure them that your decision does not reflect your own weariness or lack of motivation. Despite your assurances, however, they do seem concerned about your state of mind, which causes you to wonder again about your own motivations and decision-making abilities.

49

RELYING ON TEAM BUILDING AND CHEERLEADING

Hal McPhee inquires, "What do you think will happen to performance around here if you ease off too much?"

"I'm not suggesting we ease off performance. I just think working together in teams provides more fulfillment and enjoyment for people. We need to emphasize this dimension of our team approach."

John Solo injects, "Don't you think we've been doing that?"

"No. I don't."

"I think we have," counters Strandmeyer.

"Look. I don't want to argue semantics. I believe we need more focus on the intangible and personal benefits of team work. We need to make working here fun."

"I agree, wholeheartedly," responds Thurow.

"I think you're overreacting because you're worn out," counters McPhee.

"I am worn out but I'm not overreacting," you respond. "I think we keep our people in the dark, overprogrammed, and underappreciated. Because of our success, we have the luxury of changing that. We can make life at CyTech more enjoyable for our people and we must."

"That's fine," says McPhee, "but let's not lose our focus on performance challenges."

"Okay," you respond, "let's not."

You move forward with team building and cheerleading, trying to help employees throughout the CyTech organization appreciate the joy of teams. Even though this violates one of Katzenbach and Smith's main points—that you should never organize teams for their own sake—you strongly feel your organization needs more fun and excitement to keep it fresh and alive.

Unfortunately, in the process CyTech losses some of its edge in the marketplace as Motorola moves ahead and CyTech's performance wanes. Members of your senior team communicate with members of the board about your tiring out, and at the end of your fifth year as CEO the board suggests that you become vice chairman of the board and step down as CEO.

Sales reach $13 billion and the stock continues to climb, as shown in the table on the next page.

Selected Financial and Stock Information
(Dollars in millions, except stock price in actual dollars)

	Year ended March 31	
	This Year	Last Year
Sales	$13,010	See Chapter 45 or 46,
Profits	781	depending on which one
Profits as a % of:		you chose to get here.
Sales	6%	
Assets	12%	
Common Equity*	18%	
Market Value**	22,759	
Stock Price	89 ¼	

* Total stockholders' equity includes capital stock, surplus, and retained earnings at the company's year end. For purposes of determining profits as a percent of common stockholders' equity, all preferred stock is excluded.

** Calculated by multiplying the number of common shares outstanding by the price per common share as of March 31.

Personally, you welcome the change. You really are worn out. You've made it to the end of a decision-making track, but you can go on to other challenges if you'd like.

> - *If you want to compare how the results of your last five years of organizational decision making stack up against the other positive outcomes in* The Organization Game, *turn to Chapter 78.*
>
> - *If you want to explore the other alternatives you could have selected on this track, turn to the Chapters you didn't read the first time through:*
>   *Chapter 39, Stressing the Role of Top Management;*
>   *Chapter 40, Eliminating Pseudo Teams;*
>   *Chapter 41, Teaching Team Basics;*
>   *Chapter 42, Developing a Strong Team at the Top;*
>   *Chapter 43, Changing the Role of Top Management;*
>   *Chapter 44, Focusing on Team Building;*

Chapter 45, Continuing to Stress Team Performance;
Chapter 46, Making Performance Challenges the
Focal Point;
Chapter 47, Developing Process Guidelines for
CyTech's Teams;
Chapter 48, Introducing a Program of Team Basics
and Discipline; or

- *If you want to embark on a fresh, new track, move to:*
   Chapter 2, Building a Classic Innovative
   Organization;
   Chapter 14, Developing a Synthesis of Best Practices;
   Chapter 26, Imbuing the Culture with
   Empowerment and Accountability;
   Chapter 50, Reengineering Work Processes; or
   Chapter 62, Embracing a Revolutionary New
   Perspective.

Your decision to reengineer CyTech's work processes rests heavily on the work of Michael Hammer and James Champy, authors of the best-selling book *Re-Engineering the Corporation: A Manifesto for Business Resolution.* You ask each member of your senior executive team to read the book as background for detailed discussions about exactly how CyTech can implement the authors' concepts. Convinced yourself that the traditional approach to management, developed in the nineteenth century and refined over the last ninety years, will no longer meet the challenges of the twenty-first century, you admire Hammer and Champy's work, which, in your mind, culminates several trends such as process mapping, downsizing, flattening, delayering, empowering, and revolutionizing organizations. You especially like Hammer and Champy's focus on business processes—a collection

50

REENGINEERING WORK PROCESSES

of business activities with various inputs and an output—that organizations must redesign in order to meet the challenges of a new economy and a new global marketplace.

A few weeks later, during your first discussion with your senior executives in an off-site, full-day meeting, you quote a passage from *Re-Engineering the Corporation,* "Re-engineering isn't another idea imported from Japan. It isn't another quick fix that American managers can apply to their organizations. It isn't a new trick that promises to boost the quality of a company's product or service or shave a percentage off costs. Business re-engineering isn't a program to hike worker morale or to motivate the sales force. It won't push an old computer system to work faster. Business re-engineering isn't about fixing anything. Business re-engineering means starting all over, starting from scratch."

With that notion as the launching pad for thinking about and designing business processes at CyTech, you ask your senior executives what they thought of the book and how they would apply its ideas at CyTech. Morris Strandmeyer, vice president of production, comments first, "Their approach seems pretty extreme. Do you really think we need to take CyTech apart and put it back together from scratch?"

You respond by saying, "Morris, I want to see us move beyond the same old questions, such as: How can we do what we do faster? How can we do what we do better? How can we do what we do at a lower cost? I want to go back to the essential question: Why do we do what we do at all?"

Morris counters, "That makes it sound as if we haven't done anything right in the past."

"No, we've done a lot of things right in the past, but that doesn't mean they will be the right things for the future. We need to ask ourselves continually whether we're doing the right things, but more important, we need to ask ourselves why we're doing what we're doing. Answering that question will put us in the right frame of mind to redesign our business processes."

Predictably, Hal McPhee shares Morris's concerns, and John Solo concurs. Even though you know that Karen Walsh, Nan Thurow, and Bob Kiechel will probably favor a reengineering course, they don't enter into the discussion, leaving you to deal with Strandmeyer's, McPhee's, and Solo's objections. It's almost as if they're waiting to see how you handle the resistance, testing the depth and thoroughness of your resolve.

To defend your position by becoming philosophical, "The American management system needs to be reinvented, it's not working anymore. Most organizations today are inflexible, unresponsive, obsessed with activity, bureaucratic, lacking innovation, over staffed, and hard to change. Most companies can't pass along high costs, inefficiencies, or unresponsiveness to their customers anymore. Customers have more options than ever before. We must change our ways. We can't do things the same way anymore. We must do things differently, and, more importantly, we must do *different things.*" Silence envelops the room for more than 30 seconds, which seems like an hour as you wonder how long it's going to take to convince Strandmeyer, McPhee, and Solo.

Finally, Bob Kiechel, senior vice president of product development, comes to your aid, "I agree. Even though CyTech has worked hard to remain flexible, dynamic, and responsive to change and has employed the latest management and leadership thinking and practice, all of us have grown up with the old ways of doing things, the traditional hierarchies, the acceptance of bureaucracy, the fragmentation of work born out of a division of labor. We really do have to go further."

You take the discussion to the next step by reviewing the four keys words that Hammer and Champy use to describe business reengineering: fundamental, radical, dramatic, and processes. You hold up a chart with each of these four words defined:

Fundamental:	Ask basic questions about how the company operates
Radical:	Get to the root of things
Dramatic:	Make sweeping changes
Processes:	Become process-oriented; don't focus on tasks, jobs, people, or structures

In the months that follow, you engage in numerous additional discussions with your executive team, working through the details of exactly how reengineering will work at CyTech. You even ask Dr. Michael Hammer to spend a day with you and your executive team looking at all the conceptual options.

All the while, competitors continue to upgrade their phone-fax-computers. CyTech does likewise, introducing *PowerBase 3, 4,* and *5,* all with new chips, new designs, new wire and wireless modes, as well as other minor modifications. As the competitive environment in the industry continues to heat up, you feel that reengineering at CyTech must occur quickly if the company expects to remain at the forefront of this industry. Japanese and German competitors have been moving quickly, and you foresee a major change on the horizon. You must invent that change or be swept along by it. Your first year as CEO of CyTech comes to an end with the company posting a respectable performance, as shown here in the following table.

Selected Financial and Stock Information
(Dollars in millions, except stock price in actual dollars)

	Year ended March 31	
	1st Year	Previous Year
Sales	$6,232	$4,083
Profits	374	242
Profits as a % of:		
Sales	6%	6%
Assets	8%	9%
Common Equity*	16%	17%
Market Value**	7,426	6,123
Stock Price	29 $\frac{1}{8}$	23 $\frac{3}{4}$

* Total stockholders' equity includes capital stock, surplus, and retained earnings at the company's year end. For purposes of determining profits as a percent of common stockholders' equity, all preferred stock is excluded.

** Calculated by multiplying the number of common shares outstanding by the price per common share as of March 31.

Soon after the year end, as you continue attempting to synthesize the months of discussion, debate, analysis, and a lot of mind-stretching thought, you and your senior executives identify four options for implementing a radical change in work processes at CyTech: (1) develop a complete reengineering strategy and organization, (2) begin redesigning processes throughout the organization from the bottom up, (3) work to get everyone in the organization to embrace the concept of reengineering, and (4) adopt a small-wins strategy for launching reengineering. Each of these alternatives has advantages and disadvantages, which you and your senior team summarize in the chart on the next page.

As you review these advantages and disadvantages and ask for additional input from your executive team, you're not surprised when Hal McPhee, your chief financial officer, and Morris Strandmeyer, your vice president of production, argue for alternative number four, adopting a small-wins strategy.

It also doesn't surprise you that Nan Thurow, senior vice president of worldwide operations, favors alternative number two, redesigning processes throughout the organization from the bottom up.

Alternative	Advantage	Disadvantage
1. Developing a complete reengineering strategy and organization.	Clarifies the who and what of reengineering.	May place too much emphasis on more analysis, planning, and structuring and not enough on action.
2. Redesigning processes throughout the organization from the bottom up.	Puts the organization into the reengineering mode immediately.	People at the bottom may not have a broad enough perspective or be able to see across organization boundaries to make reengineering work.
3. Getting everyone in the organization to embrace the concept of reengineering.	A reduction of the resistance to reengineering.	The potential creation of additional fear and resistance without seeing what reengineering can really accomplish.
4. Adopting a "small-wins" strategy to launch reengineering.	Allows the company to ease into reengineering and learn to appreciate its value.	Marginal improvements may only complicate CyTech's current organizational processes.

John Solo, executive vice president for worldwide sales and marketing, argues for getting everyone in the organization to embrace the concept of reengineering, and Bob Kiechel, senior vice president of product development, along with Karen Walsh, vice president of the advanced technology lab, votes for the first alternative, developing a complete reengineering strategy and organization.

In your judgment, it will take weeks and maybe months to forge a consensus with your group, months you just cannot afford, so you elect to make this decision yourself. That's exactly what you tell your executive team, asking for their full support once you decide what to do.

As a final input to your decision making, you ask each member of your senior team to write a one-page memo putting forth his or her best arguments for the option he or she prefers. As you review the memos, you discover little new thinking in any of the arguments, but they do suggest that any one of these paths offers a potential avenue for success. What will you do?

- *If you choose to develop a complete reengineering strategy and organization, turn to Chapter 51.*

- *If you want to begin redesigning processes throughout the organization from the bottom up, turn to Chapter 52.*

- *If you see the need for getting everyone in the organization to embrace the concept of reengineering before you implement it, turn to Chapter 53.*

- *If you choose to adopt a small-wins strategy, turn to Chapter 54.*

Believing in your heart that organizations don't reengineer, people do, you decide that only a complete reengineering strategy can bring about necessary changes at CyTech. You have paid close attention to this part of Hammer and Champy's work and have asked Michael Hammer himself to offer his recommendations for developing an overall strategy and organization during his consulting engagement.

When you announce your decision, you tell your senior executives, "The people we select and how we organize them to oversee reengineering will provide the key to this endeavor." While not every one of your executive team favors this option, each quickly recognizes that he or she must play a crucial role in the reengineering effort or risk losing his or her power and influence within the organization. In the end, this self-interest impels your direct reports to support this decision wholeheartedly.

You decide to begin with selection and organization of the people who will assume responsibility for developing the reengineering strategy. You try to follow

51

DEVELOPING A COMPLETE REENGINEERING STRATEGY AND ORGANIZATION

Hammer and Champy's recommendations to find a leader who can authorize and motivate the overall reengineering effort, establish a steering committee of senior managers who can set policy, develop the organization's overall reengineering strategy, monitor its progress, and appoint a reengineering czar responsible for developing specific reengineering techniques and insuring synergy across the company's separate reengineering projects.

In addition, you anticipate developing process owners, managers with responsibility for specific processes, and reengineering teams dedicated to the reengineering of a particular process, who can diagnose the existing process and oversee its redesign and implementation. The steering committee and the reengineering czar will select these people when appropriate to do so.

You, yourself, will assume the role of the leader who authorizes and motivates the overall reengineering effort, and the six members of your executive team will form the policy-making body that develops the organization's overall reengineering strategy and monitors its progress.

Finally, you ask Bob Kiechel to serve as CyTech's reengineering czar, the one responsible for developing reengineering techniques and tools throughout the company and for gaining synergy across the company's separate reengineering projects. To give Kiechel the time to accomplish this vital mission as well as his other responsibilities, you promote Karen Walsh to senior vice president with responsibility for the advanced technology lab as well as a portion of new-product development. You ask Bob and Karen to work out the details of implementing Kiechel's shift in emphasis and Walsh's broadened responsibilities.

Kiechel seems to present the perfect profile for making reengineering work at CyTech. A former Apple executive, he also worked as director of McKinsey & Company before joining Apple, and he possesses the kind of inventive insight and quick conceptual and superior analytical capability needed to fuel successful reengineering. You send Bob Kiechel to one of Hammer and Champy's workshops while you continue preparing your other senior executives for their roles on the steering committee.

Organizationally, you must wait until the full-blown strategy has been developed before you appoint the process owners who will direct the teams that will actually reengineer CyTech's business processes.

However, just as you're beginning to see real progress on the reengineering strategy, three foreign competitors launch an industrywide price war that pushes phone-fax-computer prices below $500. Work on reengineering slows for several months as CyTech scrambles to meet the challenge of the price war. As your second year comes to an end, CyTech's sales increase, but profits as a percentage of sales decline, as shown.

Selected Financial and Stock Information
(Dollars in millions, except stock price in actual dollars)

	Year ended March 31	
	2nd Year	1st Year
Sales	$8,063	$6,232
Profits	403	374
Profits as a % of:		
Sales	5%	6%
Assets	7%	8%
Common Equity*	14%	16%
Market Value**	7,411	7,426
Stock Price	29 $\frac{1}{16}$	29 $\frac{1}{8}$

* Total stockholders' equity includes capital stock, surplus, and retained earnings at the company's year end. For purposes of determining profits as a percent of common stockholders' equity, all preferred stock is excluded.
** Calculated by multiplying the number of common shares outstanding by the price per common share as of March 31.

The board seems satisfied with your performance as CEO but appears somewhat restless about the ongoing reengineering process, with some members wondering whether you can accomplish it fast enough, whether the organization will really embrace it, and if it will produce the results you promise. You feel their watchful eyes upon you as you embark upon your third year as CyTech's CEO.

Now you must quickly decide from among four basic strategic directions for reengineering that your steering committee has offered as the most viable possibilities: (1) select a few key processes for reengineering, (2) fix several processes throughout the company, (3) reorganize the entire CyTech company to facilitate reengineering, or (4) set clear parameters for all reengineering efforts. Once again, you analyze each of these alternatives with your steering committee to determine which course of action CyTech should pursue. You summarize the advantages and disadvantages of each option as depicted on page 232.

Again, your steering committee divides along fairly predictable lines. Morris Strandmeyer, vice president of production, and Hal McPhee, chief financial officer, favor alternative four, setting clear parameters for reengineering.

Bob Kiechel, senior VP of product development and CyTech's new reengineering czar, along with Karen Walsh, senior vice presi-

Alternative	Advantage	Disadvantage
1. Selecting a few key process for reengineering.	Focuses resources on one process at a time and targets greatest needs first.	Affects only one or two processes at a time.
2. Fixing several processes.	Affects a wide range of business processes throughout the company.	May encourage process changes, but not complete reengineering.
3. Reorganizing to facilitate reengineering.	Prepares the entire organization for reengineering.	Could place too much emphasis on structure and not enough on processes.
4. Setting clear parameters for reengineering.	Allows management to define problems and formulate guidelines for reengineering processes.	May keep reengineering efforts from breaking through old boundaries and traditions.

dent of the technology lab and head of a portion of CyTech's product development team, favors alternative number one, selecting a few key processes for reengineering. That leaves Nan Thurow, senior VP of worldwide operations, favoring option three, and John Solo, executive vice president for worldwide sales and marketing, recommending option two. Once again, it's your call, and you must move decisively in the heat of the raging price war.

- *If you choose to select a few key processes for reengineering, turn to Chapter 55.*

- *If you prefer fixing several processes simultaneously, turn to Chapter 56.*

- *If you want to reorganize to facilitate reengineering, turn to Chapter 57.*

- *If you would rather set clear parameters for all reengineering efforts, turn to Chapter 58.*

Having decided that you must make it work even on the shop floor, you launch a massive campaign for reengineering everything that goes on at CyTech, which means dramatically redesigning the work flow, moving from a functional mindset to a process orientation that may combine eight different functions into one process. At a management meeting early on, Bob Kiechel expresses serious misgivings about this program and asks to speak with you privately. Behind closed doors, he admits, "I just don't think this is going to work here."

"What are you talking about? Reengineering?"

"No, I'm talking about this bottom-up approach. I think it's got to come from the top down."

"Look, I really don't like halfway or half-hearted measures. That's why I want to engage every individual in this company in the process of reengineering. If we reengineer top management but not the work that gets new products out the door, we won't accomplish anything. That means beginning reengineering at once, especially at the bottom."

Bob shakes his head, "I see two major problems with that. First, the people at lower levels in the organization just do not have a broad enough perspective to accomplish the conceptual shift necessary to redesign processes. Second, you know that many of these processes cross organizational and functional lines, making it impossible for people at lower levels in the

52

REDESIGNING PROCESSES THROUGHOUT THE ORGANIZATION FROM THE BOTTOM UP

organization to deal with the design possibilities before management does."

"Bob, we're good at overcoming such obstacles. We simply must rise to the challenge, helping our people gain a broader perspective that sees beyond the old boundaries."

"I hope you're right."

"With your help, I know we can make it work."

In the next several weeks, CyTech embarks on a flurry of activity at all levels throughout the organization—examining, redefining, and redesigning processes at all levels. Under the direction of Nan Thurow, senior VP of worldwide operations, whom you have appointed as the reengineering leader for CyTech, the company becomes a beehive of reengineering activities. People in every part of the company ignore the old work flows and start redesigning and reorganizing everything from how inventory gets handled to how customer complaints are resolved.

By midyear, most of the work processes within CyTech have been redesigned, though you admit to yourself it took much longer than you anticipated. Now you expect results to flow rapidly from all levels. About this same time, however, three foreign competitors, two Japanese and a German company, launch a price war that engulfs the entire industry in a battle for profitability and leadership. Long before you expected it, the price of phone-fax-computers drops below $500. With more and more consumers throughout the world buying their first phone-fax-computer, demand skyrockets. Suddenly, you're thrust into a mass production/mass marketing game.

During the next six months of scrambling to get costs down and to meet customer demand, you discover that the redesigned processes do not allow CyTech to move as quickly as it must to slash costs and provide consumers with the variety of products they demand. Much of the reengineering activity has produced either superficial change or chaos because the effort has lacked guidance and direction from the top. In a desperate attempt to correct the months of activity that have not resulted in the sort of rapid response CyTech needs, you hire Jim Champy's company, CSC Index, Inc., a management consulting firm that pioneered and developed the practice of reengineering, to perform an audit of CyTech's reengineering program in an effort to determine what went wrong. To your chagrin, their assessment cites the very two reasons that Bob Kiechel identified up front.

Word of CSC's assessment reaches the board of directors about the same time you close your second year's books. Sales jump to $8 billion, but profits fall substantially, causing the stock price to plummet, as shown in the following table.

Selected Financial and Stock Information
(Dollars in millions, except stock price in actual dollars)

	Year ended March 31	
	2nd Year	1st Year
Sales	$7,820	$6,232
Profits	156	374
Profits as a % of:		
Sales	2%	6%
Assets	4%	8%
Common Equity*	9%	16%
Market Value**	4,654	7,426
Stock Price	18 $\frac{1}{4}$	29 $\frac{1}{8}$

* Total stockholders' equity includes capital stock, surplus, and retained earnings at the company's year end. For purposes of determining profits as a percent of common stockholders' equity, all preferred stock is excluded.
** Calculated by multiplying the number of common shares outstanding by the price per common share as of March 31.

This poor profit performance spurs the board into action, and they vote to appoint Bob Kiechel as CyTech's new CEO, with you assuming a transition position as a member of the board. The chairman of the board tells you, "We're not firing you—we just think it's time for someone else to take the helm. Of course, I would like to keep you aboard during this trying period." Maybe you haven't been fired, but your job as CyTech's driving force has ended.

> • *You might have been able to make this decision work in real life even though Hammer and Champy would argue against this approach to reengineering. If you want to know why the author considers other options preferable, turn to:*

Chapter 51, Developing a Complete Reengineering Strategy and Organization;

Chapter 53, Getting Everyone in the Organization to Embrace the Concept of Reengineering; or

Chapter 54, Adopting a Small-Wins Strategy to Launch Reengineering.

- *If you want to begin a new decision-making track, select one of the following:*

  Chapter 2, Building a Classic Innovative Organization

  Chapter 14, Developing a Synthesis of Best Practices;

  Chapter 26, Imbuing the Culture with Empowerment and Accountability;

  Chapter 38, Pursuing a Work Team Approach; or

  Chapter 62, Embracing a Revolutionary New Perspective.

Since helping people acknowledge and accept the value of reengineering presents a formidable task, you decide to attack this problem first and foremost. John Solo, executive vice president of worldwide sales and marketing, expresses confidence in your choice and assures you that when everyone clearly understands the

53

GETTING EVERYONE IN THE ORGANIZATION TO EMBRACE THE CONCEPT OF REENGINEERING

need for reengineering, they will strongly desire to implement it throughout the organization. You agree with Solo's assessment and ask the other members of your senior team to help you get everyone else in the organization on board.

Drawing on Hammer and Champy's work, you develop a very clear message about the need for reengineering. First, you ask John Solo to help people understand how CyTech functions as a company and why it can't remain complacent with the old ways. Doing so proves difficult because CyTech has posted such a strong performance in its past. However, John tries to show that the company cannot continue such performance in the future unless it undergoes some major reengineering. Second, you paint a picture of what CyTech needs to become in the future. You personally describe to every middle manager the need for reengineering based on the reality that the marketplace, including competitors' moves and customer demands, is changing faster than CyTech itself is changing. "The new CyTech organization," you insist, "cannot look as it looks today. The way the company invents, makes, sells, delivers, and services its products must match the new realities."

Through a series of *diverse communications* by memo, meetings, and video tape throughout the organization, your entire senior team helps people understand that the CyTech of the future must address what will happen in the industry years from now, which translates into changing business processes today in order to invent a prosperous tomorrow.

For the next several months, the message goes out. John Solo holds informal meetings with employees working in facilities throughout the world. Your senior team does likewise until the message has been delivered to every nook and cranny of the organization. Unfortunately, in the process, a good deal of fear and apprehension begins to build in people about just what reengineering will do to their jobs and careers. People have just enough information to recognize the dramatic impact of reengineering, but not enough to remove the fear about job security and role changes.

Just as this fear and apprehension reaches its peak, three foreign competitors, two Japanese and one German company, launch a price war that lowers prices of phone-fax-computers to $500 and engulfs the entire industry in a battle for market position, market share, and profitability. The new competitive pressure heaps new stress and worry about job security and career development on everyone at CyTech. According to one employee, "There's been a lot of communication about the need for reengineering, but I feel like it's being shoved down my throat without any real understanding on my part about what it's going to mean for me personally."

Before you know it, the company's morale falls into a tailspin. With the company unable to respond effectively to the challenges of the price war, you quickly refocus John Solo's efforts on maintaining market share and desperately enlist the help of your other senior executives to halt the declining morale. Rumors proliferate, however, about your plans to downsize and flatten the organization. Foreign competitors eat into CyTech's position in the marketplace, causing sales to drop for the first time in the company's history, as shown here in the accompanying table.

Selected Financial and Stock Information
(Dollars in millions, except stock price in actual dollars)

	Year ended March 31	
	2nd Year	1st Year
Sales	$5,981	$6,232
Profits	120	374
Profits as a % of:		
Sales	2%	6%
Assets	4%	8%
Common Equity*	8%	16%
Market Value**	3,856	7,426
Stock Price	15 $\frac{1}{8}$	29 $\frac{1}{8}$

* Total stockholders' equity includes capital stock, surplus, and retained earnings at the company's year end. For purposes of determining profits as a percent of common stockholders' equity, all preferred stock is excluded.

** Calculated by multiplying the number of common shares outstanding by the price per common share as of March 31.

This performance convinces the board of directors that you have lost your grip on the handle of leadership, and they decide they must act quickly before the company loses further ground. After asking for your resignation, they appoint Bob Kiechel, senior vice president of product development, the new CEO of CyTech.

As you leave CyTech, you replay the last twelve months again and again in your mind, asking yourself what you would have done differently. Fortunately, in this book, you can go back and test an alternate scenario.

- *Maybe you could have salvaged this situation in real life, but even Hammer and Champy would have advised against this course of action. If you want to see why the author considers another alternative preferable, turn to:*

  Chapter 51, Developing a Complete Reengineering Strategy and Organization;

  Chapter 52, Redesigning Processes Throughout the Organization from the Bottom Up; or

Chapter 54, Adopting a Small-Wins Strategy to Launch Reengineering.

- *If you want to begin fresh with another decision-making track, choose one of the following:*

    Chapter 2, Building a Classic Innovative Organization

    Chapter 14, Developing a Synthesis of Best Practices;

    Chapter 26, Imbuing the Culture with Empowerment and Accountability;

    Chapter 38, Pursuing a Work Team Approach; or

    Chapter 62, Embracing a Revolutionary New Perspective.

As you announce your decision to adopt a small-wins strategy to launch reengineering, you meet tremendous resistance from your senior executive team, which claims that you have ignored one of the most basic points of reengineering—you can't do it incrementally. To defend your position you explain what you mean by "small

wins," the small improvements in processes and even major redesigning and reengineering of minor business processes as first steps that properly set the stage for tackling the major processes that will affect the entire company. Nevertheless, your senior team expresses grave doubts about this approach.

Bob Kiechel reminds you, "Hammer and Champy make it clear that re-engineering can't be carried out in small steps. They describe it as an all-or-nothing undertaking."

To your surprise, Karen Walsh rallies to this same banner, also referring to Hammer and Champy's book: "Great results require great ambitions. Reengineering is about making major changes. It's about doing different things, not about doing things differ-

54

ADOPTING A SMALL-WINS STRATEGY TO LAUNCH REENGINEERING

ently. This won't work if we focus on incremental change."

Even Hal McPhee and Morris Strandmeyer, who originally argued for this option, agree with Kiechel and Walsh and admit they shouldn't have voted for it. Given the strong consensus among your senior people, you decide not to justify why a small-wins strategy might work. Instead, you opt to select one of the other alternatives. You gracefully abandon your commitment to a small-wins strategy, telling your executive team that you appreciate their thinking and will discuss everything further in the morning. Now you must go back and choose one of the other alternatives.

- *If you choose to develop a reengineering strategy and organization, turn to Chapter 51.*

- *If you want to begin redesigning processes throughout the organization from the bottom up turn to Chapter 52.*

- *If you see the need for getting everyone in the organization to embrace the concept of reengineering before you implement it, turn to Chapter 53.*

Heeding Hammer and Champy's warning that reengineering involves processes, not organizations, you conclude that you must first redesign a few key processes through reengineering. To avoid confusing organizational units and business processes, you ask reengineering czar Bob Kiechel to emphasize that processes are what companies do (that is, natural business activities that make up CyTech). You also remind your steering committee that most people misunderstand the true nature of processes because they spend their time in departments or functions and rarely think about overall business processes.

55

SELECTING A FEW KEY PROCESSES FOR REENGINEERING

To give everyone a better handle on the processes that make up the business activities at CyTech, Kiechel asks the steering committee to identify the beginning and ending points for each process. They produce the following list:

- Concept to prototype;
- Procurement to shipment;
- Warehouse to customer purchase;
- Customer inquiry to resolution; and
- Customer feedback to product concept.

They then create a process map that shows how the company actually conducts its business. Although you recognize unidentified administrative and sublevel processes within each of the major processes the committee has mapped, you decide that this general view can sufficiently enable CyTech to determine which processes it should reengineer first.

243

Although launching a reengineering effort continues to receive less attention than CyTech's response to the price war, you see the silver lining in the clouds overhead: Despite the price war, CyTech's commitment to reengineering, though taking longer than expected, has laid an ideal foundation for implementation. When the year ends with mediocre performance, as shown in the accompanying table, you assure the board that future figures will amaze them.

Selected Financial and Stock Information
(Dollars in millions, except stock price in actual dollars)

| | Year ended March 31 | |
	3rd Year	2nd Year
Sales	$9,810	$8,063
Profits	491	403
Profits as a % of:		
Sales	5%	5%
Assets	7%	7%
Common Equity*	13%	14%
Market Value**	8,639	7,411
Stock Price	33 $7/8$	29 $1/16$

* Total stockholders' equity includes capital stock, surplus, and retained earnings at the company's year end. For purposes of determining profits as a percent of common stockholders' equity, all preferred stock is excluded.

** Calculated by multiplying the number of common shares outstanding by the price per common share as of March 31.

Determined to make reengineering a reality, you quickly focus on deciding whether the company should try to reengineer one process at a time or should tackle two major processes simultaneously. Immediately, you encounter another obstacle: gridlock in the steering committee. Morris Strandmeyer argues for reengineering the procurement-to-shipment process alone; Hal McPhee insists on clarifying administrative processes first; Bob Kiechel, reengineering czar and senior VP of product development, wants to reengineer the customer feedback to product concept process; while Karen Walsh, head of CyTech's advanced technology lab, naturally wants to address the concept to prototype process. John Solo, executive vice president for worldwide sales and marketing, thinks the company should reengineer the customer inquiry-to-resolution process, while Nan Thurow, senior VP of worldwide operations, thinks that the warehouse-to-customer-purchase process should come first.

Searching for a way to break this gridlock and end the debate, which has already consumed far too much time and energy, you look to the marketplace to find CyTech's next greatest challenge. When, through some aggressive competitor intelligence, you discover that Motorola plans to introduce a voice-operated phone-fax-computer within the next few months, you take this information to your senior executives, telling them, "We're barely winning the price war, and now we're going to face a major competitive move by Motorola that will turn the market upside down. I'm convinced that this threat is real. It changes everything. In light of this new information, I'm recommending that we focus all of our reengineering efforts on only one process, the concept-to-prototype process. That's the only way to beat Motorola."

You sense general approval, but just as you seem to have forged the desired consensus among your executive team, Bob Kiechel interrupts, "Like you, I have been doing some competitor intelligence as well, and I asked a few of our international sales people to find out what's on the horizon. We discovered just yesterday that several Japanese firms are planning to allow the current price war to continue cooling off only to launch another one in a couple of years. That would argue for reengineering the procurement-to-shipment process as soon as possible."

Both pieces of information fuel a lot of discussion over the next several hours, as you continue meeting until after 10:00 p.m. Without any clear consensus emerging, you realize you must make the decision yourself.

- *If you choose to redesign the procurement-to-shipment process first, turn to Chapter 59.*

- *If you choose to redesign the concept-to-prototype process first, turn to Chapter 60.*

- *If you decide to redesign both processes, turn to Chapter 61.*

To your mind, the diverse makeup of your senior team supports an approach aimed at fixing several processes at once. Predictably, each one of them favors a different area of the company or a different process as a starting point, so you wisely launch a campaign to fix those processes dearest to their hearts. However, reengineering czar Bob Kiechel warns you that this gambit may dissipate resources and energy across too many reengineering efforts. He points out that reengineering dogma argues against simply fixing a number of processes because doing so doesn't bring about the necessary fundamental rethinking. Thanking Bob for his candor, you assure him that the steering committee and your own leadership will bring to bear the necessary resources to make sure real reengineering occurs. John Solo and the others agree with your assessment and reassure you of their full support.

56

FIXING SEVERAL PROCESSES

Unfortunately, the continuing price war makes it difficult to marshal the necessary resources for reengineering, but you persist, attempting to fix as many processes as you can by making improvements in several processes, including manufacturing, inventory handling, distribution, and customer service. By year end, sales approach $10 billion, as shown in the table on page 248.

Although the board congratulates you for this performance, the members seem anxious about your endeavor to reengineer processes throughout the company. To bring them up to speed on the matter, you detail your reasons for reengineering and how it will benefit key parts of the organization, which reduces, but does not totally remove, the tension you feel as you move forward.

You put additional pressure on CyTech's reengineering efforts, but so many reengineering needs exist throughout the company that your efforts create more *bewilderment* than action. With reluctant assistance from Bob Kiechel, you select process owners and help them develop reengineering teams for 30 different processes, hop-

Selected Financial and Stock Information
(Dollars in millions, except stock price in actual dollars)

	Year ended March 31	
	3rd Year	2nd Year
Sales	$9,502	$8,063
Profits	380	403
Profits as a % of:		
Sales	4%	5%
Assets	6%	7%
Common Equity*	13%	14%
Market Value**	7,936	7,411
Stock Price	31 $\frac{1}{8}$	29 $\frac{1}{16}$

* Total stockholders' equity includes capital stock, surplus, and retained earnings at the company's year end. For purposes of determining profits as a percent of common stockholders' equity, all preferred stock is excluded.
** Calculated by multiplying the number of common shares outstanding by the price per common share as of March 31.

ing that this move will reduce bewilderment and demoralization throughout the company. However, the new reengineering efforts unearth too many problems and recommend too much radical change, causing people to express fear, resistance, and cynicism.

Your senior team begs you to cut back on the massive reengineering effort and work more diligently to cut costs, which means a singular focus on the procurement-to-shipment process. You resist their input and move forward with the campaign you've launched, meeting regularly with the process owners, but getting little support from your steering committee and even less from Bob Kiechel, your new reengineering czar. Stubbornly, you ignore the writing on the wall that's telling you you're losing the price war and failing to achieve profitability at below-$500 price levels. Worse, reengineering has stalled, as well.

Bob Kiechel, concerned about your unwavering position and what it means for the future of the company, discusses his concerns with two members of the board of directors, which eventually leads to a confrontation between you and the chairman of the board. The chairman asks you to redirect your reengineering efforts to the procurement-to-shipment process in an effort to get costs below existing levels so that the company can achieve profitability. Once again, you resist the advice, claiming that the reengineering you have launched will bring about improvements in many vital areas, including cost reduction.

While you do place additional emphasis and resources behind all processes dealing with manufacturing, it's not enough to gain profitability by the end of your fourth year as CEO. Consequently, sales reach $12 billion, but profits plummet, causing CyTech's stock price to drop below $15 per share, as shown in the following table.

Selected Financial and Stock Information
(Dollars in millions, except stock price in actual dollars)

	Year ended March 31	
	4th Year	3rd Year
Sales	$11,844	$9,502
Profits	(118)	380
Profits as a % of:		
Sales	(1%)	4%
Assets	(3%)	6%
Common Equity*	(6%)	13%
Market Value**	3,794	7,936
Stock Price	14 ⅞	31 ⅛

* Total stockholders' equity includes capital stock, surplus, and retained earnings at the company's year end. For purposes of determining profits as a percent of common stockholders' equity, all preferred stock is excluded.
** Calculated by multiplying the number of common shares outstanding by the price per common share as of March 31.

In moves it views as painful but necessary, the board votes to call for your resignation, which you reluctantly submit. Bob Kiechel takes your place. You refuse to be consoled by members of your senior team and you leave CyTech, bitter over having lost the war before you'd even begun to fight.

- *You might have turned the tide in real life, but even Hammer and Champy could have predicted this outcome. If you want to know why the author considers other options better, turn to:*

  Chapter 55, Selecting a Few Key Processes for Reengineering;

  Chapter 57, Reorganizing to Facilitate Reengineering; or

  Chapter 58, Setting the Parameters for Reengineering.

- *If you want to start a new decision-making track, pick one of the following:*

  Chapter 2, Building a Classic Innovative Organization

  Chapter 14, Developing a Synthesis of Best Practices;

  Chapter 26, Imbuing the Culture with Empowerment and Accountability;

  Chapter 38, Pursuing a Work Team Approach; or

  Chapter 62, Embracing a Revolutionary New Perspective.

After he hears your decision to reorganize to facilitate reengineering, Bob Kiechel pulls you aside and expresses his concern that such a course may keep the steering committee, as well as the process owners and reengineering teams, from focusing on processes by getting them too wrapped up in the details of reorganization. Reengineering, he points out, requires a steady focus on processes. He asks you, gently, to reconsider your decision, and you appreciate Bob's candor, honesty, and discretion so much, you agree to take the matter under advisement.

57

REORGANIZING TO FACILITATE REENGINEERING

Before taking any further action on your decision to reorganize in order to facilitate reengineering, you think long and hard about the situation. Perhaps you really did chose this path too hastily. One evening, while reviewing portions of *Re-Engineering the Corporation,* you note the caution Hammer and Champy issue not to get wrapped up in any organizational or structural diversions that will keep processes away from the core of your thinking.

While you supposed this alternative would facilitate reengineering, you now realize how it could become an end in itself, potentially diverting focus away from the right issues. You don't want to miscommunicate to anyone that reorganization and reengineering are the same thing. Reorganization deals with structure while reengineering addresses process.

The more you think about it, the more you appreciate reengineering czar Bob Kiechel's gentle prodding. Not only did he offer his feedback diplomatically, he didn't attack you in front of everyone else on the executive team.

The next day, you ask Bob to join you for lunch, during which you ask for further input and suggestions. Bob's advice mirrors your own thoughts of the previous evening, namely, that a massive reorganization to facilitate reengineering may actually communicate the opposite of what you're trying to accomplish. In fact, reorganization may prevent process owners and reengineering teams from starting over from scratch, given the fact that an overriding new organizational structure would require a lot of their attention. Bob goes further to suggest that a reorganization could take months of valuable time the company cannot afford to spend just now. When you ask him what he would recommend, he suggests selecting a few key processes for reengineering as the best alternative.

Once again, you spend the evening at home pondering the situation intensely. After a rather sleepless night, you decide in the morning to call Dr. Michael Hammer and present the problem to him. After all, he had offered to help if you run into any snags with your reengineering program.

Tracking Michael Hammer to Hilton Head Island where he's conducting a reengineering workshop for another company, you finally get a message to him, and at noon, during a lunch break, he returns your call. You briefly describe the circumstances surrounding your recent decision and share with him the input from Bob Kiechel. Hammer quickly confirms Bob Kiechel's concerns and recommends that you avoid embarking on a major reorganization, even if you think it will facilitate reengineering. He adds a couple of qualifiers to his recommendation: his lack of familiarity with everything that's going on in your company, and his brief exposure to the major issues facing CyTech during his one-day workshop. However, he does suggest that you undertake any reorganization with extreme caution.

You quickly decide to revoke your decision to reorganize and immediately reconsider one of the other three alternatives.

- *If you choose to select a few key processes for reengineering, turn to Chapter 55.*

- *If you prefer fixing several processes simultaneously, turn to Chapter 56.*

- *If you think it's wise to set clear parameters for all reengineering efforts, turn to Chapter 58.*

Because you fear that reengineering could get out of hand and not produce real, tangible results, you tell your senior team that you want to set strict parameters for the endeavor. Immediately, Hal McPhee and Morris Strandmeyer applaud your decision and quickly begin identifying the major problems that should receive immediate attention. Together they identify three problem areas: (1) a cumbersome manufacturing process the company must streamline and consolidate, (2) loose supplier arrangements and contracts CyTech must tighten and strengthen, and (3) a freewheeling customer service operation the firm should standardize.

To your surprise, Strandmeyer and McPhee take the bit in their teeth, persuading the other members of the executive team to set parameters that can direct reengineering efforts to streamlining manufacturing, tightening supplier relationships, and standardizing customer service.

Though you had not anticipated getting to an action

58

SETTING THE PARAMETERS FOR REENGINEERING

mode so quickly, you heartily applaud this turn of events. After the meeting, however, reengineering czar Bob Kiechel pulls you aside to express his concern over senior management trying to define the problems and to narrowly limiting the scope of reengineering. "This violates the very purpose of reengineering and does not let it start over from scratch," he says. "We cannot be sure that McPhee's and Strandmeyer's assumptions about what's wrong are accurate. That's why we need a process owner and a reengineering team to begin the process without the burden of any preconceived ideas, goals, or problems."

The next day you raise Bob Kiechel's concerns with Hal McPhee to elicit his reaction. He simply responds, "Kiechel's just positioning for power. Since you've made him the reengineering czar, he wants to guide this process himself, but if we don't move swiftly to solve the problems we've identified, then why bother with reengineering at all?"

After talking to Hal, you go back to Bob with McPhee's thoughts and feelings. Bob responds without any animosity toward McPhee or anyone else. "I just want to do reengineering right," he claims. "According to Hammer and Champy, reengineering must break boundaries, not reinforce them—it can't be neat and clean and clearly focused on a specific problem. It must be uncomfortable, disruptive, and without any limitations."

You ask, "Are you sure this isn't another one of those personality clashes between you and McPhee?"

Bob bristles at this suggestion. "As far as I'm concerned, it's not."

You leave Bob Kiechel's office confused, wondering which voice to heed. Finally, you decide to side with Hal because you, yourself, initially felt you should set the parameters for reengineering in order to prevent the undertaking from growing unwieldy and uncontrollable. You remind yourself that Hammer and Champy are just consultants, detached from the real decisions of a major corporation.

Consequently, you move forward with your decision to set the parameters and focus on the three problems identified by Hal McPhee and Morris Strandmeyer. In the weeks that follow, Bob Kiechel leaves CyTech to join Motorola. Stunned by his departure, you conclude that a personality conflict really did exist between Bob Kiechel and Hal McPhee. Perhaps Bob's departure is for the best.

Scrambling to meet the demands of the price war makes it difficult to get reengineering parameters set, but over the next several months you manage to appoint process owners and reengineering teams to focus on the three areas of concern identified by your senior executives. Soon the teams go to work redesigning processes within those areas. By the end of your third year as CEO, the company achieves a few more incremental improvements, though not the breakthroughs that you've been reading about at Motorola. According to stories in *The Wall Street Journal* and

Business Week and *Fortune* magazines, Motorola has slashed operating costs to one third or even half of CyTech's. Ironically, reports
have singled out Bob Kiechel as one of the key players leading the
reengineering of Motorola's processes. With the price war changing
everything in the industry, analysts criticize CyTech for not effecting
the cost reductions achieved by more agile competitors.

At year end sales climb to $10 billion, but profits decline
precipitously causing the price of CyTech's stock to fall to $18 per
share, as shown here.

Selected Financial and Stock Information
(Dollars in millions, except stock price in actual dollars)

	Year ended March 31	
	3rd Year	2nd Year
Sales	$9,810	$8,063
Profits	98	403
Profits as a % of:		
Sales	1%	5%
Assets	3%	7%
Common Equity*	6%	14%
Market Value**	4,605	7,411
Stock Price	18 $\frac{1}{16}$	29 $\frac{1}{16}$

* Total stockholders' equity includes capital stock, surplus, and retained earnings at
the company's year end. For purposes of determining profits as a percent of
common stockholders' equity, all preferred stock is excluded.
** Calculated by multiplying the number of common shares outstanding by the price
per common share as of March 31.

You receive a letter in the mail from Jack Ryan, a Michael
Hammer disciple and reengineering consultant who has been
watching the news and talking with Motorola's Bob Kiechel. In the
letter, Ryan suggests that CyTech's marginal incremental improvements demonstrate that reengineering has really not taken place.
Marginal continuous improvements, he points out, do not reflect
fundamental change. He goes on to suggest that only by reengineering now can CyTech continue to be a major player in the industry.

Somehow, word of the letter leaks to the board and to the
press. Before you know it, the chairman of the board has spoken

directly with Jack Ryan. Ryan puts his reputation on the line by telling the chairman that CyTech has not reengineered itself at all. The communication angers you, but, unfortunately, the chairman of the board, along with other members of the board, agrees with Ryan and calls for your resignation.

- *You might have salvaged this situation in real life, but you were going against the odds. If you want to know why the author considers other alternatives better, turn to:*

    Chapter 55, Selecting a Few Key Processes for Reengineering;

    Chapter 56, Fixing Several Processes; or

    Chapter 57, Reorganizing to Facilitate Reengineering.

- *If you want to begin another decision-making track, select one of the following:*

    Chapter 2, Building a Classic Innovative Organization

    Chapter 14, Developing a Synthesis of Best Practices;

    Chapter 26, Imbuing the Culture with Empowerment and Accountability;

    Chapter 38, Pursuing a Work Team Approach; or

    Chapter 62, Embracing a Revolutionary New Perspective.

With the partial support of your senior executive team (specifically Hal McPhee, Morris Strandmeyer, and John Solo), you overrule reengineering czar Bob Kiechel and select a process owner and organize a reengineering team to take on the procurement-to-shipment process. The design team consists of seven people, including the process owner, who is leading the reengineering effort. To launch the effort, you conduct an intensive three-day orientation for the new process owner and reengineering team, during which the team identifies some of the likely outcomes of their efforts: combining several jobs into one; encouraging workers to make more decisions; performing steps in the process in the natural order, not necessarily sequentially and certainly not artificially; allowing multiple versions of processes; doing work only where it makes the most sense; reducing checks and controls; minimizing reconciliation processes; letting case managers provide single points of contact; and establishing highbred centralized/decentralized operations.

Drawing upon Hammer and Champy's work, you communicate to the procurement-to-shipment team them that reengineering should bring about a fundamental change in the nature of work, including:

59

REDESIGNING THE PROCUREMENT- TO-SHIPMENT PROCESS

- Work units should change from functional departments to process teams;
- Jobs should change from simple tasks to multidimensional work;

- People's roles should evolve from control to empower;
- Job preparation should move from training to education (i.e., education should be broader than the traditional narrowly focused training);
- Performance measures and compensation programs should shift from activity to results;
- Achievement criteria should stress performance rather than ability;
- Values should become productive rather than protective;
- Managers should evolve from supervisors to coaches;
- Organizational structures should change from hierarchical to flat; and
- Executives should replace scorekeeping with leadership.

As you provide further guidance to the reengineering team, you suggest that first and foremost they should strive to understand the process completely and thoroughly. They must take into account everything about the process, what it does, how well it performs, and the critical issues that govern its performance, working through all of the details necessary to allow for appropriate redesign. The team must, you insist, work quickly to apply the appropriate principles of reengineering, and they must search out and destroy all assumptions based on past performance and past methods of doing the work. This will probably involve the creative application of technology.

During the final day of your orientation session, you again draw on Hammer and Champy's work by issuing the following guidelines:

1. You don't need to be an expert to redesign a process.
2. Being an outsider helps.
3. You must discard preconceived notions.
4. It's important to see things through the customer's eyes.
5. Teams like yours can best accomplish redesign.
6. You don't need to know much about the current process (except what it does, how it performs what it does, and the critical issues relating to its performance).
7. It's not hard to develop fresh ideas.
8. Have fun.

You also charge the team with rereading Chapter 14 of *Re-Engineering the Corporation,* making sure they avoid the stumbling blocks and the common errors identified, such as "trying to fix a process instead of changing it, settling for minor improvements and results, quitting too early, or assigning someone who doesn't understand re-engineering to lead the effort." Over the next several weeks the reengineering team works hard and fast to understand and reshape the procurement-to-shipment process. You replace Bob Kiechel with Hal McPhee as reengineering czar and ask him to monitor the team's progress every step of the way, providing the necessary leadership and drawing input from the steering committee whenever necessary.

Three months later, you receive the reengineering team's report, complete with preliminary recommendations, which include the combining of several jobs; much more worker decision making; changing the order of work steps to allow for flexibility and natural occurrence; recommending multiple versions of work performance; relocating work to take place where it makes most sense; eliminating many checks and controls; reducing the need for reconciliation of information; organizing case managers by dealer, distributor, and customer group; mixing centralized and decentralized operations; and eliminating all warehouses. Surprisingly, while this last recommendation addresses another process, namely warehouse-to-customer purchase, you find the rationale for the elimination of warehouses positively brilliant.

After reviewing the recommendations with your senior executive team, which has been functioning as the steering committee for reengineering, you find that everyone fully supports everything the reengineering team has recommended. Now, you can flash the green light to proceed.

Within weeks, CyTech adopts many of the reengineering recommendations with amazing speed and astonishing success, resulting in rapid gains in performance and reduced costs. Finally, CyTech manages to score good profits under price war conditions.

At the end of your fourth year as CEO, CyTech's sales reach $12 billion, and the stock price climbs to $65 per share, as shown in the table on page 260.

Selected Financial and Stock Information
(Dollars in millions, except stock price in actual dollars)

	Year ended March 31	
	4th Year	3rd Year
Sales	$12,176	$9,810
Profits	731	491
Profits as a % of:		
Sales	6%	5%
Assets	10%	7%
Common Equity*	17%	13%
Market Value**	16,639	8,639
Stock Price	65 ¼	33 ⅞

* Total stockholders' equity includes capital stock, surplus, and retained earnings at the company's year end. For purposes of determining profits as a percent of common stockholders' equity, all preferred stock is excluded.
** Calculated by multiplying the number of common shares outstanding by the price per common share as of March 31.

With rumors flying about a voice-operated phone-fax-computer coming soon from Motorola, you quickly turn your attention to the concept-to-prototype process in order to gain the quick benefits the company has realized with its reengineered procurement-to-shipment process. Unfortunately, Motorola's voice-operated phone-fax-computer comes to market much faster than you expected. You've only just begun orienting the new process owner and reengineering team when Motorola's new product hits the market.

In eight weeks, however, CyTech manages to reengineer the concept-to-prototype process and moves swiftly with the development of its own voice-operated phone-fax-computer. Still, Motorola gains strong recognition in the market and easily establishes itself as the leader in the industry. Nine weeks later, CyTech has developed its own voice-operated prototype three to six months earlier than originally planned, but the product still lies several weeks away from introduction into the marketplace. At midyear, CyTech finally introduces its version and begins recapturing its lost market share.

At the end of your fifth year as CEO, sales climb to $14 billion. The stock price climbs to $78 per share, as shown in the accompanying table on the next page.

Selected Financial and Stock Information
(Dollars in millions, except stock price in actual dollars)

	Year ended March 31	
	5th Year	4th Year
Sales	$14,235	$12,176
Profits	854	731
Profits as a % of:		
Sales	6%	6%
Assets	11%	10%
Common Equity*	18%	17%
Market Value**	19,859	16,639
Stock Price	77 $\frac{7}{8}$	65 $\frac{1}{4}$

* Total stockholders' equity includes capital stock, surplus, and retained earnings at the company's year end. For purposes of determining profits as a percent of common stockholders' equity, all preferred stock is excluded.

** Calculated by multiplying the number of common shares outstanding by the price per common share as of March 31.

Looking back, you decide that you should have focused on at least two processes to begin reengineering at CyTech, but learning from your mistake, you immediately launch reengineering efforts in both the customer inquiry-to-customer resolutions process and the shipment-to-customer purchase process.

You renew your employment contract as CEO with the board of directors for another five years because you see so much more to accomplish before you move on. When Bob Kiechel leaves the company for Motorola, you admit to yourself that you should not have replaced him as reengineering czar, but you resolve to learn a lesson here as well.

This marks the end of a decision-making track, but you can continue playing the game by selecting one of the following options.

- *If you want to compare how the results of your last five years of organizational decision making stack up against the other positive outcomes in The Organization Game, turn to Chapter 78.*

- *If you want to explore the other alternatives you could have pursued on this track, turn to one of the following:*

  Chapter 52, Redesigning Processes Throughout the Organization from the Bottom Up;

  Chapter 53, Getting Everyone in the Organization to Embrace the Concept of Reengineering;

  Chapter 54, Adopting a Small-Wins Strategy to Launch Reengineering;

  Chapter 56, Fixing Several Processes;

  Chapter 57, Reorganizing to Facilitate Reengineering;

  Chapter 58, Setting the Parameters for Reengineering;

  Chapter 60, Redesigning the Concept-to-Prototype Process; or

  Chapter 61, Redesigning Both the Procurement-to-Shipment Process and the Concept-to-Prototype Process.

- *If you would rather try your hand at another decision-making track, select one of the following:*

  Chapter 2, Building a Classic Innovative Organization

  Chapter 14, Developing a Synthesis of Best Practices;

  Chapter 26, Imbuing the Culture with Empowerment and Accountability;

  Chapter 38, Pursuing a Work Team Approach; or

  Chapter 62, Embracing a Revolutionary New Perspective.

With the partial support of your senior executive team (specifically Nan Thurow, Karen Walsh, and John Solo), you bypass Bob Kiechel to select a process owner and organize a reengineering team to redesign the concept-to-prototype process. You conduct an intensive three-day orientation for this process owner and the reengineering team, identifying some of the likely outcomes of their efforts: combining several jobs into one; encouraging workers to make more decisions; performing steps in the process in the natural order, not necessarily sequentially and certainly not artificially; allowing multiple versions of processes; doing work only where it makes the most sense; reducing checks and controls; minimizing reconciliation processes; letting case managers provide single points of contact; and establishing highbred centralized/decentralized operations.

Drawing upon Hammer and Champy's work, you stress that reengineering should bring about a fundamental change in the nature of work, such as:

60

REDESIGNING THE CONCEPT-TO-PROTOTYPE PROCESS

- Work units should change from functional departments to process teams;
- Jobs should change from simple tasks to multidimensional work;
- People's roles should evolve from control to empower;
- Job preparation should move from training to education (i.e., education should be broader than the traditional narrowly focused training);
- Performance measures and compensation programs should shift from activity to results;

263

- Achievement criteria should stress performance rather than ability;
- Values should become productive rather than protective;
- Managers should evolve from supervisors to coaches;
- Organizational structures should change from hierarchical to flat; and
- Executives should replace scorekeeping with leadership.

To further guide the reengineering team, you suggest first and foremost they must understand the process completely and thoroughly. They must take into account everything about the process, what it does, how well it performs, and the critical issues that govern its performance before they tackle appropriate redesign.

The design team consists of seven people, including the process owner. You encourage them to work quickly to apply the appropriate principles of reengineering, searching out and destroying all assumptions based on past performance and past methods of doing the work, and you challenge them to look for creative ways to apply technology.

During the final day of your orientation, you draw again on Hammer and Champy's work to issue the following guidelines:

1. You don't need to be an expert to redesign a process.
2. Being an outsider helps.
3. You must discard preconceived notions.
4. It's important to see things through the customer's eyes.
5. Teams like yours can best accomplish redesign.
6. You don't need to know much about the current process (except what it does, how it performs what it does, and the critical issues relating to its performance).
7. It's not hard to develop fresh ideas.
8. Have fun.

You also charge the team with rereading Chapter 14 of *Re-Engineering the Corporation*, which should help them avoid the stumbling blocks and the common errors identified there. Inspired by the challenge to make dramatic fundamental improvements in the way CyTech conceives of and develops its products, the concept-to-prototype reengineering team moves forward with great enthusiasm. As the team achieves a full understanding of the product concept-to-product prototype process, it then works to redesign the process. Several recommendations unfold over the next several weeks, making it clear that CyTech can indeed make major, substantial improvements in the way it conceives of and develops new products.

Three months into your fourth year as CEO, Bob Kiechel leaves for Motorola. His departure, while it saddens you, is overshadowed by the reengineering team's recommendations to combine research and development teams, expanding the scope of their research and development efforts and giving them more responsibility for making decisions about everything, including more simultaneous work on different products, projects, and multiple versions of the R&D process. The team also recommends more common-sense management, fewer checks and controls, minimized reconciliation, and concept customer interface managers who represent the point of view of the customer as they watch the progress of various projects through R&D. If CyTech can accomplish all this without a reengineering czar, perhaps you don't really need a new one.

As CyTech implements the recommendations from the concept-to-prototype process reengineering team, it makes astonishing advances as a whole host of new product concepts move forward quickly, some reaching the prototype stage by the end of your fourth year as CEO. The most exciting of these is a voice-operated phone-fax-computer. However, you begin to realize that CyTech has been losing the price war as it focused solely on concept-to-prototype reengineering, a misstep that has kept the company from adapting to the low price conditions and has allowed competitors to gain market share.

Sales increase less than anticipated to $11 billion, driving the stock price up to $52, based largely on the rumor that CyTech will soon introduce a major new product. The table on page 266 summarizes CyTech's fourth-year performance under your leadership.

Selected Financial and Stock Information
(Dollars in millions, except stock price in actual dollars)

	Year ended March 31	
	4th Year	3rd Year
Sales	$11,394	$9,810
Profits	456	491
Profits as a % of:		
Sales	4%	5%
Assets	6%	7%
Common Equity*	11%	13%
Market Value**	13,324	8,639
Stock Price	52 ¼	33 ⅞

* Total stockholders' equity includes capital stock, surplus, and retained earnings at the company's year end. For purposes of determining profits as a percent of common stockholders' equity, all preferred stock is excluded.

** Calculated by multiplying the number of common shares outstanding by the price per common share as of March 31.

A nervous and anxious board of directors makes it clear to you that if the voice-operated phone-fax-computer does not turn the numbers around, they will replace you as CEO within the year. Oblivious to that threat, you move forward, and three weeks after the beginning of your fifth year as CEO, CyTech introduces the *PowerBase 10,* the world's first voice-operated phone-fax-computer. The product takes the market by storm and racks up impressive sales for three months before Motorola introduces its own version. Sales reach $15 billion by the end of your fifth year, pushing the stock price to $90 per share, as shown on the opposite page.

The board of directors applauds your reengineering efforts, but as you look back you think you should have launched two or more reengineering processes at the same time. You also regret losing Bob Kiechel.

You agree to another five-year term as CEO of CyTech, vowing to make fewer mistakes in the future. Though this marks the end of a decision-making track, you can continue playing the game by choosing one of the following options.

Selected Financial and Stock Information
(Dollars in millions, except stock price in actual dollars)

	Year ended March 31	
	5th Year	4th Year
Sales	$15,002	$11,394
Profits	750	456
Profits as a % of:		
Sales	5%	4%
Assets	8%	6%
Common Equity*	14%	11%
Market Value**	22,919	13,324
Stock Price	89 $\frac{7}{8}$	52 $\frac{1}{4}$

* Total stockholders' equity includes capital stock, surplus, and retained earnings at the company's year end. For purposes of determining profits as a percent of common stockholders' equity, all preferred stock is excluded.

** Calculated by multiplying the number of common shares outstanding by the price per common share as of March 31.

- *If you want to compare how the results of your last five years of organizational decision making stack up against the other positive outcomes in The Organization Game, turn to Chapter 78.*

- *If you want to explore the other alternatives you could have pursued on this track, turn to one of the following:*

  Chapter 52, Redesigning Processes Throughout the Organization from the Bottom Up;

  Chapter 53, Getting Everyone in the Organization to Embrace the Concept of Reengineering;

  Chapter 54, Adopting a Small-Wins Strategy to Launch Reengineering;

  Chapter 56, Fixing Several Processes;

  Chapter 57, Reorganizing to Facilitate Reengineering;

Chapter 58, Setting the Parameters for Reengineering;

Chapter 59, Redesigning the Procurement-to-Shipment Process; or

Chapter 61, Redesigning Both the Procurement-to-Shipment Process and the Concept-to-Prototype Process.

- *If you want to try your luck on another decision-making track, turn one of the following:*

    Chapter 2, Building a Classic Innovative Organization

    Chapter 14, Developing a Synthesis of Best Practices;

    Chapter 26, Imbuing the Culture with Empowerment and Accountability;

    Chapter 38, Pursuing a Work Team Approach; or

    Chapter 62, Embracing a Revolutionary New Perspective.

With the full support of your senior executive team, you and Bob Kiechel select process owners and organize reengineering teams to redesign both the procurement-to-shipment and the concept-to-prototype processes. You, Bob Kiechel, and your senior executives, acting as a steering committee, provide an intensive week-long orientation for the two process owners and the reengineering teams, identifying some of the likely outcomes of their efforts, including: combining several jobs into one; encouraging workers to make more decisions; performing steps in the process in the natural order, not necessarily sequentially and certainly not artificially; allowing multiple versions of processes; doing work only where it makes the most sense; reducing checks and controls; minimizing reconciliation processes; letting case managers provide single points of contact; and establishing highbred centralized/decentralized operations.

Drawing upon Hammer and Champy's work, you remind them that reengineering should bring about a fundamental change in the nature of work:

- Work units should change from functional departments to process teams;
- Jobs should change from simple tasks to multidimensional work;

61

REDESIGNING BOTH THE PROCUREMENT-TO-SHIPMENT AND THE CONCEPT-TO-PROTOTYPE PROCESSES

- People's roles should evolve from control to empower;
- Job preparation should move from training to education (i.e., education should be broader than the traditional narrowly focused training);
- Performance measures and compensation programs should shift from activity to results;
- Achievement criteria should stress performance rather than ability;
- Values should become productive rather than protective;
- Managers should evolve from supervisors to coaches;
- Organizational structures should change from hierarchical to flat; and
- Executives should replace scorekeeping with leadership.

As you further guide the reengineering teams, you suggest that first and foremost they must thoroughly understand the process itself, taking into account everything about the process, what it does, how well it performs, and the critical issues that govern its performance. Only then can they work through all the details necessary for appropriate redesign.

Each reengineering design team consists of seven people, including the process owners who will lead the reengineering efforts. You and Kiechel encourage them to apply the appropriate principles of reengineering quickly, to search out and destroy all assumptions based on past performance and past methods of doing the work, and to look for opportunities to apply technology creatively.

During the final day of your week-long orientation, Kiechel draws on Hammer and Champy's work to issue the following guidelines:

1. You don't need to be an expert to redesign a process.
2. Being an outsider helps.
3. You must discard preconceived notions.
4. It's important to see things through the customer's eyes.
5. Teams like yours can best accomplish redesign.
6. You don't need to know much about the current process (except what it does, how it performs what it does, and the critical issues relating to its performance).
7. It's not hard to develop fresh ideas.
8. Have fun.

You charge the teams with rereading Chapter 14 of *Re-Engineering the Corporation,* which will help them avoid the stumbling blocks and the common errors identified there. The teams move forward, reengineering with great speed and energy.

Over the next several weeks, the two reengineering teams develop a thorough understanding of the two targeted processes. You and Kiechel monitor their progress every step of the way, providing the necessary leadership and drawing input from your steering committee as needed. Three months into your fourth year, you receive the procurement-to-shipment team's report, complete with preliminary recommendations, which include combining several jobs; much more worker decision making; changing the order of work steps to allow for flexibility and natural occurrence; effecting multiple versions of work performance; relocating of work so it's done where it makes most sense; eliminating many checks and controls; reducing the need for reconciliation of information; organizing case managers by dealer, distributor, and customer group; mixing centralized and decentralized operations; and eliminating all warehouses. Surprisingly, this last recommendation flows over into another process, warehouse-to-customer purchase, but you find this suggestion positively brilliant.

After reviewing the recommendations with your reengineering steering committee, you find everyone fully behind the effort. Now you can empower implementation. Within weeks, the company installs many of the reengineering recommendations with amazing speed and tremendous success, resulting in strong gains in performance and reduced costs. Just as you're congratulating yourself for major breakthroughs in performance and cost, *The Wall Street Journal* cites CyTech as one of the four winners of the two-year price war.

CyTech has won the price war, but it has also made strong headway with new-product development, as the concept-to-prototype reengineering team initiates several moves that substantially improve the way CyTech conceives of and develops new products. They recommend giving more responsibility to R&D teams for making decisions about everything, including more simultaneous work on different products, various projects, and multiple versions of the R&D process. They also suggest more common-sense management, fewer checks and controls, minimized reconciliation, and concept-customer interface managers who bring the customer's point of view to the progress of various projects through R&D.

As CyTech implements the recommendations from the concept-to-prototype reengineering team, the company moves forward quickly with a whole host of new-product concepts, some reaching the prototype stage by the end of your fourth year as CEO of CyTech. The most exciting of these is a voice-operated phone-fax-computer that your people tell you will outperform Motorola's rumored device.

At the end of your fourth year as CEO, CyTech's sales reach $14 billion, and the stock price soars to $82 per share, as shown.

Selected Financial and Stock Information
(Dollars in millions, except stock price in actual dollars)

	Year ended March 31	
	4th Year	3rd Year
Sales	$13,849	$9,810
Profits	831	491
Profits as a % of:		
Sales	6%	5%
Assets	9%	7%
Common Equity*	16%	13%
Market Value**	20,974	8,639
Stock Price	82 $\frac{1}{4}$	33 $\frac{7}{8}$

* Total stockholders' equity includes capital stock, surplus, and retained earnings at the company's year end. For purposes of determining profits as a percent of common stockholders' equity, all preferred stock is excluded.
** Calculated by multiplying the number of common shares outstanding by the price per common share as of March 31.

At the beginning of your fifth year as CEO, CyTech introduces the *PowerBase 10,* Cytech's first voice-operated phone-fax-computer. The product takes the market by storm and racks up impressive sales for three months before Motorola introduces its own version. Sales reach $17 billion at the end of your fifth year, and the stock price rises to $123 per share, as shown in the table on the opposite page.

The board of directors elects you their new chairman and praises you lavishly. Your stock options increase your net worth to over $300 million. The results flowing from reengineering have

Selected Financial and Stock Information
(Dollars in millions, except stock price in actual dollars)

	Year ended March 31	
	This Year	Last Year
Sales	$17,383	$13,849
Profits	1,217	831
Profits as a % of:		
Sales	7%	6%
Assets	11%	9%
Common Equity*	21%	16%
Market Value**	31,238	20,974
Stock Price	122 ½	82 ¼

* Total stockholders' equity includes capital stock, surplus, and retained earnings at the company's year end. For purposes of determining profits as a percent of common stockholders' equity, all preferred stock is excluded.

** Calculated by multiplying the number of common shares outstanding by the price per common share as of March 31.

enabled CyTech to win the price war, position itself for future price wars, and introduce a major technological breakthrough. No traditional organization could have accomplished anything close to what CyTech has achieved in the past few years with reengineering. You relish your new role as chairman of the board, but you work diligently to prepare a new CEO, so you can focus on other dimensions of CyTech's development and your community interests, as well as national business development and the advancement of management thought and practice.

One year later you appoint Bob Kiechel CEO of CyTech and assume your new limited role as chairman of the board, which will afford you time to explore new dimensions of your life and to spend more time with your grandchildren. You receive many honors as you step down as CEO and assume the chairmanship, but the feature article in *Time* magazine, in the issue naming you *Time*'s "Man of the Year" for revolutionizing personal computing and reengineering American business, pleases you more than anything because it captures the full extent of what you accomplished at CyTech.

Congratulations! This represents the end of a decision-making track. However, you can continue playing the game by choosing one of the following.

- *If you want to compare how the results of your last five years of organizational decision making stack up against the other positive outcomes in The Organization Game, turn to Chapter 78.*

- *If you want to explore the other options you could have selected on this decision-making track, turn to one of the following:*

  Chapter 52, Redesigning Processes Throughout the Organization from the Bottom Up;

  Chapter 53, Getting Everyone in the Organization to Embrace the Concept of Reengineering;

  Chapter 54, Adopting a Small-Wins Strategy to Launch Reengineering;

  Chapter 56, Fixing Several Processes;

  Chapter 57, Reorganizing to Facilitate Reengineering;

  Chapter 58, Setting the Parameters for Reengineering;

  Chapter 59, Redesigning the Procurement-to-Shipment Process; or

  Chapter 60, Redesigning the Concept-to-Prototype Process.

- *If you want to embark on a new decision-making track, choose one of the following:*

  Chapter 2, Building a Classic Innovative Organization

  Chapter 14, Developing a Synthesis of Best Practices;

  Chapter 26, Imbuing the Culture with Empowerment and Accountability;

  Chapter 38, Pursuing a Work Team Approach; or

  Chapter 62, Embracing a Revolutionary New Perspective.

Since you believe your industry itself will redefine communication and personal effectiveness in the twenty-first century, you decide that your approach to CyTech's organization and culture should move boldly beyond all the current practices and cutting-edge literature. If personal communications will revolutionize the way people live and work, your company should revolutionize the way its own people live and work.

62

EMBRACING A REVOLUTIONARY NEW PERSPECTIVE

You now face the obstacle of carving enough time out of the day-to-day pressures of running CyTech to conceptualize a radical new kind of organization. Formulating a conceptual foundation for something really new will take more than a few days, but you simply must take the necessary time to think things through before you approach your executive team with the challenge.

In a strikingly unusual move, you petition the board of directors for a sabbatical of 90 days, during which you will work around the clock designing a brand-new blueprint for your company. Initially disturbed by the request because of all the swift developments in the marketplace, the chairman of the board attempts to counsel you against such a leave of absence. However, you remain firmly convinced of your plan and describe it in the context of the personal communications revolution itself, "CyTech must lead the revolution by revolutionizing itself. If we don't invent our future, someone else will do it for us, and we'll just be following the herd."

Sensing that the chairman likes this line of reasoning, you continue, "The phone-fax-computer is changing the way people live and work in very fundamental ways. The impact of these changes will spread throughout the world only as the price of phone-fax-computers continues to fall. Surely, we should seize this new opportunity by applying it to the very way we do business."

After two more sessions with the chairman of the board and other members of the board, you win their approval for a 90-day sabbatical. To allay any remaining fears that CyTech might lose ground during your absence, you promise to prepare your executive team carefully prior to your departure, and you assure the board that you will remain in close contact while you're away. However, you remain committed not to get bogged down in operating issues as you immerse yourself in designing CyTech's future.

Once you make all the necessary preparations, you embark upon your sabbatical at midyear with a clear but open-ended schedule. During the first 30 days, you will read all the current literature on transformation, reengineering, power shifting, and social trends. The following list of 10 books represents your beginning point, though you expect to add other books and articles as you move forward with your thinking.

- *Re-Engineering the Corporation* (Harper Business) by Hammer & Champy
- *The Wisdom of Teams* (Harvard Business School Press) by Katzenbach & Smith
- *Control Your Own Destiny or Someone Else Will* (Currency/Doubleday) by Tichy & Sherman
- *Global Paradox* (William Morrow) by John Naisbitt
- *Visionary Leadership* (Jossey-Bass) by Burt Nanus
- *First Things First* (Simon & Schuster) by Stephen Covey
- *Life After Television* (Norton) by George Gilder
- *War and Anti-War* (Bantam) by Alvin Toffler
- *The Oz Principle* (Prentice Hall) by Connors, Smith & Hickman
- *Uncommon Genius* (Viking) by Denise Shekerjian
- *Further Along the Road Less Traveled* (Simon & Schuster) by Scott Peck

During the second 30 days, you expect to use this background to identify the very basis upon which future organizations might operate. With luck, you will synthesize the best ideas into a central organizing principle that can guide Cytech into the next century. Once you've done that, you'll spend the final 30 days developing alternatives, making sure that you're including all viable options. In the end, you plan to boil down all the alternatives to the three most viable—the ones you'll present to your senior executive team upon your return. In short, your agenda will move from study to alternatives to a set of three final options for action.

You choose Cambridge, Massachusetts, as the base for your first 30-day period because you want access to the Harvard and MIT libraries and to professors with whom you have developed a relationship over the years. With the help of a Harvard professor friend, you rent a comfortable home on Brattle Street near Harvard Square. Once you have completed the first phase in Cambridge, you will spend your second 30-day period in New Zealand on a country estate owned by the family of one of CyTech's key distributors to Asia. You know you will need isolation for this second phase of the sabbatical and know New Zealand will offer that. For the final phase, you will move to CyTech University, reserving one full wing of the main training center in order to devote the necessary resources to developing action plans for your final three viable options.

The next 90 days unfold with few changes in the planned schedule. During the first phase, you become convinced that the organizations of the future must look entirely different from the way they look now. Not only will they be flatter, more decentralized, and process-driven, they will also place much greater importance on individual contribution, productivity, and fulfillment. During the second phase, you identify the core principle that should underlie CyTech's new organization: "permanently unleashing the power of the human spirit," the implementation of which might involve any of two hundred alternatives, including focus cultures, hyper-motivation, 24-hour training, telecommuting, and horizontal networks. During the final 30 days, you boil everything down to three distinct alternatives for creating a total perspective for your company: (1) moving employees through development phases to a high productivity core group; (2) contracting with each employee instead of reporting relationships, and (3) creating an internal temporary employment function with competence centers. Each of the alternatives centers on the idea that permanently unleashing the human spirit will require a complete shift in emphasis away from behavior and action toward the inherent talent, motivation, ambition, vision, and values of the individual. Put simply: "If we can create an environment where people receive the opportunity and the resources to accomplish and become exactly what they desire, we won't have to manage behavior, standards, performance, and results artificially. Instead, we'll prepare individuals to flourish in an environment that matches their talents and desires with the key processes and purposes of the organization."

According to your new way of thinking, the new-style organization will not force people to accept any vision, values, goals, objectives, standards, or procedures they don't believe in. The job of management will shift to harmonizing individual talents, motivations, ambitions, and values with the market and customer-driven purposes and processes of the organization. For such an environment to work, it must afford people unlimited opportunity to adapt and change at will. The organization must define its purposes and processes clearly, but in such a way that will allow people to experiment and find out exactly how and where they can maximize their individual contributions, fulfillment, and results. Without question, every employee must understand that the organization must meet its goals and achieve its results in order for the individual to be able to achieve his or hers. You know that harmonizing individual and organizational desires and results won't come easily. It will require dramatically and fundamentally different ways of operating, managing and leading.

To accomplish all this, you have narrowed the possibilities to three distinct alternatives. The first alternative divides everyone in the CyTech organization into three groupings or levels. As shown in the accompanying diagram, the people in the inner core would require no supervision and would determine all their activities and priorities through an annual individual-corporation contracting process. People in the inner core must prove their ability to apply their talent, motivation, and ambition in ways that achieve their own requirements for fulfillment, progress, and well-being, as well as the purposes and results of the organization. You expect people at this level will operate at productivity levels much higher than those attained by people in traditional organizations. People at the inner core will enjoy free access to corporate resources, functioning as

Three-Level Approach

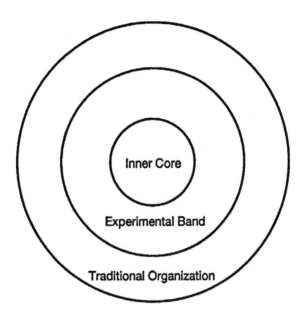

agents unto themselves as they work with teams, groups, and processes in myriad ways, guided by a flexible contracting relationship.

The experimental band represents people preparing to enter the inner core, who are still experimenting with exactly how to maximize their talent, their motivation, and their contribution. These people will be assigned to groups and teams without the full freedoms and access to resources as have the inner core, but they will be constantly working toward that end.

The outer band of employees will function in ways very similar to how CyTech currently operates with managers, projects, and a highly flexible hierarchical structure that gives people the opportunity to figure out exactly what they want to do with their careers, their lives, and whether CyTech is the right place for them to achieve their own and the organization's goals. These people will largely perform support functions for the processes that drive the CyTech organization. They will be guided and directed by people in the inner core, with assistance from those in the experimental band.

Under this alternative, everyone in the organization would know precisely where he or she stands. Initially, you expect only about 10 percent to compose the inner core, with approximately 50 percent in the experimental band and 40 percent in the outer band. In time, however, you expect an equal number of people to compose each of the three groups.

The role of management in the traditional band will conform to contemporary management thought and practice. In the experimental band, managers will provide discipline and assistance during the intense experimenting, learning, and developing processes. And in the inner core, everyone will share management responsibility through the individual contracting process. The first group will look fairly standard, the second rather innovative, and the third, quite radical by today's standards.

While you cannot currently envision the ideal final state of this kind of organization, (that is, whether all employees should eventually enter the inner core or whether the three bands should continue to exist indefinitely), you do feel that the three different groupings of people within the organization will provide the means for helping individuals reach the kind of productivity levels that will allow them to contribute far more than they ever imagined, allowing CyTech to reach objectives far beyond those of other organizations.

The second alternative involves organizing people by contract. Building on the ideas of process mapping used at General Electric and the notion of focusing on business processes presented in *Reengineering the Corporation*, this alternative emphasizes contracts and processes as the basic modes of organizing CyTech. People will

Business Processes

Employees

Contractual Arrangements

Business Processes

continue to reside and work in specific process locations, but under their own local management.

On the surface, this alternative looks like a matrix-style organization. However, the reporting relationships inherent in a matrix-style organization do not exist here. Through an annual contracting process, each employee within the CyTech organization will sit down with an officer of the company to establish a one-, two-, three-, five-, or ten-year contract for a process and a location with which that person will align. All management will occur by contract, with little distinction between peers, subordinates, or superiors.

Local process coordinators will address and resolve anything not spelled out in the contract that arises during the course of a person's work. This organization will abolish all hierarchies, with the exception of the distinction between officers and associates. During the course of day-to-day work, however, officers will apply no more leverage in the organization than an associate, except as dictated by the contractual arrangement. In other words, an officer may be working as part of a team, with an associate serving by contract as the team leader. However, company officers, perhaps five hundred in all, will shoulder the additional responsibility of spending about 25 percent of their time developing and reviewing contracts.

The locations where people work will remain completely flexible, allowing individuals to work wherever they choose and permitting movement across processes and subprocesses as determined by contractual arrangements. Everyone in this organization will function as a manager in the old sense of the word.

The holistic contracts developed with each employee will deal with everything from personal goals, spiritual well-being, family needs, development of talent, application of talent, improvement of strengths, mitigation of weaknesses, career vision, core values, life track, fulfillment and satisfaction expectations, sense of meaning, contribution to organizational purposes, and anticipated results. People working under this organizational alternative will learn to use the contract as the basis for all management and organizational processes, and they can redevelop and renegotiate their contract at any time with a company officer. Anyone who violates the intent and essence of a contract will most likely leave the company for a more suitable environment. Termination will require the consent of three company officers. New hires will also require the consent of three company officers.

All company officers will receive 50 percent of their compensation and associates 25 percent of their compensation in CyTech stock. Not only will CyTech stock be traded on the NASDAQ Stock Exchange, but the company will trade stock at any time with any associate.

The responsibility for work teams will fall squarely on the shoulders of every associate within the organization. Each individual within the company must feel empowered to do whatever it takes to fulfill his or her contract.

The third alternative would consist of two elements: competence centers and business processes. All CyTech employees would work for one of 15 to 20 competence centers organized around basic functional, technical, managerial, and skill-based capabilities. The major processes within CyTech, which would range from 6 to 12, would temporarily hire individuals from the competence centers to work on an ad-hoc basis. The 6 to 12 process heads would oversee subprocess heads. The competence centers would function like temporary service firms, making the process heads aware of capabilities and delivering the necessary people when required.

Competence Centers - Business Processes

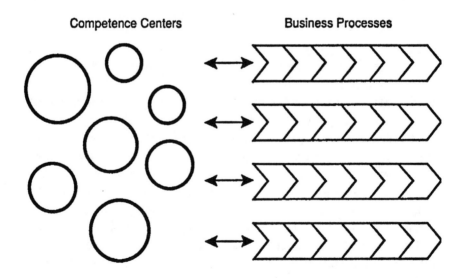

Competence Centers   Business Processes

People throughout the CyTech organization could shift competence centers in order to develop their own talents and capabilities or to learn new areas of competence. The business process heads would award compensation strictly on the basis of competence level and performance. They would take two measures into account: competence, as judged by the competence center heads, and performance, as judged by the business process heads.

The business process heads would do no traditional hiring and would maintain no long-term permanent employees, except the four to ten subprocess heads in each business process. These process heads could turn back any individual to a particular competence center whenever performance would fall below the required levels. When that occurs, the competence center heads, along with their own staff, would assess the returned individual to help redirect, redeploy or retrain them, with the objective of maximizing the productivity of the individual by aligning his or her contribution to the organization with that individual's talent, motivation, and desires.

The competence centers would function like human resource pools focused on learning, development, and preparation for deployment. The business processes where people work would focus on getting desired results, as determined by the marketplace and CyTech's customers. Business process heads would strive to obtain organizational results, while the competence center heads would work to prepare, develop, and strengthen individuals.

In this environment, an individual worker could request transfer at any time to a different business process, back to a competence center, or between competence centers. Regardless of an individual's movement throughout the organization, he or she would receive compensation based on an assessment of that individual's value to the corporation. In other words, if an individual performs well in a business process, the process head could weight that individual's contribution and determine an appropriate compensation level based on performance. An individual who takes a year to develop a particular competence in one of the competence centers would receive compensation for that development time, but would be expected to turn that competence into value for the organization through application in some business process. This approach would require a management system of *competence development* and *business process application* that would apply to everything the company does.

Each of these three alternatives intrigues you, and you develop a thorough summary of each for your executive team. Three weeks after returning from your sabbatical, you present the three alternatives to your senior executive team, which has been eagerly awaiting the results of your 90-day sojourn into the future. With a combination of video clips, overhead slides, flip charts, and handouts, you lead your team through the three options. Given the complexities of each possibility, you move slowly and you limit discussion in this initial meeting, asking each member of your senior team to study and ponder the materials and come back prepared with questions three days hence.

During the second meeting, you discover that John Solo, your executive vice president for worldwide sales and marketing, Hal McPhee, chief financial officer, and Morris Strandmeyer, vice president of production, favor the competence center and business process alternative. Nan Thurow, senior vice president of worldwide operations, leans toward the contract alternative, and Bob Kiechel, senior VP of product development, and Karen Walsh, vice president of CyTech's advanced technology lab, line up behind the three levels of employees' option.

Given the differences in orientations among your senior executives, you expected such a divergence of opinion, but you had hoped they could gradually compromise and hammer out a consensus. Unfortunately, as hard as you try to get them to move outside their own views to consider what might prove best for CyTech, each executive remains aligned with the alternative he or she initially favored.

In the meantime, your first year as CEO of CyTech comes to an end. Product updates and enhancements to the *PowerBase* line of phone-fax-computers keeps CyTech growing, but you know the future will not look so rosy unless you get one of your new organizational schemes quickly into place. For now, however, you savor the jump in sales to $6.5 billion and the rise in stock to $34, as shown in the accompanying table. With the year-end books closed, you turn your attention to the pressing decision.

Each of these organizational alternatives will create a very different organization from the one CyTech currently employs, and

Selected Financial and Stock Information
(Dollars in millions, except stock price in actual dollars)

	Year ended March 31	
	1st Year	Previous Year
Sales	$6,496	$4,083
Profits	390	242
Profits as a % of:		
Sales	6%	6%
Assets	9%	9%
Common Equity*	18%	17%
Market Value**	8,734	6,123
Stock Price	34 ¼	23 ¾

* Total stockholders' equity includes capital stock, surplus, and retained earnings at the company's year end. For purposes of determining profits as a percent of common stockholders' equity, all preferred stock is excluded.

** Calculated by multiplying the number of common shares outstanding by the price per common share as of March 31.

you must determine which one will best meet the needs of the fast-paced personal communications and computing market (see summary of strengths and weaknesses below). You tell your senior executives that you will make a final decision within the month.

Alternative	Strength	Weakness
Three Levels of Employees	High Commitment and Productivity of Inner Core	Demotivation of Employees Outside the Inner Core
Employee Contracting	Elimination of Bureaucractic Hierarchies	Potential for Anarchy and Destructive Chaos
Competence Centers and Business Processes	Effectiveness of Employee Training and Deployment	Inefficiency due to Movement Between Centers and Processes

- *If you decide to create three levels of employees with an inner core of highly productive people, turn to Chapter 63.*

- *If you prefer the employee contracting option, turn to Chapter 64.*

- *If you would rather install competence centers and business processes, turn to Chapter 65.*

When you announce your decision, Bob Kiechel and Karen Walsh approve wholeheartedly and tell you they relish trying this radical new organization approach. Certainly, you think to yourself, these two senior executives deserve a place in the inner core. But what about the others? Hal McPhee and Morris Strandmeyer seem particularly skeptical. Maybe they are not candidates for the inner core.

Now you move quickly to implement the initial stages of this new form of organization. To assist you, you engage the management consulting firm, the Hay Group, to adapt their compensation, decision-making and responsibility-level classification methods for categorizing employees to your new philosophy. As you bring them up to speed on your thinking (of course, you require them to sign a nondisclosure agreement), you feel heartened by their enthusiasm for your experiment.

Within a few short weeks, the Hay Group consultants, along with internal CyTech teams, have begun interviewing all employees in the company, using a sophisticated assessment instrument to determine: (1) the alignment between their current jobs at CyTech and their psychological and personality profiles, (2) the

63

CREATING THREE LEVELS OF EMPLOYEES

balance between personal and professional accomplishment in their lives, (3) the spiritual well-being of each employee as determined by relative peace of mind, confidence, contentment with the course of their lives, and (4) the record of demonstrated performance and contribution to the goals and purposes of the company. They also weigh numerous other items, including education, competence, potential, and ability, and they evaluate each individual in terms of his or her level of talent, motivation, ambition, desire, and determination to succeed in personal and professional pursuits.

At the same time, the marketplace turns upside down as three foreign competitors launch a price war that engulfs the entire industry. However, you refuse to let this turn of events halt work on the new organizational thrust. Instead, you charge Morris Strandmeyer and Nan Thurow to reduce manufacturing and operating costs dramatically so John Solo and Bob Kiechel can fulfill customer demand at under-$500 prices. Your unwavering commitment to the future inspires your senior team and people throughout the organization.

Six months later, the company's current 30,000 employees have undergone the initial assessment process and have been categorized in one of the three groupings: the traditional organization, the experimental band, and the inner core. People who scored a high level of alignment between their psychological profiles and their current responsibilities at CyTech, who exhibited well-balanced lifestyles, high levels of fulfillment and spiritual well-being, and track records of impressive performance at CyTech fell into the inner core.

Every member of your senior executive team made it into the inner core, with the exception of Hal McPhee, your chief financial officer, who scored low on lifestyle and spiritual well-being issues and clearly possesses a number of frustrations with his job. Of CyTech's 30,000 employees, 2,800 move into the inner core, with almost 16,000 in the experimental band, and more than 11,200 in the traditional organization.

With the assessment complete, you move quickly to establish management structures for each of the bands. Anyone in the inner core will share management responsibility and enjoy maximum flexibility within the organization, whereas those in the experimental band will operate under a slightly more structured process-oriented approach, and those in the traditional organization will work within a more hierarchical framework. The latter are primarily involved in support service activities.

You then launch a massive communications campaign designed to inform everyone throughout the company about the new organizational philosophy and the enhanced opportunity for people to move at their own speed and according to their own preferences to maximize their own contribution, fulfillment, and financial well-being, coupled with the performance of the company. You take pains to stress the increased opportunities, freedom, and flexibility that this new categorization can offer everyone in the organization. With specific help from Bob Kiechel and Karen Walsh, you develop a clear path for individuals to move from one category to the next.

You purposely spend the majority of your time with the core inner group, asking those with management responsibility for the other two groups of employees to encourage individuals to move into the inner core group as quickly as possible.

Most of CyTech's business process activities continue as before, with emphasis on cutting costs, but the added dimension of the three levels of employees stimulates problem solving and productivity gains beyond your expectations. While Hal McPhee complains that you've created unnecessary confusion by setting up different classes of people within the organization, raising artificial boundaries and barriers between them, you discover quite the opposite. In fact, those in the inner core swiftly become symbols and models throughout the organization. Their general balance and spiritual well-being and alignment with what they're doing and their increasing levels of fulfillment and satisfaction and contribution become beacons for the myriad people in the organization yearning for successful advancement.

You do experience a high turnover in the traditional organizational group as many people look for a different environment in which they will feel more comfortable, but you use this opportunity to develop a new approach to hiring that will attract people eager to join the core inner group.

Within a few months, the productivity of those in the inner core continues to climb at an amazing rate as they unleash their power to get results, pursuing creative initiatives that reduce costs, streamline operations and stimulate sales. Propelled by their energy, CyTech introduces new lower-cost versions of the *PowerBase,* at prices under $400, which enables CyTech to seize the lead position in the price war. Competition furiously continues in the industry, but you believe that your new approach to organization will allow CyTech to leapfrog any and all competitors.

You complete your second year as CEO of CyTech with sales reaching $10 billion, and the stock price climbing to $62 per share, as shown in the accompanying table on the following page.

Selected Financial and Stock Information
(Dollars in millions, except stock price in actual dollars)

	Year ended March 31	
	2nd Year	1st Year
Sales	$10,188	$6,496
Profits	509	390
Profits as a % of:		
Sales	5%	6%
Assets	8%	9%
Common Equity*	16%	18%
Market Value**	15,841	8,734
Stock Price	62 ⅛	34 ¼

* Total stockholders' equity includes capital stock, surplus, and retained earnings at the company's year end. For purposes of determining profits as a percent of common stockholders' equity, all preferred stock is excluded.

** Calculated by multiplying the number of common shares outstanding by the price per common share as of March 31.

You work hard to nurture people from the experimental band into the inner core, and you charge your training and development people to respond with maximum flexibility to the individual needs of people, grouping them according to similar needs and desires as much as possible.

Just as you're beginning to see rapid movement of people into the inner core group, Motorola drops its prices below $350 in an effort to attack CyTech's leadership position. Scrambling to get costs. down even further so CyTech can reach profitability for its phone-fax-computer at the new below-$350 price, you look to the inner core group of people to do so within weeks. Their response astounds you, as now more than 3,000 inner core employees redesign CyTech's operating system, tapping the resources they need to reengineer key business processes. Almost overnight, a variety of experimental manufacturing processes spring into existence.

Many of these experiments reduce costs and improve the technical merits of CyTech's *PowerBase* products, resulting in the introduction of a whole new generation of phone-fax-computers throughout the year, each at a different price point and each representing a different approach to cost improvement. Some outside analysts initially express dismay over what appears to be runaway flexibility at CyTech, but in every case, product quality surpasses that of previous models. The variety of products available to the marketplace strengthens rather than weakens CyTech's position.

At the end of your third year as CEO, sales jump to $14 billion, with stock trading at $98 per share, as shown below:

Selected Financial and Stock Information
(Dollars in millions, except stock price in actual dollars)

	Year ended March 31	
	3rd Year	2nd Year
Sales	$14,321	$10,188
Profits	859	509
Profits as a % of:		
Sales	6%	5%
Assets	9%	8%
Common Equity*	17%	16%
Market Value**	24,900	15,841
Stock Price	97 $^{11}/_{16}$	62 $^{1}/_{8}$

* Total stockholders' equity includes capital stock, surplus, and retained earnings at the company's year end. For purposes of determining profits as a percent of common stockholders' equity, all preferred stock is excluded.

** Calculated by multiplying the number of common shares outstanding by the price per common share as of March 31.

Clearly, your new organizational philosophy has taken hold beautifully, but you now face another decision point: How many people should move into the inner core? You have discovered the inner core attracts people, especially new hires, so much they will move heaven and earth to join that group.

However, this welcomed trend poses a serious dilemma. Should CyTech attempt to move all of its people into the inner core, or should it maintain the three original groupings to protect the integrity of the inner core and prevent it from getting watered down? Already you have received reports of individuals moving into the inner core without having developed the necessary inner core attributes. The pressure to make such a move has become so great that individuals have figured out ways around the assessment system and have entered the inner core before they're really ready to work there. You ask Bob Kiechel if you should tighten the screws. "Perhaps," he says, "but on the other hand, if people believe that it is too difficult to enter into the inner core, they will cease to feel motivated to do so and may either leave the organization or fall to even lower levels of productivity."

Just as you're grappling with this decision, another major problem erupts as you learn that a group of almost two hundred former CyTech employees has filed a class action suit against CyTech for discriminatory employment practices. Applying their own analysis of the inner core group, they claim to have proven that CyTech's process favors certain types of individuals with certain types of educational backgrounds, to the detriment of minorities.

You see several alternatives: (1) you can heed the lawsuit and work to move everyone in the organization into the inner core group; (2) you can ignore the law suit and maintain the three levels of employees indefinitely; (3) you can try to deflect the lawsuit by abandoning your philosophy but actively relying on the inner core to form your management structure for the future; (4) you can hire outside experts, including legal counsel and management consultants to guide you through the maze; (5) or you can do nothing, waiting to see what occurs naturally over the course of the coming year.

- *If you choose to make the inner core available to every employee of CyTech, turn to Chapter 66.*

- *If you decide to maintain the three bands of employees in order to protect the integrity of the inner core, turn to Chapter 67.*

- *If you decide to back off your current organizational thrust and return to a more traditional organizational form, relying on the inner core as your key managers in the future, turn to Chapter 68.*

- *If you decide to hire outside experts, including legal advisers, human resource specialists, and management consultants to work through the maze brought on by the lawsuit, turn to Chapter 69.*

- *If you decide to do nothing and wait to see what the next twelve months will bring, turn to Chapter 70.*

This decision disappoints everyone on your senior executive team except Nan Thurow, who loves the idea. Individual contracts will, she agrees, promote the sort of freedom that should characterize new organizational forms. You move into action quickly by asking your training and development people and human resources de-

64

partment to develop a general employee contract based on your goal of unleashing individual talent and fulfilling individual desires consistent with CyTech's business goals. You ask Nan Thurow to identify the major processes within the company and to work with CyTech's current directors (the level below vice presidents) to identify managers who might oversee various facilities or offices.

Within a matter of weeks, Nan Thurow defines CyTech's major processes using the process-mapping technique developed at General Electric. She comes up with a list of potential location managers who will monitor contract fulfillment in each geographical location, just

BASING THE ORGANIZATION ON INDIVIDUAL CONTRACTS

as your human resource and training and development people complete an initial draft of the new individual contract, which outlines expected results, anticipated timetable, team and process assignments, and budgeted resources.

After appointing Nan Thurow COO under the new organizational scheme, you reassign the other five executives on your senior team and an additional nine directors to head the fourteen processes. You also promote six middle managers to serve as regional executives to whom the location managers will report.

The new organization sets aside all current compensation methods as each employee enters into a contract with one of the newly

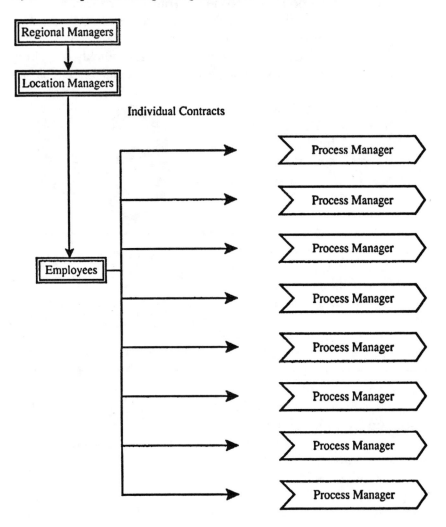

designated five hundred officers. To speed this process, all individuals with the title of director and above (that is, vice presidents, directors, and senior vice presidents) become corporate officers capable of contracting with associates throughout the organization.

In the midst of all this activity, three foreign competitors, two Japanese and a German firm, thrust the entire industry into a massive price war, with the price of phone-fax-computers dropping below $500. With this shocking development in the marketplace, which occurs two to three years earlier than you expected, you wonder whether you should continue with your organizational vision for the future or put your efforts on hold while you guide CyTech through this crisis.

The advantage of continuing with the organizational change agenda lies in its promise of better future results. However, doing so could offer a disadvantage of lost time as the company battles to work out all the difficulties and confusion a top-to-bottom reorganization entails.

On the other hand, if you focus strictly on getting costs down so that CyTech can show a profit at the below-$500 price level for its *PowerBases,* you must surely set aside the distraction of the organization change for the moment. On the down side, such a move would communicate a lack of confidence on your part in the sweeping changes you've undertaken. People might think that when the going gets tough, you'll resort to the old ways of doing business. Why should they embrace the new organizational environment if it doesn't work in a crisis? On the up side, you might lose the price war if you don't bring all resources to bear on it at the exclusion of all else.

However, before you can fully consider this decision, Hal McPhee, John Solo, and Morris Strandmeyer inform you they're leaving to launch a new joint venture between Apple Computer and Microsoft. You beg them to stay, but they decry your new organizational approach, accusing you of purposely cutting them out of the decision making with your current course of action.

After several days of discussion, McPhee, Solo, and Strandmeyer convince you to abandon your present course of action and select their preference, competence centers and business processes. In exchange for such a reversal of direction, the three executives will remain at CyTech.

Relieved that you could prevent three key executives from leaving, you quickly shift gears to implement the new alternative. Thankfully, Nan Thurow supports you 100 percent, even though she favored the individual contract approach. She recognizes the importance of keeping McPhee, Solo, and Strandmeyer.

- *Turn to Chapter 65, Establishing Competence Centers and Business Processes.*

The fact that the majority of your senior executive team voted for this alternative strongly influences your decision to establish competence centers and business processes as the main thrust of the new organizational scheme. The three who voted for this alternative—McPhee, Solo, and Strandmeyer—will be crucial to CyTech's future success, regardless of the company's organizational direction. Pleased with the full support of McPhee, Solo, and Strandmeyer, you award them responsibility for all the company's business processes. In turn, you charge Karen Walsh, Nan Thurow, and Bob Kiechel with responsibility for managing the competence centers, a move they applaud with excitement and enthusiasm.

While the scope of this shake-up surprises the board, they agree with your argument that the three executives you have selected to focus on business processes can accomplish the task most quickly, while the three chosen to manage the competence centers should certainly do that job most ably. In the end, the board comes to accept your program because you've assigned the division of labor so wisely. It all makes sense on paper.

65

ESTABLISHING COMPETENCE CENTERS AND BUSINESS PROCESSES

In the weeks and months that follow, you set about obliterating all of CyTech's old hierarchical reporting relationships. By July 1, everyone in the organization has become a temporary employee in one of ten business processes: Research and Innovation; New Product Development; Procurement; Production; Marketing; Sales; Distribution; Customer Service; Administrative Services; or Strategy Formulation.

While it will take months to get the competence centers fully functioning, you quickly turn CyTech's major training and development facility into the competence hub for the organization, designating other locations throughout CyTech's far-flung facilities as remote competence centers. Immediately, you give people the opportunity to move in and out of business processes or back into more intensive competence development. Happily, the three executives you have placed over the business processes begin quickly turning nonperforming employees back to the competence centers. Doing so clearly addresses performance problems more quickly and more effectively than under the old system. As you had hoped, people rise to the challenge, accepting new responsibility for the development of their careers and acquiring needed competence and skills to move their careers forward.

By October the organization is humming along with unprecedented efficiency and effectiveness. However, you must accomplish much more, ironing out all the bugs in the new system of competence centers and business processes, such as balancing the flow between centers and processes that naturally occur as the new organizational form takes hold. In the midst of all this activity, three foreign competitors throw a major wrench in the works by engulfing the industry in a price war that drops the prices of phone-fax-computers below $500.

With this new development in the marketplace coming two to three years earlier than you expected, you now wonder whether to put your organizational development efforts on hold while you address this crisis, or to continue building the competence centers and making temporary employment in the business processes work even better.

You know CyTech must cut its operating costs substantially in order to make a profit at prices below $500. Can the new organizational philosophy and environment enable people to meet the challenge? Will it overburden them? As you weigh your options, you feel pressure from the board to set aside the new organizational initiatives, at least temporarily. However, your six direct reports send you the opposite message: "Proceed at full energy with the new perspective."

As you juggle these two views, the year comes to an end with sales reaching $9 billion, as shown in the accompanying table.

Selected Financial and Stock Information
(Dollars in millions, except stock price in actual dollars)

	Year ended March 31	
	2nd Year	1st Year
Sales	$9,402	$6,496
Profits	470	390
Profits as a % of:		
Sales	5%	6%
Assets	8%	9%
Common Equity*	16%	18%
Market Value**	13,206	8,734
Stock Price	51 $^{13}\!/_{16}$	34 $^{1}\!/_{4}$

* Total stockholders' equity includes capital stock, surplus, and retained earnings at the company's year end. For purposes of determining profits as a percent of common stockholders' equity, all preferred stock is excluded.

** Calculated by multiplying the number of common shares outstanding by the price per common share as of March 31.

Early in April of your third year as CEO, you finally must decide whether or not to move forward with the new organizational vision. You carefully weigh the choices.

- *If you decide to continue actively and aggressively implementing the competence centers and the process groups, turn to Chapter 71.*

- *If you want to put all organizational development on hold while waging the price war, turn to Chapter 72.*

When Karen Walsh convinces you that CyTech should afford every employee the opportunity to move into the core, you immediately gear up to do just that, focusing all the efforts of human resources, training, and development on preparing people throughout the organization to enter the inner core.

On the plus side, this decision provides a defense against the current lawsuit, which could represent the mere tip of an iceberg if you continue with the three original groups. In fact, your corporate general counsel believes that a demonstrated effort to give all employees the opportunity to become part of the inner core would undermine the logic behind the lawsuit.

You establish a target of three years for getting everyone into the inner core, with large groups of CyTech employees transferring into the inner core during each of those years. To support this goal, you hire one hundred new human resource counselors over the next six months, each of whom will prepare people throughout the organization to work on issues of psychological-type identification, alignment with job goals, development of balance between personal and professional life, spiritual development, and the attainment of a high level of fulfillment and satisfaction.

66

MOVING EVERY EMPLOYEE INTO THE INNER CORE

The impact of this move on the organization astonishes you as people throughout the organization seize this opportunity to strengthen their lives and become more fulfilled both at work and at home. However, in the midst of all this, Motorola introduces a voice-operated phone-fax-computer earlier than expected. The new machine takes the market by storm, and CyTech simply cannot respond swiftly enough to the competitive challenge. You quickly realize that while the company has grown in satisfying directions, it has, in the process, taken its eye off the marketplace and its customers.

All of the recent organizational initiatives have prepared people to move into the inner core and accomplish spectacular results in the future, but all that potential could go to waste if it does not allow CyTech to introduce its own version of the voice-operated phone-fax-computer.

Once again, you turn to those already in the inner core, relying heavily on Karen Walsh in particular to round up those people with product-development experience and challenge them to do whatever it takes to get a voice-operated phone-fax-computer to market.

Karen reports that the core R&D people have been working on a variety of projects during the last 18 months, but have not given a voice-operated phone-fax-computer top priority. Instead, they have targeted enhancements such as user creation and production of multimedia and high-definition display screens over the existing phone-fax-computer.

When you lay down the challenge of developing a voice-operated *PowerBase,* you come up against the fact that people in the core R&D group no longer respond to commands from the top because the new organizational philosophy has so strongly emphasized personalized directions, which management cannot easily shift. While you did not anticipate this down-side to the new organizational form, you reaffirm in your belief that in the long run people should chart their own course without undue influence from competitor moves. The current crisis, far from eroding your confidence, rekindles your faith that CyTech's people will respond to customers and developments in the marketplace. Karen Walsh supports this view, saying, "Our people will rise to the challenge. They'll see the trend themselves. After all, trends always guide our R&D projects."

You tell your board of directors that CyTech will introduce its own voice-operated machine within 18 months and that meanwhile other enhancements already underway will fuel the company's growth and profitability. Unfortunately, the board cannot easily accept your position as the stock price drops to below $50 per share and sales at the end of your fourth year as CEO plunge to $11.5 billion, as shown in the accompanying table.

Selected Financial and Stock Information
(Dollars in millions, except stock price in actual dollars)

	Year ended March 31	
	4th Year	3rd Year
Sales	$11,561	$14,321
Profits	462	859
Profits as a % of:		
Sales	4%	6%
Assets	7%	9%
Common Equity*	13%	17%
Market Value**	12,464	24,900
Stock Price	48 $\frac{7}{8}$	97 $\frac{11}{16}$

* Total stockholders' equity includes capital stock, surplus, and retained earnings at the company's year end. For purposes of determining profits as a percent of common stockholders' equity, all preferred stock is excluded.

** Calculated by multiplying the number of common shares outstanding by the price per common share as of March 31.

However, remaining steadfast in your convictions, which has removed the threat of the lawsuit, you continue moving people into the inner core, asking them to focus on those initiatives that will bring back CyTech's technological leadership. You also continue pushing for cost improvements as the price of non-voice-operated phone-fax-computers settles below $300 per unit.

As the next year unfolds, you discover that pushing people into the inner core faster than they should go there damages the productivity of those people already working in the inner core. An alarming number of misjudgments, misappropriation of funds, and misallocation of resources occurs throughout the company as too many people obtain too much freedom without the perspective and the attributes you originally intended those in the inner core to exhibit. Some workers lack the strategic savvy to properly deploy readily accessible resources, while others fail to assume accountability for their choices or prove unable to make good judgments about people. As a result, sales continue to decline over the course of the year and new-product introductions get bogged down as the inner core grows paralyzed by virtual anarchy within its ranks.

A few months before the conclusion of your fifth year as CEO,

Karen Walsh leaves for Motorola, abandoning ship just when the company needs her most. The board asks for your resignation. As you leave CyTech, you wish you'd done things differently.

- *In real life you might have produced better results with this option, but the author believes this option was doomed to fail from the beginning. If you want to consider other alternatives you could have selected, turn to one of the following:*

    Chapter 67, Maintaining the Three Groupings of Employees Indefinitely;

    Chapter 68, Backing Off by Disbanding the Inner Core;

    Chapter 69, Hiring Outside Legal, Human Resource, and Management Experts; or

    Chapter 70, Doing Nothing.

- *If you want to begin fresh on a new decision-making track, pick one of the following:*

    Chapter 2, Building a Classic Innovative Organization

    Chapter 14, Developing a Synthesis of Best Practices;

    Chapter 26, Imbuing the Culture with Empowerment and Accountability;

    Chapter 38, Pursuing a Work Team Approach; or

    Chapter 50, Reengineering Work Processes.

Given the diversity of human beings and the range of their inherent abilities, you decide you must allow for that fact by maintaining the three original groupings of people. One group will accommodate people coming in and trying to determine exactly how they're going to contribute to the organization, identifying their talents and capabilities and working out the balance in their lives. The second grouping will serve those experimenting with different ways to develop their sense of how they want their lives to unfold and how they expect to contribute to CyTech's goals. And the third grouping (inner core) will unleash the power of people who have aligned "who they are" and "what they do" and have balanced their lives spiritually, mentally, and physically.

You know that this course will create legal problems, but you welcome the chance to defend your philosophy, even in a court of law. You believe so deeply in your ideas, you feel confident that you can demonstrate to any body that participation in the inner core should be restricted to those who have won membership through merit and performance. Bob Kiechel's total support helps cement commitment to this decision among the rest of the senior team.

You set to work immediately, demonstrating with compelling examples how the high performance of the inner core can drive the company to unparalleled heights as ever greater freedoms and opportunities flow from that high performance and vice versa. Performance begets freedom, and freedom, in turn, heightens performance. No frivolous lawsuit can dispute that equation. You've

67

MAINTAINING THE THREE GROUPINGS OF PEOPLE INDEFINITELY

embarked on a journey of radical change and you fully expect detractors and second-guesses, but time, you know, will prove you right.

In the months that follow, the distinctions among the three groupings of employees becomes even more pronounced throughout the organization. CyTech's legal department works hard to communicate to every individual that he or she can move toward the inner core at any time, regardless of his or her tenure with the company, regardless of his or her skills, and regardless of his or her current pay level.

You make it clear in your own communications to employees that these groupings do not erect barriers that keep people out or visit rewards to a small elite group. Rather, they put in place a system within which anyone who performs can gain ever more freedom to accomplish even more. In a speech to all employees, you say, "Getting to the inner core requires a price, but getting there also offers great benefits and rewards that could not come about without the associated higher level of productivity. Creating the opportunity for people to arrive at a point where they can experience the highest possible productivity, get properly paid for it, and win additional freedom to seek new opportunities, that's what this company's all about."

You tell people throughout the organization in meeting after meeting as you travel around the world to all of CyTech's facilities, "Opening the inner core indiscriminately to all people throughout the organization without establishing the necessary requirements and demands would destroy the inner core's ability to accomplish more. If you want to become a producer at CyTech, you can do so any time, any place, throughout this organization. The company has drawn you a map, but only you can make the journey."

Boarding a plane in Tokyo, you get word that Motorola will introduce a voice-operated phone-fax-computer within the next few weeks. Though you hadn't expected this development so soon, you turn to your inner core of people, numbering nearly 4,000 now, to tackle the challenge of getting CyTech's own voice-operated machine to market ahead of schedule.

You know that R&D has not made a voice-operated machine a top priority, choosing instead to add the creation and production of multimedia and high-definition display screens to existing products, but you also know that CyTech must respond to this development in the marketplace because it will no doubt take the market by storm. To speed the company's response, you hire the executive recruiting firm of Korn/Ferry to find a group of R&D people somewhere in the world, from one or several companies, who understand voice-operating technology and can add that knowledge to CyTech's inner core.

You carefully outline CyTech's organizational philosophy over the last 18 months to the Korn/Ferry recruiters, emphasizing the assessment the company uses to identify people in the inner core. Understanding the urgency of your need, the executive recruiters work diligently to locate 12 candidates, from which you hire 6 to form the nucleus of CyTech's new voice-operated-technology R&D core team. As the new hires enter the organization, they respond enthusiastically to the unprecedented levels of resources, and they quickly chart a course to meet Motorola's challenge.

Strengthened by individuals in the experimental band who have been striving to gain admission into the inner core, the new R&D team develops a voice-operated prototype within two months. After debugging the machine and making necessary improvements, the team enables CyTech to introduce its voice-operated *PowerBase 10* just three weeks after Motorola introduces its own version.

As CyTech and Motorola battle for market share in the new voice-operated market segment, which quickly grows larger than the non-voice-operated market, you witness the real strength of CyTech's inner core. In less than 90 days, the voice-operated R&D team, having spontaneously grown to 24 people working on three different projects, introduces an upgraded *PowerBase* 100 with a dramatically expanded vocabulary and a much more sensitive voice-detecting mechanism. The *PowerBase 100* immediately dominates the market and CyTech's sales soar to $17 billion, with stock jumping to $124 per share, as shown on the following page.

Fortune magazine, describing you as "the mastermind behind the premier twenty-first century company," publishes a cover story that captures the sentiment of the board of directors, they appoint you chairman of the board and ask you to begin grooming a replacement for yourself over the next year. About this same time, CyTech's attorneys win the original lawsuit, establishing a clear precedent for three levels of employees and a company's right to

Selected Financial and Stock Information
(Dollars in millions, except stock price in actual dollars)

	Year ended March 31	
	4th Year	3rd Year
Sales	$17,085	$14,321
Profits	1,196	859
Profits as a % of:		
Sales	7%	6%
Assets	11%	9%
Common Equity*	22%	17%
Market Value**	31,684	24,900
Stock Price	124 ¼	97 ¹¹⁄₁₆

* Total stockholders' equity includes capital stock, surplus, and retained earnings at the company's year end. For purposes of determining profits as a percent of common stockholders' equity, all preferred stock is excluded.

** Calculated by multiplying the number of common shares outstanding by the price per common share as of March 31.

protect an inner core of high producers with extraordinary freedoms and opportunities won by high productivity and performance.

Over the next several months, you prepare Bob Kiechel to take your place as CEO, so you can turn your attention to strategic acquisitions and the continuing development of CyTech's unique organizational perspective. By the end of your fifth year as CEO, just as you're preparing to install Kiechel as your heir, sales reach $20 billion, an unimaginable milestone five years earlier. See table on opposite page.

You eagerly look forward to your new job and the next wave of advancement at CyTech. You also take great pleasure in seeing the net value of your stock options rise above $500 million. Congratulations! This represents a stunningly successful end of a decision-making track, but you can keep playing the game, if you wish.

Selected Financial and Stock Information
(Dollars in millions, except stock price in actual dollars)

	Year ended March 31	
	5th Year	4th Year
Sales	$20,196	$17,085
Profits	1,616	1,196
Profits as a % of:		
Sales	8%	7%
Assets	12%	11%
Common Equity*	25%	22%
Market Value**	39,971	31,684
Stock Price	156 $\frac{3}{4}$	124 $\frac{1}{4}$

* Total stockholders' equity includes capital stock, surplus, and retained earnings at the company's year end. For purposes of determining profits as a percent of common stockholders' equity, all preferred stock is excluded.
** Calculated by multiplying the number of common shares outstanding by the price per common share as of March 31.

- *If you want to compare how the results of your last five years of organizational decision making stack up against the other positive outcomes in The Organization Game, turn to Chapter 78.*

- *If you want to explore other alternatives on this track turn to one of the following:*
  Chapter 64, Basing the Organization on Individual Contracts;
  Chapter 65, Establishing Competence Centers and Business Process;
  Chapter 66, Moving Every Employee into the Inner Core;
  Chapter 68, Backing Off by Disbanding the Inner Core;
  Chapter 69, Hiring Outside Legal, Human Resource, and Management Experts;

> *Chapter 70, Doing Nothing;*
> *Chapter 71, Continuing to Implement the Competence Centers and Business Processes;*
> *Chapter 72, Setting Aside Your Organizational Initiatives to Focus on the Price War Crisis;*
> *Chapter 73, Moving the Competence Centers Toward More Specialization; or*
> *Chapter 74, Moving the Competence Centers Toward More Generalization.*

- *If you wish to explore another decision-making track, select one of the following:*

> *Chapter 2, Building a Classic Innovative Organization*
> *Chapter 14, Developing a Synthesis of Best Practices;*
> *Chapter 26, Imbuing the Culture with Empowerment and Accountability;*
> *Chapter 38, Pursuing A Work Team Approach; or*
> *Chapter 50, Reengineering Work Processes.*

Convinced not only that you can never win the current lawsuit but that CyTech has already gained great benefit from having identified over 3,000 inner core people who can serve as management building blocks for the future, you quickly disband the three classifications of employees and work with your human resources people to make sure the 3,000 plus inner core people move onto a special high-potential development track within the company.

Karen Walsh objects to this move, saying, "I can't believe you'd buckle under to external pressure, especially from a bunch of lawyers!" Kiechel and Thurow agree. The others seem ambivalent. But you disregard Karen's reaction, chalking it up to naivete. A lawsuit really could do more damage than she realizes, putting off customers, future employees, and the business press.

You move forward with the plan to deploy the core people over the next several years with a program for grooming them as the key managers of the future. You ask Nan Thurow to oversee the development of a program for training and tracking these individuals and, in several meetings with the full senior executive team, she parcels out assignments for each of your direct reports.

68

BACKING OFF BY DISBANDING THE INNER CORE

Because you believe the lawyers for the plaintiffs in the lawsuit will use CyTech's change in policy as evidence of wrongdoing, you decide to settle the lawsuit out of court for $20 million. Four new lawsuits emerge in the wake of this settlement, but your attorneys settle these as well. It appears you have brought the crisis to a successful conclusion.

As you cast your gaze back to the marketplace and CyTech's new-product strategy, you discover that Motorola plans to introduce a voice-operated phone-fax-computer in three weeks. This startling news comes many months earlier than CyTech's competitive intelligence had originally suggested, and CyTech stands at least a year away from introducing its own version of the machine. But you challenge your executive team to focus the entire organization on this challenge.

To your dismay, you find that disbanding and dispersing the inner core of employees has pleased most everybody in the company except members of the inner core itself—whose morale has been shattered. Many of them have begun looking for jobs outside CyTech, and several of the most promising have already left. Ironically, the most gifted engineer in the area of voice-recognition accepts a job at Motorola. In her exit interview, she tells Bob Kiechel, "When the company made the decision to disband the inner core, I couldn't help thinking of how John Galt felt in Ayn Rand's *Atlas Shrugged.* The company has shortchanged the real producers by catering to society's needs."

When the Motorola voice-operated phone-fax-computer hits the market, it wins immediate market share, causing CyTech's sales to plummet and the stock price to drop to $43 per share by the end of your fourth year as CEO, as shown in the accompanying table.

Selected Financial and Stock Information
(Dollars in millions, except stock price in actual dollars)

	Year ended March 31	
	4th Year	3rd Year
Sales	$11,481	$14,321
Profits	230	859
Profits as a % of:		
Sales	2%	6%
Assets	3%	9%
Common Equity*	6%	17%
Market Value**	10,996	24,900
Stock Price	43 $\frac{1}{8}$	97 $\frac{11}{16}$

* Total stockholders' equity includes capital stock, surplus, and retained earnings at the company's year end. For purposes of determining profits as a percent of common stockholders' equity, all preferred stock is excluded.

** Calculated by multiplying the number of common shares outstanding by the price per common share as of March 31.

The chairman of CyTech's board tells you it's time to turn the reins over to someone else, suggesting that the fiasco over the three levels of employees created too much baggage for you to continue operating successfully as CEO of the company. You argue your case but soon realize that you cannot change his mind. You resign.

- *In real life you might have avoided this outcome, but the author believes this choice made little sense from the beginning. To see why, you may choose one of the other options:*

  Chapter 66, Moving Every Employee into the Inner Core;

  Chapter 67, Maintaining the Three Groupings of People Indefinitely;

  Chapter 69, Hiring Outside Legal, Human Resource, and Management Expert; or

  Chapter 70, Doing Nothing.

- *If you want to begin a new decision-making track, turn to one of the following:*

  Chapter 2, Building a Classic Innovative Organization

  Chapter 14, Developing a Synthesis of Best Practices;

  Chapter 26, Imbuing the Culture with Empowerment and Accountability;

  Chapter 38, Pursuing a Work-Team Approach; or

  Chapter 50, Reengineering Work Processes.

Soon after you announce your decision to bring in an outside team of legal, human resource, and management experts to handle the lawsuit and help you decide whether to continue with the company's three levels of employees, CyTech's people begin citing this move as a sign of weakness and uncertainty at the top. Since you expected this reaction, you do not let it dissuade you because you firmly believe you need the advice of experts to help you make crucial decisions about the company's future. Oddly, just as people begin losing their confidence in you, you begin questioning the allegiance of your senior executive team, especially Strandmeyer and McPhee, and their ability to do anything but represent their own limited points of view.

It takes much longer than you expected for the legal, human resource, and management experts to study the situation and devise a set of alternatives. In the meantime, Motorola introduces a voice-operated phone-fax-computer much earlier than expected, taking the market by storm and strongly eroding CyTech's sales and profits. Still months away from introducing your own voice-operated phone-fax-computer, you strive to buoy up sales of existing *PowerBases*, but the additional expenditures on marketing and sales only cut into profits. CyTech's stock price drops precipitously to $22 per share as you conclude your fourth year as CEO. See table on page 318.

In an attempt to win back the confidence of CyTech's board of directors and employees, you take the alternatives flowing out of

69

HIRING OUTSIDE LEGAL, HUMAN RESOURCE AND MANAGEMENT EXPERTS

Selected Financial and Stock Information
(Dollars in millions, except stock price in actual dollars)

	Year ended March 31	
	4th Year	3rd Year
Sales	$10,289	$14,321
Profits	103	859
Profits as a % of:		
Sales	1%	6%
Assets	3%	9%
Common Equity*	5%	17%
Market Value** 5,674	24,900	
Stock Price	22 ¼	97 ¹¹⁄₁₆

* Total stockholders' equity includes capital stock, surplus, and retained earnings at the company's year end. For purposes of determining profits as a percent of common stockholders' equity, all preferred stock is excluded.

** Calculated by multiplying the number of common shares outstanding by the price per common share as of March 31.

the analysis of the legal, human resource, and management experts into an open forum for decision making. For many members of the board and employees, this is just one more sign of your lack of leadership, representing the final straw that leads to your eventual ouster. The board begins looking for your replacement, someone that can meet the challenge laid down by Motorola and stop the spiraling decline at CyTech.

It turns out that Bob Kiechel, frustrated with the paralysis that has seized CyTech in recent months, had already gone behind your back to the board of directors, convincing them that he could marshall a group of people to develop a prototype of a CyTech voice-operated machine within weeks. In a sudden move, the board replaces you. Ironically, the board justifies its action on the basis of Bob's belief that the three-tiered organizational approach with three different groups and a vibrant inner core should continue guiding CyTech's future, regardless of the lawsuit. In his first week as CEO, Bob dismisses the outside group of experts, announces his intention to maintain the inner core, and vows to defend these moves, even if he must do so in a court of law.

You scoff at Kiechel's optimism, but several months later, you read in *The Wall Street Journal* about CyTech's comeback driven by "a new and improved voice-operated phone-fax-computer and an amazingly innovative organizational approach." Bob Kiechel gets all the credit, while you get only a chance to rethink your last decision as CEO.

- *You might have succeeded with this choice in real life, but in this game, you've reached a bitter conclusion. If you want to try your hand at reversing this outcome, turn to:*

   Chapter 66, Moving Every Employee into the Inner Core;

   Chapter 67, Keeping the Three Groupings of People Indefinitely;

   Chapter 68, Backing Off by Disbanding the Inner Core; or

   Chapter 70, Doing Nothing.

- *If you would like to embark on a new decision-making track, start anew at one of the following:*

   Chapter 2, Building a Classic Innovative Organization

   Chapter 14, Developing a Synthesis of Best Practices;

   Chapter 26, Imbuing the Culture with Empowerment and Accountability;

   Chapter 38, Pursuing a Work Team Approach; or

   Chapter 50, Reengineering Work Processes.

Your decision to do nothing but wait out the crisis astounds your senior executive team, and McPhee complains to the board of directors. You slowly recognize yourself that doing nothing makes little sense. What were you thinking? Have you grown too weary to fight? Should you retire early? Despite these troublesome questions, you conclude that waiting for a few months can't hurt because the company has been turning in a steady performance and more time will give you more data on which to act.

70

DOING NOTHING

Fortunately for you, however, Nan Thurow, your senior vice president of worldwide operations, invites you to lunch and carefully and gently tells you that she thinks you've made a big mistake. "Waiting to see how the lawsuit turns out won't prove you were right or wrong about the three groupings," she advises. "The three employee groupings are a brilliant organizational form, even though I didn't think at first they would work. You simply can't let your good work stagnate. You must continue forward. If you don't, you ought to step aside and let one of us continue."

You know Nan wants the best for everyone, so you listen closely as she continues, "I've been frank with you because I care about you and this company. I have always admired you for doing what you think is best for all of us, and I don't want to see you leave under this cloud." Finally convinced that Nan has put the situation in its proper perspective, you take her advice and choose one of the other alternatives that you had considered earlier.

- *If you want to move forward by making the inner core available to every employee, turn to Chapter 66.*

- *If you decide to maintain the three bands of employees in order to protect the integrity of the inner core, turn to Chapter 67.*

- *If you wish to back off your current organizational thrust and return to a more traditional organizational form, tapping the inner core for future key managers, turn to Chapter 68.*

- *If you would rather hire a group of outside experts, including legal advisers, human resource specialists, and management consultants to work through the maze brought on by the lawsuit, turn to Chapter 69.*

Once you make this decision, it turns out that continuing to stress competence centers and business process groups with the temporary services approach does allow CyTech to find new ways to reduce costs in all aspects of the procurement, inventory, manufacturing, packaging, and shipping processes. Morris Strandmeyer, John Solo, and Hal McPhee perform brilliantly as they administer CyTech's redefined business processes, while Bob Kiechel, Karen Walsh, and Nan Thurow make the competence centers a vital force for change. Using personalized contracts to guide competent people into key business processes, CyTech builds cross-functional teams that address the processes with lightning quickness, breaking down the traditional barriers between functions to create a seamless, continuous flow of work. At the same time, the competence centers beef up their cost-reduction training courses, drawing on the best talent in the country and putting the employees assigned to the various business processes through crash courses. The new organizational philosophy works brilliantly as the company implements a variety of new initiatives for reducing costs, many of which bring about impressive gains.

71

CONTINUING TO IMPLEMENT THE COMPETENCE CENTERS AND BUSINESS PROCESSES

By the end of your third year as CEO, sales reach $12 billion. The stock price jumps to $74 per share and CyTech's profits look healthier than ever. CyTech is clearly winning the price war and emerging as one of the most dominant competitors in the industry, as shown in the following table.

Selected Financial and Stock Information
(Dollars in millions, except stock price in actual dollars)

	Year ended March 31	
	3rd Year	2nd Year
Sales	$11,975	$9,402
Profits	838	470
Profits as a % of:		
Sales	7%	5%
Assets	11%	8%
Common Equity*	21%	16%
Market Value**	18,839	13,206
Stock Price	73 $7/8$	51 $13/16$

* Total stockholders' equity includes capital stock, surplus, and retained earnings at the company's year end. For purposes of determining profits as a percent of common stockholders' equity, all preferred stock is excluded.
** Calculated by multiplying the number of common shares outstanding by the price per common share as of March 31.

People throughout CyTech have become comfortable with the new organizational approach as they see greater clarity in their job purposes and relish the opportunity to move from one temporary assignment to another. They also express a new sense of personal growth and satisfaction as their competence grows and they achieve higher and higher results in the business processes they tackle. Morale climbs to new heights and productivity skyrockets as CyTech prepares to introduce several new *PowerBases* in the next few months with some models selling for below $400. You worry now, however, that the company's preoccupation with cost reduction has made the company too myopic, given rumblings about innovations and technological breakthroughs, particularly from Motorola, which plans to market a voice-operated phone-fax-computer by midyear. Not only must CyTech respond to this challenge, introducing its own version in a timely manner, but the company now faces a larger question: Should the competence centers at CyTech encourage more specialization in a variety of arenas, or should the competence centers stress generalization? The former would create more diversity, but the latter might enable people to transfer more easily from one key process to another.

As you consider these two alternatives and mull over the implications of each, your senior team uses the current challenge to further their own positions. Morris Strandmeyer, John Solo, and Hal McPhee argue for more generalization, while Bob Kiechel, Karen Walsh, and Nan Thurow push for more specialization. The latter group thinks specialization will allow CyTech to address and resolve specific, technical challenges with highly dedicated and trained teams. You, however, think doing so might create too much complexity that would require an inordinate amount of coordination among the specialists.

The former group believes more generalization will enable the company to draw from a larger pool of people who can move to vital business processes as necessary with a better overall picture of what needs to be done. However, you fear that a lack of specialized expertise at critical junctures might thwart solutions to specific, sticky problems.

Given the upcoming challenge of Motorola's voice-operated phone-fax-computer, you must now choose between these two options, both of which seem to make sense.

- *If you decide to move the competence centers toward specialization, turn to Chapter 73.*

- *If you conclude that the competence centers should move toward more generalization, turn to Chapter 74.*

After wrestling with the issue of the price war, you finally decide to table any further development of competence centers and business processes within CyTech until you've resolved this particular crisis. You freeze all movement from competence centers to business processes and *vice versa*. Then you drain the competence centers by assigning everyone into CyTech's business processes, where they will work feverishly on cost reduction until the company has come out a winner. You tell your senior executive and the entire CyTech organization that you will resume the competence centers and business processes program with temporary assignments as soon as the price war passes. You ask Nan Thurow and Morris Strandmeyer, your senior vice president of operations and your vice president of production, to move the organization into a crisis mode focused solely on finding new ways to reduce costs so that CyTech can reach an acceptable level of profitability at unit prices below $500.

The abrupt change in emphasis throws the organization into disarray. Many people conclude that you never really believed with all your heart in the new organizational ap-

72

SETTING ASIDE YOUR ORGANIZATIONAL INITIATIVES TO FOCUS ON THE PRICE WAR CRISIS

proach, and that causes them to lose heart, as well. You can foresee resistance to any future development of the competence centers and business processes, resistance that will set you back to square one if and when CyTech survives the price war. Ironically, your six senior executives increasingly resent your decision to table the new organizational approach, eventually complaining to the board of directors about the high frustration among employees, your ambivalence and, most important, CyTech's increasing vulnerability in the marketplace.

Although your senior executives rarely go out of their way to make contact with the board, in the normal course of business activities they do attend board meetings and the usual social events involving board members that inevitably gives them the opportunity to discuss their views on the company's progress. CFO Hal McPhee argues his views in these settings most vocally, strongly questioning your effectiveness as CEO. Concerned about the circumstances, CyTech's chairman of the board approaches you with the recommendation that Hal McPhee take over as CEO, while you become vice chairman of the board. His rationale: "You've taken CyTech a long way, but we now think it's time for someone else to run the show under your guidance."

You reluctantly accept the change in assignment, though it appears you have been sent out to pasture, largely because of your recent ambivalence regarding CyTech's organizational form. Not surprising, Hal McPhee takes full advantage of the competence centers, the business process groups, and the temporary employment assignments as the means to win the price war. While CyTech's stock price was hovering around $62 per share when you left office as CEO, it climbs to $98 per share by the end of the year under McPhee's aggressive and unwavering leadership. See the table on the accompanying page.

Convinced that you were robbed of your rightful claim to CyTech's success, you begin to look elsewhere for another CEO assignment.

Selected Financial and Stock Information
(Dollars in millions, except stock price in actual dollars)

	Year ended March 31	
	3rd Year	2nd Year
Sales	$11,233	$9,402
Profits	674	470
Profits as a % of:		
Sales	6%	5%
Assets	10%	8%
Common Equity*	19%	16%
Market Value**	25,005	13,206
Stock Price	98 $\frac{1}{16}$	51 $\frac{13}{16}$

* Total stockholders' equity includes capital stock, surplus, and retained earnings at the company's year end. For purposes of determining profits as a percent of common stockholders' equity, all preferred stock is excluded.

** Calculated by multiplying the number of common shares outstanding by the price per common share as of March 31.

- *You might have been able to avoid getting put out to pasture in this scenario, but you did underestimate the negative impact of tabling a substantial shift in organizational approach. If you want to see why the author thinks the other alternative is better, turn to Chapter 71.*

- *If you want to begin a new decision-making track, select one of the following:*

  Chapter 2, Building a Classic Innovative Organization

  Chapter 14, Developing a Synthesis of Best Practices;

  Chapter 26, Imbuing the Organization with Empowerment and Accountability;

  Chapter 38, Pursuing a Work Team Approach; or

  Chapter 50, Reengineering Work Processes.

During your fourth year as CEO, CyTech's emphasis on competence centers and business processes keeps the company at the forefront of the price war. With the crisis abating, you now lay the groundwork for increasing specialization in the competence centers, even though you keep the entire organization waging the price war. By year's end, sales climb to $13 billion, profit grows to 8 percent of sales, and the stock price is $101 per share, as shown in the table on page 332.

As you move the competence centers toward specialization, you and your senior executive team assemble a number of temporarily assigned teams charged with the goal of bringing CyTech's voice-operated phone-fax-computer to the market as quickly as possible. While the idea of a voice-operated phone-fax-computer has attracted media speculation for some time, CyTech has done little real work on it until now. The new specialization can, you think, turn all the speculation into a working prototype within months. With this objective in mind, you ask Hal McPhee to assign temporary work teams to focus on the

73

MOVING THE COMPETENCE CENTERS TOWARD MORE SPECIALIZATION

vocabulary base of the voice-operated machine: one group works on voice sensitivity, another on the transfer of voice sounds to digital output. You also ask John Solo to assign a group to work on the test sequence that every operator who buys a voice-operated machine must perform in order to activate his or her machine. Finally, you urge Morris Strandmeyer to assign one team to design the new look and feel of the voice-operated device and another to incorporate a

Selected Financial and Stock Information
(Dollars in millions, except stock price in actual dollars)

	Year ended March 31	
	4th Year	3rd Year
Sales	$13,832	$11,975
Profits	1,107	838
Profits as a % of:		
Sales	8%	7%
Assets	13%	11%
Common Equity[*]	27%	21%
Market Value[**]	25,786	18,839
Stock Price	101 $\frac{1}{8}$	73 $\frac{7}{8}$

[*] Total stockholders' equity includes capital stock, surplus, and retained earnings at the company's year end. For purposes of determining profits as a percent of common stockholders' equity, all preferred stock is excluded.
[**] Calculated by multiplying the number of common shares outstanding by the price per common share as of March 31.

new high-powered chip to make it all work. Various other temporary work groups begin tackling voice-keyboard transferability, as well as voice-keyboard combination functions. To augment the talent and expertise applied by these special work teams, you ask Bob Kiechel, Karen Walsh, and Nan Thurow to develop parallel competence groups to further the necessary specialized training and resource deployment.

In the weeks and months that follow, each one of CyTech's temporarily assigned teams performs beautifully, drawing upon the increasingly specialized competence centers to reach high levels of productivity. Clear mandates established through their temporary work contracts, focused business process management, and exceptional competence training set the stage for success, but when it comes to pulling all of these specialized teams together to create a working prototype of CyTech's voice-operated machine, you run into a number of problems, such as combining voice recognition with vocabulary management functions, and integrating design and technical requirements, that bog down the process. You work day and night to resolve the problems, but you fail to do so until after the Motorola version has already been on the market for four weeks.

Finally, a full two months after Motorola introduced its machine, CyTech fields its own voice-operated phone-fax-computer. CyTech plays catch-up until the end of the year when sales reach $15 billion and CyTech stock climbs to $119 per share, as shown here.

Selected Financial and Stock Information
(Dollars in millions, except stock price in actual dollars)

	Year ended March 31	
	5th Year	4th Year
Sales	$15,303	$13,832
Profits	1,071	1,107
Profits as a % of:		
Sales	7%	8%
Assets	11%	13%
Common Equity*	21%	27%
Market Value**	30,360	25,786
Stock Price	119 $\frac{1}{16}$	101 $\frac{1}{8}$

* Total stockholders' equity includes capital stock, surplus, and retained earnings at the company's year end. For purposes of determining profits as a percent of common stockholders' equity, all preferred stock is excluded.

** Calculated by multiplying the number of common shares outstanding by the price per common share as of March 31.

Given this performance, you decide to reexamine the issue of specialization versus generalization. While CyTech has done well, you believe it could have done more. Wishing to prove it so, you sign another contract to remain as CEO for three more years. This marks the end of a decision-making track, but you can keep playing *The Organization Game* by picking one of the following options.

- *If you want to compare how the results of your last five years of organizational decision making stack up against the other positive outcomes in The Organization Game, turn to Chapter 78.*

- *If you want to review the other alternatives you could have pursued on this track, turn to one of the following:*

Chapter 63, Creating Three Levels of Employees;

Chapter 64, Basing the Organization on Individual Contracts;

Chapter 66, Moving Every Employee into the Inner Core;

Chapter 67, Maintaining the Three Groupings of People Indefinitely;

Chapter 68, Backing Off by Disbanding the Inner Core;

Chapter 69, Hiring Outside Legal, Human Resource, and Management Experts;

Chapter 70, Doing Nothing;

Chapter 72, Setting Aside Your Organizational Initiatives to Focus on the Price War Crisis;

Chapter 74, Moving the Competence Centers Toward More Generalization.

- *If you would like to start the game over, turn to one of the following:*

  Chapter 2, Building a Classic Innovative Organization

  Chapter 14, Developing a Synthesis of Best Practices;

  Chapter 26, Imbuing the Culture with Empowerment and Accountability;

  Chapter 38, Pursuing a Work Team Approach, or

  Chapter 50, Reengineering Work Processes.

To your delight, CyTech's competence center-business process innovation keeps the company near the head of the pack in the continuing price war. With the war abating, you begin shifting the competence centers toward generalization, though you do so slowly in order to keep everyone focused on decisively winning the price war.

By the end of your fourth year as CEO, sales reach $14 billion as profits and the stock price hit new heights, as shown in the table on the following page.

To address the challenge of introducing a voice-operated phone-fax-computer within the next few months, you develop CyTech's first generalized temporary work groups dedicated to the various elements of the innovation business processes. With a charge to maximize the communication between groups, you ask Hal McPhee, John Solo, and Morris Strandmeyer to make sure that each new team consists of generalists capable of seeing the full picture of how CyTech will develop its voice-operated phone-fax-computer and

74

MOVING THE COMPETENCE CENTERS TOWARD MORE GENERALIZATION

get it to the marketplace in the most streamlined, effective, and profitable manner possible. CyTech scientists and engineers have been working on the voice-operated option for several years, but only recently have the technology and the chip power become sufficient to make a voice-operated machine viable.

At the same time, you guide Nan Thurow, Bob Kiechel, and Karen Walsh to quickly move the competence centers toward

Selected Financial and Stock Information
(Dollars in millions, except stock price in actual dollars)

	Year ended March 31	
	4th Year	3rd Year
Sales	$14,425	$11,975
Profits	1,154	838
Profits as a % of:		
Sales	8%	7%
Assets	13%	11%
Common Equity*	28%	21%
Market Value**	27,571	18,839
Stock Price	108 $\frac{1}{8}$	73 $\frac{7}{8}$

* Total stockholders' equity includes capital stock, surplus, and retained earnings at the company's year end. For purposes of determining profits as a percent of common stockholders' equity, all preferred stock is excluded.

** Calculated by multiplying the number of common shares outstanding by the price per common share as of March 31.

generalized training in order to provide each business process with more generalist-oriented employees. You ask them to work closely with the other three members of the senior team to monitor each of the business process groups over the course of the next several months. During that time, your choice to focus on a more generalized approach proves highly successful, as the generalist work teams meld together in a harmonious effort that produces a CyTech prototype of a voice-operated phone-fax-computer within seven weeks. These same groups, with the assistance of additional groups set up along the way, quickly test the market, work out all the bugs, and make sure the unit meets the needs of customers. With lightning speed, which even surprises you, CyTech introduces a new line of phone-fax-computers called *PowerVoice* simultaneously with Motorola's offering. The race for market share begins.

Almost immediately, the reviews of the two products rate CyTech's *PowerVoice* higher than Motorola's *Talk Mate*, and CyTech quickly takes the lead in the marketplace as customers all over the world rush to get their hands on a new *PowerVoice*. CyTech's manufacturing facilities throughout the world are pushed to their limits as demand for the new product soars. New versions and upgrades will come on line continuously during the next several months.

By the end of your fifth year as CEO, sales reach $17 billion and stock climbs to $139 per share, as shown below:

Selected Financial and Stock Information
(Dollars in millions, except stock price in actual dollars)

	Year ended March 31	
	5th Year	4th Year
Sales	$17,467	$14,425
Profits	1,398	1,154
Profits as a % of:		
Sales	8%	8%
Assets	14%	13%
Common Equity*	28%	28%
Market Value**	35,460	27,571
Stock Price	139 $\frac{1}{16}$	108 $\frac{1}{8}$

* Total stockholders' equity includes capital stock, surplus, and retained earnings at the company's year end. For purposes of determining profits as a percent of common stockholders' equity, all preferred stock is excluded.

** Calculated by multiplying the number of common shares outstanding by the price per common share as of March 31.

The new organizational form works like clockwork as the competence centers grow in strength and the business processes peopled by temps become powerhouses of performance, making it possible for every CyTech employee to grow, develop, and achieve levels of productivity never dreamed possible. Several business magazines feature you on their covers as CEO of the year, and CyTech becomes a model for organizations throughout the world.

You create a new profit center to meet the many requests of executives, managers, and organizations throughout the world who are turning to CyTech for training. You call the profit center, which opens the company's competence center expertise to as many people as possible, *"PowerShare."* You expect the *PowerShare* profit center itself to reach $1 billion in revenues within three years.

Riding the crest of the wave, you become chairman of the board and announce your decision to step down as CEO within two years in order to focus on new and different dimensions of your life. You prepare John Solo to take your place as CEO.

Many people urge you to run for government office so you can do for the public sector what you did for CyTech. You resist that advice, however, and look forward to new adventures outside the world of organizations and management.

Congratulations! You have successfully come to the end of a decision-making tract, but you can continue playing the game by choosing one of the following options listed on the accompanying page.

- *If you want to compare how the results of your last five years of organizational decision making stack up against the other positive outcomes in The Organization Game, turn to Chapter 78.*

- *If you want to explore other avenues on this track, turn to:*

  Chapter 63, Creating Three Levels of Employees;

  Chapter 64, Basing the Organization on Individual Contracts;

  Chapter 66, Moving Every Employee into the Inner Core;

  Chapter 67, Keeping the Three Groupings of People Indefinitely;

  Chapter 68, Backing Off by Disbanding the Inner Core;

  Chapter 69, Hiring Outside Legal, Human Resource, and Management Experts;

  Chapter 70, Doing Nothing;

  Chapter 72, Setting Aside Your Organizational Initiatives to Focus on the Price War Crisis;

  Chapter 73, Moving the Competence Centers Toward More Specialization.

- *If you would like to play the game again, select one of the following:*

  Chapter 2, Building a Classic Innovative Organization;

  Chapter 14, Developing a Synthesis of Best Practices;

  Chapter 26, Imbuing the Culture with Empowerment and Accountability;

  Chapter 38, Pursuing a Work Team Approach; or

  Chapter 50, Reengineering Work Processes.

The results cited in the Thermo Electron article rivet your attention: "Thermo's sales, which were running about $200 million a year when the spin-outs began a decade ago, are expected to hit about $1.2 billion this year. The company's stock, then a split adjusted $5.85 per share, now stands at $57 on the New York Stock Exchange in a sharp run-up in the past two years." You reread the whole article about Thermo Electron several times, thinking about its possible applications to CyTech. One paragraph in particular captures your imagination: "Employees can score big gains, too. Dream up a great idea at Thermo, and you aren't rewarded with just a pat on the back or even just a bonus; you might get to run your own public company. A spin-out gives new entrepreneurs working capital, rewards them when they do well, and forces accountability when they don't."

75

FOLLOWING IN THERMO ELECTRON'S FOOTSTEPS

This is exactly what you want CyTech to accomplish. From the Inn on Alameda, the hotel where you're staying in Santa Fe, you call George Hatsopolous, Thermo Electron's 66-year-old founder and chief executive officer to set up a time when you can visit with him and members of his senior executive team.

Three weeks later, you're sitting in the offices of Thermo Electron in Waltham, Massachusetts, talking with George Hatsopolous and three of his senior executives. You have brought Bob Kiechel and Hal McPhee, as well as two analysts from your personal staff. George and his executives sketch the histories of each of the subsidiaries the company has spunout over the last ten years: Thermetices, Thermo Instrument Systems, Thermo Process Systems, Thermo Power, Thermo Cardio Systems, Thermo Valtech, Thermo

Trex, Thermo Fibertek, and Thermo Lase. These subsidiaries offer product lines that range from bomb detectors and smokestack monitors to mammography machines and artificial hearts to imaging technology and electric power plants fueled by almond shells, and even "sense strips" for homes and offices.

As you leave Thermo Electron after this first meeting, George leaves you with these parting words: "There's no better way to stimulate creativity than to see the guy next to you getting $500,000 in options for a great idea."

As you travel back to CyTech headquarters, you discuss with Hal McPhee and Bob Kiechel ideas for implementing this approach at CyTech. Then you continue brainstorming with the rest of your senior executives when you return, and together you boil down your choices to two options: Watch for the next spin-out opportunity to begin implementing the Thermo Electron approach at CyTech; or divide up the company immediately into what could have produced spin-out opportunities during the last few years. The advantage to the former option stems from the time it affords CyTech to move into this approach slowly working out the details surrounding one spin-out at a time. On the negative side, this tactic would take the company longer to make this organizational form an active and functional force at CyTech. Of course, the advantage to immediately pinpointing several potential spin-outs lies in the quickness with which it will launch CyTech into this new organizational form, though it might not allow sufficient time to work out the bugs and problems that will inevitably arise.

In the midst of grappling with this decision, your fourth year as CEO comes to an end with sales reaching $12 billion and the stock price increasing to $76 per share, as shown in the accompanying table on the next page.

Selected Financial and Stock Information
(Dollars in millions, except stock price in actual dollars)

	Year ended March 31	
	4th Year	3rd Year
Sales	$12,001	See Chapter you read last to
Profits	721	identify last year's performance.
Profits as a % of:		
Sales	6%	
Assets	9%	
Common Equity*	17%	
Market Value**	19,334	
Stock Price	75 $^{13}\!/_{16}$	

* Total stockholders' equity includes capital stock, surplus, and retained earnings at the company's year end. For purposes of determining profits as a percent of common stockholders' equity, all preferred stock is excluded.

** Calculated by multiplying the number of common shares outstanding by the price per common share as of March 31.

Soon after the new year commences, you resolve to make a firm decision about how to implement a Thermo Electron-style approach at CyTech.

- *If you decide to implement the Thermo Electron approach gradually, beginning with the next spin-out opportunity, turn to Chapter 76.*

- *If you choose to speed up the implementation of the Thermo Electron organizational approach by immediately pinpointing several spin-out possibilities, turn to Chapter 77.*

You decide that a gradual implementation of the Thermo Electron organizational approach will best meet the needs of CyTech, allowing it to meet its current challenges as well as paving the way for new ones in the future. In consultation with your senior executive team, you identify the voice-operated phone-fax-computer as the next best spin-out opportunity because you know that almost every competitor in your industry has been working on a prototype and you suspect that Motorola may actually introduce such a machine in the next few months. You ask Hal McPhee to keep the organization focused on reducing costs, making it more and more profitable for CyTech to sell phone-fax-computers at prices below $500, and you instruct Bob Kiechel to direct the company's future attention to the spin-out of CyTech's voice-operated phone-fax-computer business.

76

GEARING UP FOR THE NEXT SPIN-OUT OPPORTUNITY

Assembling the group of people that have been working on the voice-operated machine, you present them with the Thermo Electron approach that, not surprisingly, captures their imaginations and greatly stimulates their motivation. You immediately arrange for key personnel at CyTech to meet with counterparts at Thermo Electron to figure out exactly how to structure the new spin-out. Within a few short weeks, you have laid the necessary groundwork and launch a new company, CyVoice, with 60 percent of the stock owned by CyTech and 40 percent to be sold via an IPO (Initial Public Offering) administered by Merrill Lynch. The initial 250 CyVoice employees quickly expand to over 1,000 as the new company prepares for initial testing weeks before you dreamed possible.

After the device passes its tests with flying colors, CyVoice introduces a new line of phone-fax-computers called *VoicePower*, three months before Motorola introduces its own. The response from the marketplace proves extraordinary as sales skyrocket and CyVoice racks up the most phenomenal sales growth record in U.S. business history, going from $0 to over $2 billion in 14 months.

By the end of your fifth year as CEO of CyTech, sales reach $15 billion for CyTech and $2 billion for CyVoice. CyTech's stock soars to $115 per share, with CyVoice's stock sitting at $60 per share, as shown here:

Selected Financial and Stock Information
(Dollars in millions, except stock price in actual dollars)

	Year ended March 31	
	5th Year	4th Year
Sales	$16,283*	$12,001
Profits	1140	721
Profits as a % of:		
Sales	7%	6%
Assets	11%	9%
Common Equity	20%	17%
Market Value	29,389	19,334
Stock Price (Cy Tech)	115 ¼	75 ^{13}⁄₁₆
Stock Price (Cy Voice)	59 ⅞	—

* Includes 60 percent of CyVoice's sales and profits.

Interestingly, you find that the separation of the voice-operated phone-fax-computer business from CyTech allows the rest of the CyTech organization to produce phone-fax-computers at lower and lower prices, with some models selling for under $350, which continues to fuel sales despite the huge new customer demand for the voice-operated machines.

As you look forward to the coming year, you identify three more spin-out opportunities: multimedia-based phone-fax-computers, a high-definition display screen phone-fax-computer, and a new artificial intelligence computer. CyTech's future couldn't look brighter.

- *If you want to compare how the results of your last five years of organizational decision making stack up against the other positive outcomes in The Organization Game, turn to Chapter 78.*

- *If you want to see what would have happened if you had pursed the other alternative on this track, turn to Chapter 77, Moving Immediately to Implement a Thermo Electron Style of Organization.*

- *If you want to begin another decision-making track, turn to one of the following chapters:*
  Chapter 2, Building a Classic Innovative Organization
  Chapter 14, Developing a Synthesis of Best Practices;
  Chapter 26, Imbuing the Culture with Empowerment and Accountability;
  Chapter 38, Pursuing a Work Team Approach;
  Chapter 50, Reengineering Work Processes; or
  Chapter 62, Embracing a Revolutionary New Perspective.

Congratulations! This marks the end of a decision-making track, but you can keep playing the game by choosing one of the following options.

You quickly identify five different potential spin-outs to launch within the next few months. They include a low-end phone-fax-computer, a voice-operated machine, a high-end sophisticated phone-fax-computer, a teleconferencing version, and a children's notepad. CyTech currently produces all of these products, with the exception of the voice-operated machine, so your program actually turns into a virtual breakup of CyTech.

Not surprisingly, this massive effort overloads your finance and legal departments, requiring you to pull in the services of Merrill Lynch, Goldman Sachs, Morgan Stanley, and a few other smaller investment banking firms to arrange for the public offerings for each of the five new entities. Rather than motivating CyTech people to high productivity and creating excitement about the opportunities available in these new spin-out companies, the situation engulfs the organization in confusion. Employees wonder about the wisdom behind the split-up, worrying whether they should remain with CyTech or move to one of the spin-out companies.

In the midst of the confusion, CyTech loses its leadership in the price war as a competitor drops the price of phone-fax-computers below $300. The company also makes little, if any, progress on the voice-operated machine as departments,

77

IMMEDIATELY IMPLEMENTING A THERMO ELECTRON STYLE OF ORGANIZATION

groups, and individuals labor over the decision of where to move within the organization. The investment banking firms also run into so much difficulty making the multiple IPOs (Initial Public Offering) work, they advise you to sequence the public offerings of each of the five new spin-outs, a move that greatly lengthens the process and further engulfs the CyTech culture in chaos and confusion.

Before you reach the end of your fifth year as CEO at CyTech, the chairman of the board asks for your resignation, as competitors acquire major positons in two of the two spin-out companies due to declining stock prices after the IPOs. To shore up eroding financial resources, CyTech sells off portions of its own stock in the two spin-out companies, eventually giving control to the acquiring competitors.

After you leave the company, year-end results show a precipitous drop in sales due to the selling of spin-out stock. The following table tells the story.

Selected Financial and Stock Information
(Dollars in millions, except stock price in actual dollars)

	Year ended March 31	
	5th Year	4th Year
Sales	$10,377	$12,001
Profits	721	
Profits as a % of:		
Sales	3%	6%
Assets	5%	9%
Common Equity*	9%	17%
Market Value**	19,334	
Stock Price	49 $\frac{1}{2}$	75 $\frac{13}{16}$

* Total stockholders' equity includes capital stock, surplus, and retained earnings at the company's year end. For purposes of determining profits as a percent of common stockholders' equity, all preferred stock is excluded.

** Calculated by multiplying the number of common shares outstanding by the price per common share as of March 31.

As you look back, you realize that you misapplied the Thermo Electron organizational concept by using it as a means to split up the company rather than to fuel spin-outs.

- *In real life you might have avoided this unfortunate turn of events, but you really did misapply the spin-out concept. If you want to see why the author considers the other alternative preferable, turn to Chapter 76.*

- *If you want to start a new decision-making track, turn to one of the following:*

    Chapter 2, Building a Classic Innovative Organization

    Chapter 14, Developing a Synthesis of Best Practices;

    Chapter 26, Imbuing the Culture with Empowerment and Accountability;

    Chapter 38, Pursuing a Work Team Approach;

    Chapter 50, Reengineering Work Processes; or

    Chapter 62, Embracing a Revolutionary New Perspective.

Caution: Your experience playing *The Organization Game* will be enhanced if you wait to read this chapter after you have come to the end of a decision-making track, (that is the successful completion of five full years as CEO of CyTech).

By this point, you have traveled down one or more five-year decision-making tracks and should have enhanced your organizational thinking and decision-making ability. In writing this book, I intended more than anything else to broaden, deepen, and strengthen your organizational awareness and competence, but, even more, I wanted to entertain and inspire you with the challenges, dilemmas, and inevitable choices business people face every day throughout our global economy. At a minimum, I hope playing *The Organization Game* has given you a stronger appreciation of the importance of accurate and sufficient information upon which to base your organizational perceptions and judgments.

In the entire book, I have included a total of 27 negative outcomes, ranging from absolute disaster to minor failure, and 17 positive outcomes, ranging from spectacular triumph to marginal success. You may have already encountered one or more of the 27 negative outcomes, but to give you a quick overview of how the 17 positive outcomes compare to one another, you can find the number of the chapter you just completed (which represents the end of a decision-making track) ranked on the following page according to the market value of CyTech's stock at the end of five years.

78

A RANKING OF THE SUCCESSFUL OUTCOMES

Ending Chapter	Market Value	Stock Price
67	$39,971	156 $\frac{3}{4}$
74	$35,460	139 $\frac{1}{16}$
61	$31,238	122 $\frac{1}{2}$
73	$30,360	119 $\frac{1}{16}$
76	$29,389	115 $\frac{1}{4}$
48	$25,819	101 $\frac{1}{4}$
32	$24,704	96 $\frac{7}{8}$
36	$23,651	92 $\frac{3}{4}$
10	$23,561	91 $\frac{13}{16}$
60	$22,919	89 $\frac{7}{8}$
49	$22,759	89 $\frac{1}{4}$
24	$21,882	85 $\frac{13}{16}$
25	$21,882	85 $\frac{13}{16}$
59	$19,859	77 $\frac{7}{8}$
33	$16,766	65 $\frac{3}{4}$
6	$11,632	44 $\frac{1}{8}$
7	$8,250	32 $\frac{1}{2}$

Now that you know how your initial choices in *The Organization Game* stack up, put your organizational thinking skills to the test again by choosing one of the options at the end of the chapter you just finished. When you reach the end of another decision-making track, you can return to this chapter to compare your results. Good luck on your next adventure!